Higher Education in India

The International Engagement

Higher Education in India

The International Engagement

V T Patil

AUTHORSPRESS

Worldwide Circulation through Authorspress Global Network
First Published 2010
by
Authorspress
E-35/103, Jawahar Park
Laxmi Nagar, Delhi-110 092
e-mail: authorspress@yahoo.com

Higher Education in India: The International Engagement
ISBN 978-81-7273-517-3

Printed in Shri Krishna Offset Press

PREFACE

Universities today are key drivers of internationalisation and global communication with regard to intellectual property and knowledge production. Parallel to the processes of globalisation and the advent of the knowledge economy, internationalisation has become a major trend in higher education, and a major force in the globalised marketplace. For many countries, higher education is now an important export sector, with many university campuses attracting international students from around the world. Licensing production, in the form of franchising degree provision to international partners, is beginning to mutate into foreign direct investment as universities set up campuses in other countries. Driven by advances in information and communication technologies and the growing hegemony of English as the world's common language, higher education is following the classic pattern of globalisation familiar in international business.

The role of interactions between systems of higher education has increased as the interactions between individuals, institutions, and countries around the world have accelerated. This includes the inter-connectedness of economies, environments, technologies, political, and other systems. These interactions around the world require a look at education systems beyond an individual nation-state and from the perspective of the nation-state of those forces beyond its borders. Internationalisation of higher education is one of the ways a country responds to the impact of globalisation yet, at the same time respects the individuality of the nation.

The new regime under WTO where competence is the cardinal principle of success in international operations has made it abundantly clear that the country should exploit its excellent potential in higher education and training facilities and prepare itself to export the Indian brand of education to foreign countries.

Policy planning and evolving strategies for this task are somewhat new for the country. But, this is an opportunity which cannot be missed by India, as it offers interesting possibilities for strengthening of the nation's talent and resourcefulness. The Indian universities have not been able to take advantage of the possibilities that internationalisation offers for improving the quality of education, promoting Indian culture in different countries, and deriving political or economic benefits. In the context of recent national and international developments, in all major areas—it is imperative that we take up the task of internationalisation of our higher education seriously.

Although the higher education system in India has grown in a remarkable way to become one of the largest system of its kind in the world, the system has many issues of concern at present, like financing and management including access, equity and relevance, reorientation of programmes by laying emphasis on health consciousness, values and ethics and quality of higher education together with the assessment of institutions and their accreditation. These issues are important for the country, as it is now engaged in the use of higher education as a powerful tool to build a knowledge-based information society of the 21st century.

This book discusses the concept and development of, and the rationales for the internationalisation of higher education. The impacts of globalisation and the knowledge economy upon the internationalisation of higher education are examined, particularly in the Indian context. I am quite certain that this publication will help in giving a new direction aimed at the 21st century expectations to the Indian higher education system and accelerate its pace of development to meet the needs and aspirations of the society at large. I would like to thank Authorspess, New Delhi for bringing out this useful publication in time.

V T Patil

CONTENTS

1. INDIA'S GROWING HIGHER EDUCATION SECTOR

In today's world, the education sector in India has been a dramatic turn for the better, growing exponentially, especially in the domain of higher education. With communication and information technology revolution, the scope for raising educational standards has widened. Internet in education has a much wider role in extending education to a globalised world, and the recent trends in the knowledge sectors indicates the advantage enjoyed by India in the area. Concrete measures are required to mainstream India into the knowledge sector boom.

Higher Education Worldwide

Two parallel developments in the world economy are worth noting, especially for their influence on provisioning of higher education: the growth of the Internet and consequently, e-education and, second, the expanding role of World Trade Organisation (WTO) in determining the trends in world economics.

Advantages of Internet in Education

With instant information so readily available at the press of a button, the Internet has changed the way the lifestyle of the world. Even school children search the web for study material to support their homework. Today, academicians do not need to spend much time on library research poring over bulky tomes and taking copious notes. They have the facility of faster and surer access to a much wider range of information through the Internet, not just to read but to print or save or forward to others as might suit their purpose. Internet research has now become an essential study tool in all higher education courses in developed countries.

The Internet has also streamlined administrative procedures and processes of universities worldwide. Any modern university, management school or institute today has its own website on which courses offered are listed. Students apply for admission online which reduces paperwork and increases administrative efficiency. They receive e-notifications regarding admission, course schedules, and billing procedures, which they can pay online, as well as their results.

Teachers prefer to receive tutorials online, which not only lends itself to faster transmission, but also avoids the difficulty in reading a manuscript. Similarly, some teachers not only put up their course material on the website, but also their lectures, which can be heard online such that students who were unable to attend can also benefit from them. The faculty and students remain connected through e-mail on which students receive instructions, send essays/assignments, fix appointments, etc. All students are expected to have their own laptop or notebook computer.

A traditional Western university still has face-to-face lectures, but it also offers online courses especially during the summer break. While such courses have the obvious disadvantage of the absence of personal interaction, they facilitate discussion through setting up of chat rooms. Such online courses and discussions have often proved to be more rewarding than regular classroom interactions as they allow for students and teachers from different parts of the world to converge.

Universities that have online facilities and which do not require physical infrastructure, have facilitated greater accessibility to education than ever before. While popular perception values a degree from a regular college over one from an online college, the greatest advantage of an online university or college is that a student need not commute or live on campus. This is especially true for certain kinds of courses designed to cater to the needs of students who do not have financial backup or family support. As acquiring specialised degrees is directly related to better jobs, re-engineering e-education at tertiary level has a great advantage. As jobs become more and more insecure and mid-life career changes more frequently, the need for online education is increasing overtime.

Globalisation and Higher Education

According to the results of a special survey, *Higher Education: Free degrees to fly*, higher education is already a global business. The days when higher education was a matter of national policy and government regulation are rapidly fading. Higher education provisioning is now globalised and in many ways, a commercialised affair. According to Andreas Schleicher of OECD, a Paris-based 'Think Tank', the numbers studying abroad were statistically negligible two decades ago. According to the International Finance Corporation (IFC), the growth is now soaring: 2 million university students-approaching 2 per cent of the world's total of around 100 million studying outside their home country in 2003.

Since the late 1990s the higher education market is growing by 7 per cent a year. *The Economist Survey* on higher education further indicates that annual fee income alone is estimated at $ 30 billion. Private companies have entered the education business as a profit-making venture and even government-controlled universities are seeking independence from governmental authority. However, many countries, including India, continue to control the fee structure of their universities causing financial stress to foreign students, who have to cough out higher fees than local students. This has resulted in many universities openly soliciting entry of foreign students. To facilitate this process they have even tailored their courses to international requirements besides appointing agents abroad and publicising the offers widely in the media.

Hence a university is no longer a viable place for studies. Universities are now actively pursuing students, especially foreign ones using a wide variety of strategies to market their courses. The student is now the customer or client. With globalisation, Universities are spreading their reach beyond geographical and political borders. The British, Australian and American universities are setting up campuses in Singapore, China and the Gulf. Universities realise that they can examine many more students than they can teach. Hence many of them are collaborating with other institutions or franchises to teach their courses under their brand name without getting involved in the direct business of imparting the education.

The example of Professional Training Colleges best illustrates this point. The growth of such colleges worldwide shows a rising desire for professional qualifications, a new need for mid-career education and finally, the increasing acceptance of professionally qualified candidature in the job market. Very often the costs incurred in preparing for the examination outstrip the stipulated entrance fee for the examination itself.

Role of WTO and GATS

While generally higher education is viewed as a public good, the prevailing argument in the WTO Secretariat is that higher education is akin to 'private consumption' directly benefiting the consumer by way of higher income. In April 2002, Universities from Latin American countries, Portugal and Spain adopted a Declaration at the III Summit of Iberian and Latin American Universities in Porto Alegre, Brazil in which they declared education as a 'public good' and requested their governments not to make any commitment on this issue within the framework of WTO. However, over time the perception of higher education as a commercial service is gaining acceptance. The WTO Secretariat in September 1998 mentioned that with the rapid changes in higher education 'education also exists as a private consumption item with a price determined freely by the providing institutions'. As a result, they have stated that more and more paying students including foreign students are attracted to these institutions.

WTO has also adopted the Principle of Most Favoured Nation which implies that each party 'shall accord immediate and unconditionally to services and service providers of any other party, treatment no less favourable than it accords to the service and service providers of any other country.' This means that, if a country allows a foreign institution of a country to provide distance education services, all other countries can request to have the same treatment. Similarly, if subsidy is given to one, others can request the same advantage.

Another important issue of Global Agreement in Trade & Tariffs (GATS) and WTO, the notion of National Treatment, implies an obligation to treat both foreign and domestic service suppliers in the same manner. It has been contended that this would imply, if implemented rigidly, that a foreign educational institution of, say, distance education, can demand subsidies similar to those received by public universities in an individual country.

The World Conference on "Higher Education in the Twenty-First Century: Vision and Action" held at UNESCO Headquarters in Paris from October 5 to 9, 1998 was attended by nearly 5,000 participants representing 180 countries. It adopted an Action Plan for reforms in the field of higher education. Its main theme was that higher education must serve the interest of sustainable development and help build a better society.

As demands for higher education grow the world over, the governments are also finding it difficult to provide adequate budgetary allocation. GATS covers educational services of all types for all countries whose educational systems are not exclusively provided by public sector or those systems that have a commercial purpose. Hardly any country has education exclusively in the public sector domain and therefore, almost all the world's educational systems come within the purview of GATS.

The GATS covers four types of services. These are:

- Cross-border supply of services from territory of one member to another member. Distance education falls in this category.
- Consumption of a service abroad by the citizens of a member country on the territory of another member country. The most common example is undertaking studies abroad.
- Commercial presence of service supplier of a member country on the territory of another member country, enabling the supplier to provide a service in that territory. This includes activities carried out by foreign universities or other institutions in another country.
- Presence of natural persons enabling a form of trade resulting from mobility of people from one member country who supply a given service in another country. In education this would imply courses offered by foreign teachers.

These are the four categories of services defined under GATS/WTO. Any barrier in its free flow is considered to be 'non-tariff barrier'. The goal of free trade is to remove these barriers in order to gain from further liberalisation. In the sector of education these generally refer to government regulations, exchange controls, nationality requirements of students and teachers, non-recognition of equivalent qualifications, and rules regarding use of resources and subsidies. Higher education services now figure in India's offer on liberalisation in trade in services that the Commerce Ministry submitted to WTO in August 2005.

E-Education

Apart from commercial business concerns, existing universities and colleges as well are interested in entering the education industry aggressively. Private companies like Kaplan, BPP and Apollo Group already run successful education business ventures. Kalpan is a big education company owned by the same company that runs the *Washington Post* newspaper. BPP, its British rival, has entered into deals with British universities so that students enrolled into their professional courses can earn degrees from the Boston Post-Graduate University. University of Phoenix, the first university to offer a full time on-line degree is owned by the Apollo Group.

Sixteen of the world's better ranking universities have got together and set up a $ 50 million joint venture called Universitas 21 Global, an online MBA business school. These universities include McGill, British Colombia, Virginia, Edinburgh, Sweden and Melbourne of Australia. This $ 50 million project has been established in collaboration with a private company called Thomson Learning, an educational and training service division of the Thomson Corporation.

University as 21 Global aims to tap markets of potential students from UAE, Singapore, Malaysia, India, Korea and China. It has already enrolled professionals from 45 countries for its graduate programme. It has also offered an M.Sc. in Tourism and Travel Management recently. The online degree of Universities 21 has been well received in the world market and the degree certificate awarded by it bears the crest of all the 16 top-ranked participating universities.

In India is online education, very crucial for the Indian population, is heavily dependent on reliable high-speed Internet coverage. As a prerequisite to expansion of online education services, it is essential that various parts of the country be connected with high speed Internet. As more and more cities in India are coming within the ambit of high speed cyber-network, the concept of e-education, especially at higher levels, should be viewed seriously.

E-learning, however, as additional support to existing courses, is already highly successful in the West. Internet base e-tutoring or on-line tutoring is catching up in India as well. Tutor-Vista, a company set up in Bangalore, provides Indian teachers in English, Maths, Physics, Chemistry and Biology for 3rd to 12th grade students in UK and the US charging less than half the local rates. The session is interactive with use of head phones and microphone.

E-learning is not only inexpensive, but also convenient. It has clearly percolated even to the school level. It also does not force the student to relocate or forgo earnings from full time or part time employment that the student may be engaged in. Unfortunately, India's education policy has largely missed out on taking advantage of this technological revolution in education.

India needs to focus more on good quality, market based e-learning courses and Internet cafe/schools with programme structures that are relevant to the Indian context. Libraries must be equipped with computers that support high-speed internet connectivity. To bridge the digital divide we need all-night net libraries or late night accessibility at least, at a monthly charge, of course. Such internet cafes could be provided under private or cooperative licences in residential areas including slums. Personnel trained in computers and e-learning tools could man these edu-cafes and help students make better use of the facilities. The cost of e-learning, while market driven, could perhaps be subsidised through need-based scholarship schemes.

High speed Internet connection is an essential prerequisite to widespread e-learning. In India, a cheap hand-held computer designed by Indian scientists was launched in 2004 after a delay of three years. The Simputer is a low-cost portable alternative to PCs, by which the benefits of IT can reach the common man.

A wind-up computer machine and with a wifi wireless Internet connection, it may well be within the reach of the Indian student community even in remote locations with poor electric supply. While the academic community has not reacted positively to globalisation, many developed governments see it as an opportunity to expand its educational services.

International brands in consumer products are being embraced on a global scale with transnational institutions taking account of local legal codes, currencies, local tastes, habits, customs and adjusting to a new international order. Communication through Internet and e-commerce has led to improved transacting business. The rise of global authorities like WTO & GATS and their Dispute Resolution Mechanism has far reaching consequences for globalisation. Further, WTO's 'enforceable global commercial code' has made a real impact. It has facilitated incremental freedom for transnational capital 'to do what it wants, where and when it wants'.

For a public service such as education GATS at Doha was a stepping stone so that there is no discrimination against foreign corporations entering the service market. Further, after the fizzling of the dot.com bubble, corporations are looking forward to other service sectors for investments, education being one of them.

North Anglia is exporting services to Russia, Ukraine as well as running schools and local educational authority services in the UK itself. Wigan & Leigh has 15,000 students in 26 countries including 10 campuses in India. Many British universities have franchised operations and deal with other colleges and universities outside the UK. University Schools of Education generate income through consultancies that have advised countries like Chile, Poland, and Romania on how to restructure the school system.

Higher Education System in India

Education in India is seen as one of the ways to upward social mobility. Good education is seen as a stepping stone to a high flying career. Education System in India currently represents a great paradox. On the one hand we have IIMs & IITs that rank among the best institutes in the world and on the other hand there are number of schools in the country that don't even have the basic infrastructure. Even after more than 50 years after independence we are far away from the goal of universal literacy. But on a positive note, Indian professionals are considered among the best in the world are in great demand. This signifies the inherent strength of Indian education system.

The Educational structure in India which operates at all conceivable levels from pre-school to post doctoral is of monumental proportions. According to a World Bank report there are more than 7,40,000 formal schools; more than 3.6 million teachers are working on full time basis; there are more than 175 Universities offering under graduate and post graduate courses and about 6000 colleges affiliated to these universities.

The educational structure in India is generally referred to as the Ten + Two + Three (10+2+3) pattern. The first ten years provide undifferentiated general education for all students. The +2 stage, also known as the higher secondary or senior secondary, provides for differentiation into academic and vocational streams and marks the end of school education. In +3 stage, which involves college education, the student goes for higher studies in his chosen field of subject.

Since independence, the Government of India has focused on providing full policy support and substantial public funds to create one of the world's largest systems of higher education. These institutions, with some rare exceptions, have however, not been able to maintain the high standards of education or keep pace with developments in the fields especially in knowledge and technology.

Over time, financial constraints with exploding population, and a very high demand from primary and secondary education has led to the deterioration in the financial support provided by the government. On top of this, an overall structure of myriad controls with a rigid bureaucracy has stifled its development. In terms of higher education, however, on the science and technology side, India has however built up the largest stock of scientists, engineers and technicians.

In India both public and private institutions operate simultaneously. In 2000-01, of the 13,072 higher education institutions, 42 per cent were privately owned and run catering to approximately 3.1 million out of total 8.4 million of students enrolled into higher education. It is also likely that most of the growth in the rapidly expanding higher education sector took place in private unaided college or in self-financing institutions.

Since grant-in-aid to private colleges is becoming difficult, many governments/universities have granted recognition/ affiliation to unaided colleges and many universities have authorised new 'self-financing' courses even in government and aided colleges. It is felt that as of now more than 50 per cent of the higher education in India is imparted through private institutions, mostly unaided.

Deemed Universities

Government has created 221 universities of which there is also the concept of deemed university. This status is given by UGC to colleges of exceptional excellence. There are 39 deemed universities plus seven open universities. There are 9,703 colleges in India that provide mostly bachelors or sometimes master's level of education. Of these, only 550 are engineering and technical colleges, 655 medical and 600 management institutions.

Where universities are concerned, only the central or state government can open a new university, and that too by legislation in the parliament or state. Universities are empowered to award their own degrees and take affiliate colleges. But UGC is empowered under its Act to grant institutes of excellence 'Deemed University' status which they have done in 39 cases. There are, however, no private universities so far. A Private Universities' Bill has been proposed in the Parliament, but has not been approved so far. All self-financing colleges, therefore, have to also seek affiliation with a university.

UGS's Role in Education

All of India's higher education is thus managed by the UGC and the various Councils. The UGC, established by a statute 1952, has been empowered to promote and coordinate university education in India and also approve grants to them.

Vocational Education: Vocational education is one of the streams of higher education. For this a network of public and private polytechnics and vocational institutions exists, controlled and supervised by the councils specialising in each discipline. There are nearly 10 million students in 6,500 such institutions.

In a recent innovation, vocational curriculum has been introduced at the bachelor's degree level by permitting one of three subjects to be a vocational one. A number of subjects have been introduced including agriculture-related activities. Nearly 1,500 colleges have been given facilities for vocational education.

Research and Development: While R&D centres have been established in many disciplines, giving recognition to centres of excellence in different subjects has led to the establishment of Centres of Advance Studies (CAS), Department of Special Assistance (DSA) and Inter-University Research Centres of internationally comparable standards.

The objective of these centres is to provide quality inputs in higher education and research areas. Further, to cut costs of undertaking good research, especially in sciences, Inter-University Centres in nuclear science, crystal growth, astronomy and astrophysics, social sciences and humanities have been formed.

India has taken a leading role in commercial R&D which within the scope of higher education has gained greater importance. It has been stated that 150 international firms have set up R&D centres in India and in 2004 US patents office granted over 1,000 patents to Indian units of US companies. Indian companies have also started to increase their R&D budgets.

The demand for high quality researchers will require expansion of postgraduate research and PhDs in Indian institutions of higher learning. According to Saikat Chaudhory, a Management Professor at Wharton, India needs to improve its research atmosphere in its universities. This is perhaps, already happening. If we look at that the CSIR, the number of US patents granted to it has jumped to 196 in 2005 from just 6 in 1990–1. SPREAD – Sponsored Research and Development of the ICICI Technology Financing Group is helping finance commercial R&D. Similarly, Nirma Labs provides up to Rs 20 lakhs as grant. We need to expand such support to R&D activities.

Open University System: With the establishment of the Indira Gandhi National Open University (IGNOU) now there are seven open universities in India offering over 500 courses. IGNOU has about 11,87,100 students on its rolls.

Modern communication technology can be harnessed to effectively provide education through this medium. A distance education council has been set up and a common pool of programmes is available for sharing.

Open universities can be highly cost effective as the cost of teaching through distance education comes down to a third of the traditional system. Their close relationship with the industry is specially helpful to those who cannot afford a regular university degree due to high cost or lack of time as they are already employed.

Distance education with new information and communication technology promises to expand the frontiers of higher education as never before. This is because it costs 66 per cent less and the students need not leave their homes or profession. The Internet and satellite technology are being put to use to further the cause of distance education. The Indian Space Research Organisation (ISRO) is launching a dedicated satellite for educational purposes.

Public Funds for Higher Education

India has developed one of the largest systems of higher education in the world with over 230 universities and 6,500 vocational colleges catering to about 10 million students. Most of these are publicly funded although some may be privately run. The financing of higher education, however, is often reprioritised due to competing demands for budgetary funds from primary and secondary education sectors.

In the government plan outlay the share of higher education doubled for 9 per cent in the first five-year plan to 18 per cent in the second. It increased to 25 per cent in the fourth but has now come down to 15 per cent in the seventh five-year plan. In the eighth five-year plan it was around 8 per cent. It may be stated that the non-plan expenditure in education is huge compared to plan expenditure.

On the source of funding, the share of government expenditure increased from 49 per cent in 1950-51 to 76 per cent in 1986-87. The share of non-government sector, which in India is largely student fees, declined from 36 per cent in 1960s to less then half of what it was in 1950s. The share of 'other sources' that is, voluntary donation, endowments etc. also declined. The issue of raising fees in government-aided colleges and vocational institutions was bogged down by politics. As a result, this source which could potentially provide approximately 20 per cent of the funds is currently funding barely 3 per cent of the cost of education.

In order to combat the resource crunch in higher education other sources of financing besides the government have to be developed so that the massive expenditure required to expand, improve and bring it to world standards could be carried out. With an expanding middle class and globalisation this is possible provided innovative policies are formulated and implemented.

Open University System

The advances in information and communication technology provide great opportunities to enhance teaching and learning in higher education by both on-campus and distance education. Even disabled students who are denied access to traditional institutions, and all those who require updating of their knowledge and life-long education can now be benefited by the modern facilities of communication. They also provide increased access to information sources and facilitate communication among researchers and teachers and the building of networks of institutions and scholars.

Through the open universities and distance learning initiatives, mechanisms are in place to upgrade skills at regular intervals and develop new competencies. People's needs of lifelong learning are constantly expanding. Higher education institutions are offering learning opportunities to satisfy these diverse demands. Ready access and flexibility are the hallmarks of these initiatives.

The Open University System was initiated in the country to augment opportunities for higher education as an instrument of democratising education and also to make it a lifelong process. The first open university in the country was established by the state government of Andhra Pradesh in 1982. In 1985, the central government established the Indira Gandhi National Open University (IGNOU).

Indian Gandhi National Open University

The IGNOU designed, developed and delivered high quality academic programmes in the Humanities, Sciences and Social Sciences as well as in professional areas like Computer Applications, Education, Engineering, Management, Nursing and Tourism. The University has currently -101 programmes comprising 900 courses to offer. Most of the University's programmes are structured on modular pattern, leading to the award of certificates, diplomas and degrees.

The enrolment in the university has been rising rapidly. From less than 4,000 students in 1987, the enrolment rose to over 1,60,000 in 1998 and is currently about 13,11,145 The University has a vastly heterogeneous student body: demo-graphically diverse (age, gender, region, social background, etc.); educationally dis-advantaged (most of them without the traditional qualifications for entering into higher education and who have had no other opportunities to make up for the lost time); and economically weak (large majority belonging to low and lower middle income groups). Most of these students are in the lower rungs of their career looking for opportunities to improve their qualifications, professional competence and/or in acquiring new skills.

The University has demonstrated that modern communication technologies can be effectively harnessed in providing access to educational opportunities and that high technology need not necessarily be a high cost medium. The University has, at its inception, set up Audio-Video production facilities with the generous support provided by the Governments of UK and Japan. These facilities were substantially augmented with a major grant given by the Government of Japan. The current Electronic Media Production Centre is a state-of-the-art technological facility that significantly enriches the university's learning packages. The media packages of the university are transmitted on the nation-wide television network as well as through selected radio stations. A dedicated, satellite-based tele-conferencing network is being developed on an experimental basis in cooperation with the Indian Space Research Organisation for providing interactive teaching- learning support to distance education programmes offered by open universities in India.

EDUSAT the first Indian satellite built exclusively for serving the educational sector is a collaborative project of Ministry of Human Resource Development (MHRD), Indira Gandhi National Open University (IGNOU), Department of Space Indian Space Research Organisation (ISRO). It is mainly intended to meet the demand for an interactive satellite-based distance education system for the country. It strongly reflects India's commitment to use space technology for national development, especially for the development of the population in remote and rural locations.

For the delivery of various services to its students, the IGNOU has developed a nation-wide network of 48 Regional Centres 6 Sub-Regional Centres and over 1,271 Study Centres, all over India. The Study Centres and Work Centres are located generally with existing educational or training institutions who have made their facilities and services available to the IGNOU students.

Distance Education Council (DEC)

The IGNOU is also a national level apex body for distance education. Distance Education Council (DEC) has been established as a statutory authority under the IGNOU Act. The DEC is responsible for promotion, coordination and maintenance of standards of open and distance education system in the country.

The apex body role envisages the establishment and development of an Open University Network by sharing the intellectual and physical resources within the distance education system among different institutions and enriching the system by extending its outreach, on the one hand, and ensuring the quality standards of its programmes of education and training, on the other. In discharging its responsibility, the Distance Education Council also provides development funding to open universities and distance education institutions from the funds placed at its disposal by the Central Government. The DEC has been supporting all the State Open Universities (SOUs) since eighth plan and Distance Education Institutions (DEIs) of conventional universities since ninth plan.

Presently, there is one National Open University (IGNOU), eleven (SOUs) and a number of DEIs in different states.

Open University Network

The Distance Education Council (DEC) has taken several initiatives to develop the Open University Network. The programmes developed and produced by IGNOU are extensively used by the State Open Universities in the country. Efforts have also been made to evolve common standards for the products as well as processes (programme structure, credits, examination, grading, etc.) to facilitate student mobility across programmes as well as institutions through systems of credit transfer. Steps have also been initiated of credit transfer. Steps have also been initiated to frame norms and standards for the design, development and delivery of programmes in specific fields and to ensure their quality.

Cost Effectiveness and Pertinence

The Open University programmes have proved to be highly cost-effective. The current indications are that their cost is much lower than the cost normally incurred by the traditional system on comparable programmes. The open universities arrive at lower costs through economies of scale since a part of its fixed cost will get distributed over a larger number of students.

The open universities in the country have generally developed their programmes and courses with a view to ensure that they are relevant to the economic and employment needs. Most of their programmes are very different from those offered by the traditional universities. They are designed and developed in several modules to assist the potential students to choose such modules as they perceive, are relevant to their needs. On their part, the universities have also sought to diversify their course provisions and developed high quality multi-media open learning curriculum designed to meet the academic, technical and vocational needs of diverse student groups. A notable feature of these programmes especially those in the technical, vocational and professional areas is the close linkages with the industry and other employer groups, not only in designing and preparing the learning packages, but also in the delivery of various services to the students at the work place.

Knowledge Economy in India

India's higher education policy of the 1950s focusing on schools of excellence, especially in technology and sciences, has finally paid off rich dividends. The creation of IITs, IIMs, Schools of Science, Schools of Law, a large number of advanced training and research institutions are now flourishing.

India can be proud of the fact that doctors trained in India have been the backbone of the British Medical Service for many decades. Indian scientists have found positions of importance in research laboratories of the US and other developed countries. But it is the IIT engineers who finally struck gold during the dot.com boom of the 1990s and brought the final recognition and testimony for Indian competence.

Of about 140,000 graduates of IIT so far, roughly 40,000 have gone to the US. They have been given the credit of creating 150,000 jobs and $80 billion in market capitalisation. The states of Virginia and Maryland declared the month of May 2005 as IIT-Indian American Heritage Month. Further, 55 US Members of the House of Representatives co-sponsored Resolution 227 honouring 'the economic innovation attributable to graduates of the Indian Institute of Technology'. With so much of admiration and brand equity for Indian technology and knowledge sector, it is time for India to cash in on its advantage.

There is a lesson to be learned from the United States and its economy. One of its great strengths has been its educational system – especially institutes of higher learning, as well as its research laboratories. For example, Colombia University is credited with 47 Nobel Prizes.

Companies like Microsoft, Hewlett-Packard (where Silicon Valley really began), Yahoo and Google were each started by university students. Venture Capital as a financial engine for encouraging pioneering innovation started in the US. The Patent registration system of the US remains one of the best.

India's Great Strength

With Indian economy showing rising trends, the IIT graduates increasingly prefer to return or remain in the country. It is stated by some that Bangalore today has 150,000 software engineers compared to 130,000 in Silicon Valley. According to

Computerwise, the top 50 global IT service firms alone target raising India's headcount from 173,000 in September 2004 to 500,000 by end of 2005.

NASSCOM reports suggest that India had a total of 650,000 IT professionals in 2002, and by February 2005, they were to rise to 813,500. According to Brainbench Inc., India ranked behind the US in the number of certified software professionals (145,517 against 194,211) The Indian figure was 30 times larger than Europe's top country Germany (4802) and one hundred times Chinas (1325).

India, therefore, does have an overwhelming lead in software. Further, leading US IT firms have their CMM Level 5 certification in India, rather than in the US. The high technology leadership of the US is now coming under threat from India. In a paper published by Richard Freeman of Harvard University quoted by Sheshabalaya, the employment at General Electric Company's Global Research Headquarters in New York is being surpassed by their own facility, the Welch Centre at Bangalore. Similarly, IBM cut its jobs in the US and Europe but recruited more in India.

Surprisingly, in just two years, the Indian R&D Centres of Bell Laboratories, the world's largest research organisation, filed more patents than the US Labs. In August 2006, India announced 1,312 applications for drug patents, a record second only to the US. It is 25 per cent higher than Germany which is the third in ranking, and ahead of Britain, Japan, etc.

India, is therefore, now in a leading position of the scientific and financial research revolution. This is also confirmed by the massive market value of IT firms on US stock markets which indicate that the investment community endorses this view. According to current thinking an estimated $356 billion worth of global financial services will relocate to India in the next five years, producing a cost saving of $ 130 billion for top 100 financial service firms.

Apart from R&D and scientific research, Indian commercial research market has further widened to financial and economic research. It has been said that Wall Street is also outsourcing white-collar jobs to India as a reaction to the local scandals, which erupted in 2002 and 2003. Already McKinsey & Co. and AT Kearney Inc., have shifted bulk of their research to India.

J.P.Morgan, Moran Stanley, Deutsche Bank, etc. are all considering the same.

With reference to healthcare tourism in India, McKinsey & Co's forecast that India will earn $2 billion a year by 2012. Peter Dracher has noted that the Indian medical schools in New Delhi are the best in the world. Indian hospitals already treat over 150,000 foreign patients a year and India is emerging as one of the most sought after medical destinations in Asia for offshore patients. The 30 hospitals under the Apollo Group are believed to have over the period treated 60,000 foreigners. Escorts Heart Institute and Research Centre has a large number of foreigners coming in every year looking for high quality cardiac care. The cost of treatment and surgery is 25 per cent that of the UK.

In more fundamental research, Mosanto has set up a massive R&D facility within the Indian Institute of Science, Bangalore. Indian biotech firm, Shanta Biotechnics, stunned the scientific community with r-DNA based hepatitis vaccine. Work on genetically modified food is going on full swing in India. The Institute of Genomics and Integrative Biology (IGIB), based in New Delhi, has discovered these new genes of SARS virus.

The biggest company in the world—General Electricals—has announced that their R&D centre at Bangalore will take up 30 projects underway in the US. Oracle, the famous software company has 7,000 employees in India, mostly engineers.

As *Business Week* has reported, 'Unlike China, India's significant cheap labour is not a pool of factory workers, but a huge crop of scientists'. In the same view, Singapore Prime Minister has reportedly stated that while China has become the world's factory floor, India has become its IT and back office! However, China lags behind India in the global market for IT. According to analysts the world's outsourcing business is currently about US$ 20 billion and India holds about 90 per cent of it while China earns only $ 600 million. But this should not lead to complacency.

Now, sixty years after independence, still India is again at the crossroads. With a large population still under the poverty line, and a very large number of illiterates, school education, both primary and secondary, is inadequate considering the entire population. The dichotomy lies in the fact that we also have the largest pool of scientific and knowledge workers. We produce 400,000 engineers a year compared to around 60,000 in USA. We have had great success in entering the service sector through new communication technology for not only low-end backroom service work, but also top end R&D.

We have to grow the present advantage to our advantage. Our unique selling point is the pool of skilled manpower, which we need to continue to grow to maintain our competitive edge. Further, Bangalore may have come up as a rival to Silicon Valley, but it is congested and wages and attrition rates are rising. We need to develop another twenty Bangalores in locations which are cheaper. We can only do this when our supply of skilled manpower continues to grow, keeping wages stable and moving more and more Indians into the mainstream of economic growth.

Mainstreaming India

India today is definitely on par with the top knowledge economies of the world. Extensive fundamental and applied research is being undertaken here. The world's biggest multinational companies are not only opening their backroom offices, but also their R&D centres in India. This trend is apparent not just in software development but in other sectors as well, such as the financial sector, medical sector, biotech and others. By mid-1990s, almost 180 of Fortune 500 companies were outsourcing to India.

World famous names like Citicorp, Honeywell, Motorola, Sprint, Oracle, Digital Equipment, Verizon, Huges, Duet Technologies, Cisco Systems, Texas Instruments, Computer Associates, Pentafour, Eco Soft, British Telecom, SAP, Philips, Siemens, Yahoo, Google, Accenture, Sun Microsystems, Ericsson, IBM, 12 Technologies, HP, Intel, Microsoft, Nortel, etc., have all set up R&D facilities in India or have tied up with Indian companies or academic or research institutions. The cost advantage for higher research is huge. An Indian chip design engineer costs Rs. 13.5 lakh a year compared to Rs 67–90 lakh in the US.

At the India Today Conclave 20051, Professor Jagdish Bhagwati, eminent International Trade Economist of Colombia University, stated that with the high level of skilled diaspora, which grew up at the expense of Indian exchequer, the Brain Drain template has been discarded and we no longer think of skilled migration as a threat. However, it is, he further stated that skilled Indian Diaspora is huge and growing. Indians are next only to the Jews in affluence as the richest ethnic minority in the US. He then introduced the concept of 'Trojan Horse'.

The main advantage is that with people of Indian origin will hold offices in critical decision-making capacities in the US and other developed countries increasing the market acceptability for outsourcing to India. Further, this is done by both ethnic Indians and other nationalities, who see Indians doing well in their countries. It is, therefore, to India's advantage to supply skilled manpower to the West as well as develop our own knowledge-based economy.

In order to be capable of continuing support to such a large influx of R&D, and backroom office functions from the world's service sector, we need to gear up our higher education institutions to meet the growing demand for qualified persons.

India has been fortunate to offer to the world a pool of skilled, scientific, English-speaking manpower immediately after the communication boom through development of Internet and satellite communications.

At a time when India's higher education policy was under attack from the traditional advocates of the concept that 'over-education' leads to educated unemployment, this came as a happy and welcome development. Converting this liability to our advantage through development of new communication technology has been a triumph to reckon with.

As India grows into a knowledge-providing superpower, we need to provide a steady supply of quality knowledge workers with the requisite qualifications.

India has an unprecedented opportunity to become the backbone to global enterprises by delivering 'end solutions'. This is based on a study *Beyond Cost Reduction: Risks & Rewards of Services Sourcing,* conducted by H. Wadhwa and Harpreet Khurana at the Columbia Business School. The study provides an idea about the potential of 'Knowledge hubbing' out of India. However, as more high-end processes are outsourced to India, attrition at India centres is becoming an increasing problem. This is a manifestation of the shortage of quality skilled manpower availability in India. Unless the issues involved in providing higher education and increasing its accessibility, especially in subjects and areas where it is required most are tackled seriously, we will fall behind and lose our lead.

NASSCOM President, Kiran Karnik, says that Indians have neglected certain disciplines like econometrics and operations research. Many brighter students are moving away and we need to bring them back. The growing knowledge process outsourcing provides service on research on subjects such as intellectual property, financial analyses, business and market in telecom, pharmaceutical, automotive and financial service sectors.

The World Bank in its latest report 'India and the Knowledge Economy; Leveraging Strength and Opportunities' has concluded that India has made enormous strides in its economic and social development in the past two decades, but it can do much more to leverage its strengths in today's knowledge based global economy.

With the right kind of government policy incentives, the country can increase its economic productivity and the well being of its population by making effective use of its knowledge. It needs to make its education more 'demand driven' to meet the emerging needs of the economy and to keep its highly qualified people within the country.

This means upgrading the quality of all higher education institutions, not just a few world class ones like the IITs. In order to make education demand driven we need to allow private sector to enter higher education by loosening bureaucratic holds and putting an accreditation system in place for private providers of both higher education and vocational training. This will also involve university and industry participation, which is currently lacking. Dependence on distance learning technologies needs to be increased substantially.

India needs to maintain and enhance its competitive advantage of abundant, high quality and cost effective human resources. It needs to ensure the right mix of technical, business and functional skills in the work place to meet the needs of individual business segments. Indian software companies are now increasingly concerned over brain-drain, since there is now substantial internal demand to be met. It has been felt that India may not be able to produce enough number of good engineers and IT professionals to meet the expected growth in IT in the coming years.

Therefore, there is a need for rapid expansion of suitable training opportunities at home. Fortunately for India many private IT training institutes are offering focused training to young professionals such as NIIT and the Internet Training Centre Initiative for Developing Countries, developed by ITU and CISCO Systems. India, therefore, cannot afford to be complacent about its current position in the Global IT market, and needs to revamp its higher education and technical training.

India would soon lose its competitive edge unless it increased its pool of trained manpower in requisite skills and keep the wages down. In fact there is a fear that some BPO centres might close down in India due to poor turnover, higher attrition rate and even higher wages than some other countries. Brightview, an Internet service provider, is shifting its operations to South Africa. Grupo Santander of Spain, owners of Abbey National Bank of UK, view their India operations as costly failure because of 'language difficulties'. This is likely to have an impact on other companies as well.

In contrast to the policy environment within which we are functioning, our competitor governments are clearly taking much more active interest in catching up with the crest in the knowledge sector growth curve. China has reportedly decided to set up dozens of IIT-like engineering schools and 20 Harvard-like universities. India remains suspicious of foreign universities and resents their intrusion into the country. This needs liberating education from the clutches of government control.

References

Blackwell, Fritz, *India: A Global Studies Handbook,* United States of America: ABC-CLIO, Inc., 2004.

Elder, Joseph W., "Caste System", *Encyclopedia of India (vol. 1)* edited by Stanley Wolpert, 223-229, Thomson Gale, 2006.

Suri R.K., Kalapana Rajaram, "Infrastructure: S&T Education", *Science and Technology in India,* Spectrum, New Delhi, 2008.

Prabhu, Joseph, "Educational Institutions and Philosophies, Traditional and Modern", *Encyclopedia of India (vol. 2)* edited by Stanley Wolpert, 23–28, Thomson Gale, 2006.

Setty, E.D. and Ross, E.L., "A Case Study in Applied Education in Rural India", *Community Development Journal,* 22 (2): 120–129, Oxford University Press, 1987.

Sripati, V. and Thiruvengadam, A.K., "India: Constitutional Amendment Making The Right to Education a Fundamental Right", *International Journal of Constitutional Law,* 2 (1): 148–158, Oxford University Press, 2004.

Vrat, Prem, "Indian Institutes of Technology", *Encyclopedia of India (vol. 2)* edited by Stanley Wolpert, 229-231, Thomson Gale, 2006.

2. ROLE OF ICTS IN HIGHER EDUCATION

The power of information technology has been greatly enhanced by communication technology. Hence, connectivity (through wireless, cell phone technology or over cables) is the crucial feature that allows access to the internet and the World Wide Web. These common platforms have stimulated an explosion of social software and cloud services that have made the internet a highly interactive medium and created new dynamics in computer use. As computing power and communications have grown mobile devices play an increasingly important role, notably in the developing world.

While computing power continues to increase in speed costs are being driven down, thus allowing computer users to operate more complex programmes and graphic-rich applications. These improvements, coupled with the expansion of broadband internet connections, facilitate richer entertainment and learning environments, including virtual worlds and an increasing use of internet telephony and video-conferencing. Connectivity that only a few years ago regularly used dial-up connections over hard-wired telephone lines has been rapidly moving over to coaxial cable connections in industrialised countries and to 3G connections via cellular networks in both industrialised and developing countries.

The constant expansion of the availability of computers and access to the internet has boomed the availability of cloud computing. Cloud computing, or the provision of services online to computer users, includes services such as folders for data and a host of programmes that exist on the internet which can used by users from any internet-connected computer. Those interested in harnessing ICTs for development focused more on getting personal computers into the hands of learners around the world.

Meanwhile, students are using mobile technology liberally for personal purposes, while their instructors have little idea of how the technology could be applied to improve teaching and learning.

Today's students adopt a different approach and use technologies like cell phones and computers with which their teachers (digital immigrants) still need to come to terms. Educators need to know more about the virtual worlds that their students move in so that they can better understand how to interact with them in ways that make sense to digital natives. It is remarkable that cloud services have started to become truly useful and show potential for freeing users from having to own their own computer. With cloud computing, users are able to save a document on a computer in a computer lab, edit it from their internet-enabled cell phone, format it on their home computer and publish it to the internet for public viewing or sharing with their class.

The potential for hand-held devices have made computing truly portable by inventing improved touch-sensitive screens that help to predict what the user is typing on the small screens, communicate wirelessly with the internet, transmit data wirelessly to printers and other people devices. Synchronising via the cloud and directly with other devices and computers now enable these devices to be linked effectively between computers where they are available.

This technology often called social networking, has allowed people to meet, interact and share ideas and interests with one another. These applications have become popular and have already made in roads into informal learning settings. Now there is considerable interest in the use of social networking in formal education, especially in open and distance learning.

With growing interest in social dimensions of learning the institutions have adopted virtual learning environments (VLEs), which incorporate collaboration and communication tools such as wikis, blogs, forums and chat.

More recently, publicly available web-based social networking tools such as Facebook, GoogleDocs, Delicious, and Flickr have also been adopted in teaching and learning. Since 2004 the Virtual University for the Small States of the Commonwealth has been developing course materials using a combination of face-to-face and cloud computing approaches, allowing them to engage with each other despite the vast distances between them.

There has been intense competition in some Higher Educational Institutions (HEIs) between Free Open Source Software (FOSS) and proprietary software each side presenting this as an all-or-nothing choice, but the sensible approach is to use what is appropriate when it is appropriate. Free software is not free to run (free is used as in 'free speech' rather than 'free beer') and proprietary software may be suitable, but too expensive to buy there should be a total cost review of ownership calculation, including the cost of servers, programming and IT support staff time, when comparing the suitability of software. The ability to integrate data usage between multiple computer programmes without having to re-write the programming is important.

ICTs in Education

Today education uses computers in teaching rather than earlier audio-visual media. This is because the strength of computers is their power to manipulate words and symbols—which is at the heart of the academic endeavour. There is a trend to introduce e-learning or online learning both in courses taught on campus and in distance learning. Whether e-learning improves quality or reduce cost depends on the particular circumstances. ICTs in general and e-learning in particular have reduced the barriers to entry to the higher education business. ICTs should be introduced in a systematic manner that brings clarity to the business model through cost-benefit analyses.

With the intent of becoming learning societies built on knowledge, higher education has a signal role to play in development strategies in the pursuit of such aspirations. No knowledge economy can function without ICTs. Therefore, it is imperative that higher education institutions afford their graduates the literacy and competencies that their future work environments are likely to demand of them. Furthermore, being ICT-rich gives an HEI a competitive advantage in recruiting students.

In many countries, demand for higher education far outstrips supply, and governments and institutions are turning more and more to the use of ICTs to bridge the access gap.

Impact of ICTs on Teaching

Conventional teaching has emphasised content. For many years course have been written around textbooks. Teachers have taught through lectures and presentations interspersed with tutorials and learning activities designed to consolidate and rehearse the content. Contemporary settings are now favouring curricula that promote competency and performance. Curricula are starting to emphasise capabilities and to be concerned more with *how* the information will be used than with *what* the information is.

The moves to competency and performance-based curricula are well supported and encouraged by emerging instructional technologies. Such curricula tend to require:

i) access to a variety of information sources;
ii) access to a variety of information forms and types;
iii) student-centred learning settings based on information access and inquiry;
iv) learning environments centred on problem-centred and inquiry-based activities;
v) authentic settings and examples; and
vi) teachers as coaches and mentors rather than content experts.

Contemporary ICTs are able to provide strong support for all these requirements and there are now many outstanding examples of world class settings for competency and performance-based curricula that make sound use of the affordances of these technologies. For many years, teachers wishing to adopt such curricula have been limited by their resources and tools but with the proliferation and widespread availability of contemporary ICTs, many restrictions and impediments of the past have been removed. And new technologies will continue to drive these forms of learning further. As students and teachers gain access to higher bandwidths, more direct forms of communication and access to sharable resources, the capability to support these quality learning settings will continue to grow.

Another way in which emerging ICTs are impacting on the content of education curricula stems from the ways in which ICTs are dominating so much of contemporary life and work. Already there has emerged a need for educational institutions to ensure that graduates are able to display appropriate levels of information literacy, "the capacity to identify and issue and then to identify, locate and evaluate relevant information in order to engage with it or to solve a problem arising from it". The drive to promote such developments stems from general moves among institutions to ensure their graduates demonstrate not only skills and knowledge in their subject domains but also general attributes and generic skills. Traditionally generic skills have involved such capabilities as an ability to reason formally, to solve problems, to communicate effectively, to be able to negotiate outcomes, to manage time, project management, and collaboration and teamwork skills. The growing use of ICTs as tools of every day life have seen the pool of generic skills expanded in recent years to include information literacy and it is highly probable that future developments and technology applications will see this set of skills growing even more.

Impact of ICT on Learning

Just as technology is influencing and supporting what is being learned in schools and universities, so too is it supporting changes to the way students are learning. Moves from content-centred curricula to competency-based curricula are associated with moves away from teacher-centred forms of delivery to student-centred forms. Through technology-facilitated approaches, contemporary learning settings now encourage students to take responsibility for their own learning .In the past students have become very comfortable to learning through transmissive modes. Students have been trained to let others present to them the information that forms the curriculum. The growing use of ICT as an instructional medium is changing and will likely continue to change many of the strategies employed by both teachers and students in the learning process.

Student-centred learning

Technology has the capacity to promote and encourage the transformation of education from a very teacher directed enterprise to one which supports more student-centred models. Evidence of this today is manifested in:

i) The proliferation of capability, competency and outcomes focused curricula.

ii) Moves towards problem-based learning.

iii) Increased use of the web as an information source, internet users are able to choose the experts from whom they will learn The use of ICT in educational settings, by itself acts as a catalyst for change in this domain. ICTs by their very nature are tools that encourage and support independent learning. Students using ICTs for learning purposes become immersed in the process of learning and as more and more students use computers as information sources and cognitive tools, the influence of the technology on supporting how students learn will continue to increase.

Supporting knowledge construction

The emergence of ICTs as learning technologies has coincided with a growing awareness and recognition of alternative theories for learning. The theories of learning that hold the greatest sway today are those based on constructivist principles. These principles posit that learning is achieved by the active construction of knowledge supported by various perspectives within meaningful contexts. In constructivist theories, social interactions are seen to play a critical role in the processes of learning and cognition. In the past, the conventional process of teaching has revolved around teachers planning and leading students through a series of instructional sequences to achieve a desired learning outcome. Typically these forms of teaching have revolved around the planned transmission of a body of knowledge followed by some forms of interaction with the content as a means to consolidate the knowledge acquisition. Contemporary learning theory is based on the notion that learning is an active process of constructing knowledge rather than acquiring knowledge and that instruction is the process by which this knowledge construction is supported rather than a process of knowledge transmission.

The strengths of constructivism lie in its emphasis on learning as a process of personal understanding and the development of meaning in ways which are active and interpretative. In this domain learning is viewed as the construction of meaning rather than as the memorisation of facts. Learning approaches using contemporary ICTs provide many opportunities for constructivist learning through their provision and support for resource-based, student centered settings and by enabling learning to be related to context and to practice. Any use of ICT in learning settings can act to support various aspects of knowledge construction and as more and more students employ ICTs in their learning processes, the more pronounced the impact of this will become.

Any place learning

The concept of flexibility in the delivery place of educational programmes is not new. Educational institutions have been offering programmes at a distance for many years and there has been a vast amount of research and development associated with establishing effective practices and procedures in off-campus teaching and learning. Use of the technology, however, has extended the scope of this activity and whereas previously off-campus delivery was an option for students who were unable to attend campuses, today, many more students are able to make this choice through technology-facilitated learning settings. The scope and extent of this activity is demonstrated in some of the examples below.

In many instances traditional classroom learning has given way to learning in work-based settings with students able to access courses and programmes from their workplace. The advantages of education and training at the point of need relate not only to convenience but include cost savings associated with travel and time away from work, and also situation and application of the learning activities within relevant and meaningful contexts.

The communications capabilities of modern technologies provide opportunities for many learners to enrol in courses offered by external institutions rather than those situated locally. These opportunities provide such advantages as extended course offerings and eclectic class cohorts comprised of students of differing backgrounds, cultures and perspectives.

The freedoms of choice provided by programmes that can be accessed at any place are also supporting the delivery of programmes with units and courses from a variety of institutions,

There are now countless ways for students completing undergraduate degrees for example, to study units for a single degree, through a number of different institutions, an activity that provides considerable diversity and choice for students in the programmes they complete.

Anytime learning

In concert with geographical flexibility, technology-facilitated educational programmes also remove many of the temporal constraints that face learners with special needs. Students are starting to appreciate the capability to undertake education anywhere, anytime and any place. This flexibility has heightened the availability of just-in-time learning and provided learning opportunities for many more learners who previously were constrained by other commitments.

Through online technologies learning has become an activity that is no longer set within programmed schedules and slots. Learners are free to participate in learning activities when time permits and these freedoms have greatly increased the opportunities for many students to participate in formal programmes.

The wide variety of technologies that support learning are able to provide asynchronous supports for learning so that the need for real-time participation can be avoided while the advantages of communication and collaboration with other learners is retained.

As well as learning at anytime, teachers are also finding the capabilities of teaching at any time to be opportunistic and able to be used to advantage. Mobile technologies and seamless communications technologies support 24×7 teaching and learning. Choosing how much time will be used within the 24×7 envelope and what periods of time are challenges that will face the educators of the future.

The continued and increased use of ICTs in education in years to come, will serve to increase the temporal and geographical opportunities that are currently experienced. Advancements in learning opportunities tend to be held back by the ICT capabilities of the lowest common denominator, namely the students with the least access to ICT. As ICT access increases among students so too will these opportunities.

Benefits and Challenges

Adapting to various changing learning and course management systems is useful in generating and managing a variety of student support services and products, such as course outlines, digitally recorded classroom material, discussion groups, laboratory manuals and lab assignments, lecture notes, live lectures for later viewing and reviewing, links to course specific websites, online tutorials, supplementary readings, and virtual office hours for teacher-student consultations. Virtual libraries, wherever they exist, are especially useful to students as they reduce costs of acquiring expensive textbooks, journals and reference material. Tools are also now available on the internet to assist both teachers and students to manage writing assignments to detect and avoid the pitfalls of plagiarism and copyright violations.

ICTs in teaching is beneficial by way of quality and quantity of educational provision. While using ICTs in teaching has some obvious benefits, ICTs also bring challenges. The high cost of acquiring, installing, operating, maintaining and replacing ICTs are some drawbacks. While potentially of great importance, the integration of ICTs into teaching is still in its infancy and in developing countries it has a particularly high opportunity cost because installing them is usually more expensive in absolute terms than in industrialised countries whereas, in contrast, alternative investments (e.g., buildings) are relatively less costly.

Institutions with inexperience in procuring institution-wide hardware and software and attendant services may end up with wares that are outdated and subject to unworkable but binding supplier contracts. Using unlicensed software can be very problematic, not only legally but in the costs of maintenance, particularly if the pirated software varies in standard formats. Also lack of capacity in equipment maintenance can pose serious implementation problems. Clear policies and procedures for procuring computer hardware and software are necessary to tide over such problems.

A related issue is the readiness of students to learn online. Limited ICT resources may cause institutions to put their energies into making their students ICT literate as a foundation step but the lack of enhanced teaching methods may lead to inferior learning outcomes for students.

INTRODUCING E-LEARNING

Fearing that the introduction of e-learning in education would transform the organisation and delivery of higher education, it prompted significant investments in starting up new virtual universities. However, generally these virtual universities and e-learning experiences have failed to sustain the desired levels and are unable to survive without massive government support. In its 2005 report, the OECD concluded that ICT in higher education had more impact on administrative services than on teaching. The reports attributed the failure of e-learning to its inability to be relevant to local needs and cultures.

E-learning/online education need not discontinue but requires a re-conceptualisation so that it achieves the required balance. On the one hand it must recognise the importance of the effective interaction of students with content, fellow students and teachers/tutors during the learning process. On the other hand, if it is not to increase institutional costs there must be some substitution of capital for labour, as occurs in traditional open and distance learning (ODL). For this reason HEIs that already operate through ODL (e.g. open universities) can more easily introduce e-learning cost-effectively than those that try to introduce it onto classroom teaching.

There must be a paradigm shift from an emphasis on stand-alone courses and resource-based learning to a process that promotes interaction, communication, collaboration and construction. However, the economic success of e-learning must be based on a learning system that cuts costs through specialisation and division of labour. Introducing e-learning without increasing institutional costs is a serious challenge, particularly for public institutions.

Need for Generating Policies

In response to increased demand for higher education, many countries are witnessing the mushrooming of higher education institutions, both private and public. Nationally, where the infrastructure exists, many institutions working together could tap into an ICT network to facilitate collaboration and sharing to cut down on costs and optimise the returns gained in the use of ICTs. UNESCO Bangkok has developed an *ICT-in-Education*

Toolkit that governments can use in drafting ICT policies in education.

Besides enabling telecommunications and ICT policies, governments and higher education institutions will need to develop strategies for effective ICT and media deployment and sustainability. The radio for instance, is a relatively less costly medium that has not been fully exploited in some jurisdictions for educational purposes is the radio. Recognising the potential reach of this medium, 27 tertiary education institutions in Nigeria have received government licences to operate *campus radios* for teaching, research and entertainment.

Institutions must first set up training workshops in the areas of ICT procurement, contracting and the total cost of owning particular systems, which includes acquisition, installation, power supply, maintenance, allied material and equipment, replacement, training, recycling, etc. Such training should have a technology plan that includes long-term budgeting or funding scenarios, acquisition, maintenance, replacement and possible sharing, at least coordination, of ICT usage with other institutions. In developing internal capacity in the use of ICT in teaching, learning, and research, teachers need to be involved in designing particular ICT initiatives to ensure their relevance and effectiveness. It would be prudent to test the efficacy of a technology at, say, the departmental level before deploying it institution-wide. Such piloting, if successful, will reassure institutional policy-makers of the soundness of the technology in facilitating improved teaching and, on the part of students, more and better learning outcomes. But this must not lead to each department adopting its own IT solutions as students appreciate having some consistency in the platforms (say for e-learning) that they will find in different parts of the HEI.

Drawbacks

The most common drawbacks in introducing ICTs into teaching are:

i) installing learning technology without reviewing student needs and content availability;

ii) imposing technological systems from the top down without involving faculty and students;

iii) using inappropriate content from other regions of the world without customising it appropriately; and

iv) producing low quality content that has poor instructional design and is not adapted to the technology in use.

Serious consideration should be given to content preparation before deciding on the most appropriate way to deliver it to students so that it fosters more and better learning. Institutional policies and procedures for adopting and adapting technology must be in place and faculty and students involved in at least assessing content *vis-a-vis* the technological mode to deliver it. Training should be introduced to ensure that the implications of technology adoption and use are clearly understood and accounted for in short and long-term planning.

A new dynamic is that institutions are adopting cloud services which are of three basic kinds:

i) free social software;

ii) free online services; and,

iii) subscription online services.

Subscription services may sometimes represent good value because users can buy only what they need without having to run and maintain their own servers.

Promise of Open Educational Resources

Open Educational Resources (OERs) are educational materials and resources offered freely and openly for anyone to use and under some licenses to re-mix, improve and redistribute. In Africa, for example, one of the most successful collections of OERs are those developed and disseminated by the Teacher Education in Sub-Saharan Africa (TESSA) Consortium. It has 18 member institutions in nine African countries. TESSA has developed a wide variety of audio and text materials that provide support to primary school teachers and teacher educators in Africa. MIT's Open Courseware project and the UK Open University's OpenLearn site are the best known examples of open content in higher education in the industrialised world.

Worldwide, OERs have great potential for improving the cost-effectiveness of e-learning, since the creation of high quality courses is a costly process. However, institutions that specialise in eLearning, such as the Asian e-University, now find that most of the quality content that they need is already available as an OER somewhere, and all they need do is find it and adapt it to their own context and needs. However, they should develop appropriate policies and train their staff about the related technical, pedagogical and legal issues if to take full advantage of OERs.

ICTs for Promotion of Education for All

Information and Communication technologies have opened up a whole range of facilities to burden one's horizon of learning, especially in the higher education sector. The Jomtien Conference on 'Education for All' focused on the following six objectives to be achieved by the participant countries:

i) Widening the scope of early childhood care and development activities;

ii) Universal primary education by the year 2000;

iii) Improvement in learning achievement;

vi) Reduction of adult illiteracy rate to one-half its 1990 level by the year 2000, with sufficient emphasis on female literacy;

v) Expansion of provisions of basic education and training in other essential skills required by youth and adults; and

vi) Increased acquisition by individuals and families of the knowledge, skills and values required for better living, and sound and sustainable development.

UNESCO and UTLP adopted a broad concept of basic education including adult education with literacy and non-formal alternatives to schooling. The Conference also identified four principal requirements for achieving the above objectives which are:

i) Developing a supportive policy context;

ii) Mobilising resources;

iii) Building national technical capacity; and

iv) Strengthening international solidarity.

None of the objectives have been achieved in full because of the failure to meet these requirements, yet progress has nevertheless been made at least in the following six ways:

i) Remarkable growth in achieving enrolment, and participation targets for basic education at all levels of education including early childhood care and education;

ii) Large reductions in some countries in inequities, notably in the area of gender, disability and ethnic minorities;

iii) Large reductions in a small number of countries in volumes and/or rates of adult illiteracy;

iv) Better policies, frameworks, legislation and resources in several countries to pursue one or more of the EFA target directions;

v) Greater involvement of non-government organisations, community groups and parents in decision making, action programmes and the use of child care and education facilities;

vi) Significant improvements in educational information and in analytic and evaluative capacity.

Achieving Education for All

Higher education is determines to a large extent the state of the education system of the country, especially its quality. The World Conference on Higher Education in its Article 1 proclaimed as one of the missions and functions of higher education "to contribute to the development and improvement of education at all levels, including through training of teachers."

Achieving education for all should therefore be one of the goals of the higher education system. However, in reality higher education has been involved mainly with human resource development for the modern economic sector, serving the elites of the society and producing elites. Institutions of higher education (IHEs) in developing countries have mostly kept to their traditional functions and objectives. It has hardly concerned itself with other levels and types of education except through some *ad hoc* individual efforts without any institutional mechanism. Paradoxically, the foundation for education has been ignored making the whole education system weak and fragile.

Higher education has an important role to play through its graduates and postgraduates who should provide leadership roles in education as researchers, teachers, consultants and managers, who should create and apply new knowledge and innovations, and who should provide analytical perspectives on development problems and service to public and private sectors.

Higher education through its research training and service programmes, could contribute to build national technical capacity and contribute to strengthening international solidarity. In particular, to promote basic education for all, could improve access and equity in basic education, its quality and relevance, and improve its efficiency and management. However, it must be remembered that even for higher education to be successful in undertaking the above tasks, a supportive policy context for itself is needed. This would call for extensive and intensive reform in higher education. The role of higher education has to be developmental and transformative instead training individuals for the labour market. As such its management has to be improved so that it can function efficiently with, at least, minimum basic resources. The development of basic education and literacy should be an explicitly recognised function of higher education as instruction, research and public service. An institutional framework for the development of basic education is essential within the institutions of higher education.

Learning through ICTs

We take the same broad definition of ICT to include radio, television, satellite, fixed and mobile telephone, fax, computers and CD-ROMs and the internet, as used by DFID. The ICTs can be divided into two groups: traditional or old ICTs (namely, radio and TV) and the new ICTs. Learning through new ICTs is also called e-learning. Recent studies show the enormous potential of e-learning, especially in industrialised countries.

Learning materials and syllabi for all courses were being put on the internet for anyone to use—recognising the power of the internet and that knowledge is for sharing. E-learning has the following advantages:

i) Access to the learning programme any time convenient to the learner.
ii) Learners can be at any place to log on.
iii) Asynchronous interaction providing participants and tutors with time to prepare their responses leading to succinct and to-the-point interaction and on-track, thoughtful and creative conversations.

iv) Group sessions creating shared electronic conversations which can be more thoughtful and permanent than voice conversation. Aided by group coordinators, these sessions can be powerful for learning and problem solving.

v) New educational approaches can be used. For example, faculty from anywhere in the world, faculty teams with different specialities can be put together and innovations of teachers can be shared among themselves for improvement and adaptation.

vi) Recently developed intelligent computer-assisted instruction (ICAI) programmes are able to generate and solve problems, diagnose students' misconceptions, select appropriate teaching strategies and carry on dialogues with students based on in-depth studies by researchers on how people think, learn and solve problems.

Unfortunately these advantages are beyond the realms of most developing countries, where power and telecommunication facilities are poor, where resources and well trained teachers are scarce and where television and other forms of distance education cost more. One has to look for alternatives while being watchful not to 'miss the bus' with the new ICTs.

There are four ways ICTs can support basic education:

i) Supporting education in schools,

ii) Providing non-formal education for out-of-school children and adults,

iii) Supporting pre-service distance education of teachers and their in-service professional development, and

iv) Enhancing the management of schools.

Supporting education in schools

ICTs can provide access to information sources, enable communications, create interacting learning environment and promote change in the methods of teaching with improvement in quality and access to up-to-date and relevant materials there will been offsetting some costs of textbooks. However, the improvement in quality resulting from the new ICTs is yet to be justified with the cost in developing countries. Radio continues to be still the most cost-effective ICT for enhancing quality in school education. However, with the falling cost of hardware, maintenance and internet access, and increasing extension of telecommunications and power infrastructure, it is expected that the benefits of using new technology in the schools of developing countries will exceed the costs.

Supporting non-formal education for out-of-school children and adults

Empirical evidence demonstrates that radio and television, the traditional ICTs, are cost-effective means to reach out-of-school children and adults in the regions of conflict and for refugees. For who cannot go to school for remoteness and/or for opportunity costs, radio and television are more likely to widen access than the new ICTs which may not be available to them. However, basic education is more successful when delivered in the mother tongue and traditional ICTs may be less economic because of the small number of learners. The possibility of two-way communications with new ICTs makes them more attractive where the target group have easy access to them, for example, in peri-urban areas.

Supporting pre- and in-service teacher education

There is a high demand for teacher which necessitates the rapid supply of trained teachers. Distance education of teachers is an essential medium to achieve education for all. Radio and television still remain popular means because of low costs. However, teacher education availing of new ICTs are increasingly becoming popular because of the possibilities of the 'multiplier effect', greater interactivity between students and tutor, opportunities for learners to proceed at their own pace, at any place and at any time, the possibilities of combining video, audio and texts to improve delivery and quality of instruction, and finally the possibilities of establishing teacher resource centres with access to power and telecommunications equipped with computers and internet facilities.

Enhancing educational management

New ICTs are more useful in this field. Computer software programmes are being used in timetabling and school management to improve the use of staff time, student time and space, thus reducing costs significantly. This requires only a few computers and hence ICTs in schools can improve quality with less cost. Old ICTs are still cost-effective for provision of education to out-of-school children and youth in developing countries. New ICTs have a very large potential for teacher education in larger quantity and better quality. A combination of old ICTs to widen coverage and access to new ICTs to provide interactivity can be cost-effective for teacher education. If a nationwide network of community learning centres equipped with computer laboratories with broadband access and trained staff to access online distance learning and to provide tutoring support could be set up in developing countries until a computer is available at home, there are possibilities for these countries to take advantage of the benefits of e-learning.

ICTs for Enhancing Educational Quality and Accessibility

India in recent decades has been focusing on the development of its educational sector. Higher education drives the competitiveness and employment generation in India. However, the overall state of higher education is dismal in the country. There is a severe constraint on the availability of skilled labour. There exist socio-economic, cultural, time and geographical barriers for people who wish to pursue higher education. Innovative use of ICT can potentially solve this problem.

Economic and social development in any country depends on good education of the citizens of a nation. Therefore it is necessary to find ways to make education of good quality, accessible and affordable to all, using the latest technology available. In the last two decades there has been a rapid development of ICT. ICT has changed the dynamics of various industries as well as influenced the way people interact and work in the society. Internet usage in home and workplace has grown exponentially. ICT has the potential to remove the hurdles that are causing the problems of low rate of education in any country. It can be used as a tool to overcome the issues of cost, less number of teachers, and poor quality of education as well as to overcome time and distance barriers.

India with its billion-plus population and a high proportion of the young has a large formal education system. The demand for education in developing countries like India has skyrocketed as education is still regarded as an important bridge of social, economic and political mobility.

The challenges before the education system in India can be said to be of the following nature:

i) *Access to education:* There are infrastructure, socio-economic, linguistic and physical barriers in India that deny people who wish access to education.

ii) *Quality of education:* This includes infrastructure, teacher and the processes quality.

iii) *Resources allocated:* Central and state governments reserve about 3.5 per cent of GDP for education as compared to the 6 per cent that has been aimed.

There exist drawbacks in general education in India as well as all over the world like lack of learning materials, teachers, remoteness of education facilities, high dropout rate, etc. Thus, the participation rates of the Indian population in education, and especially in higher education, are quite low.

In the current information society, people have to access knowledge via ICT to keep pace with the latest developments. In such a scenario, education, which always plays a critical role in any economic and social growth of a country, becomes even more important. Education increases the productive skills of the individual and also his earning power. The various kinds of ICT products available and having relevance to education, such as tele-conferencing, e-mail, audio conferencing, television lessons, radio broadcasts, interactive radio counselling, interactive voice response system, audio cassettes and CD-ROMs, etc., have been used in education for different purposes.

Today ICTs, include laptops wirelessly connected to the internet, personal digital assistants, low cost video cameras, and cell phones. All these have become affordable, accessible and integrated in large sections of the society throughout the world. It can restructure organisations, promote collaboration, increase democratic participation of citizens, improve the transparency and responsiveness of governmental agencies, make education and health care more widely available, foster cultural creativity, and enhance the development in social integration.

ICT can be used as a tool in the process of education in the following ways:

i) *Informative tool:* It provides a vast amount of data in various formats such as audio, video, documents.

ii) *Situating tool:* It creates situations, which the student experiences in real life. Thus, simulation and virtual reality is possible.

iii) *Constructive tool:* It manipulates the data and generates analysis.

iv) *Communicative tool:* It can be used to remove communication barriers such as that of space and time.

The following mediums are used for the delivery and for conducting the education process:

i) *Voice:* Instructional audio tools that include interactive technologies as well as the passive ones.

ii) *Video:* Instructional video tools that include still images, prerecorded moving images, and real-time moving images combined with audio conferencing.

iii) *Print:* Instructional print formats that include textbooks, study guides, workbooks and case studies..

The creation of digital resources like digital libraries allow the students, teachers and professionals to access research material and course material from any place at any time. Such facilities allow the networking of academics and researchers and hence sharing of scholarly material. This avoids duplication of work.

ICT used in education develops higher order skills such as collaborating across time and place and solving complex real world problems. It improves the perception and learning skills of the student. Thus, ICT can be used to prepare the workforce for the information society and the new global economy.

The web and the internet are the core ICTs to spread education through e-learning. The components include e-portfolios, cyber infrastructures, digital libraries and online learning object repositories. All the above components create a digital identity of the student and connect all the stakeholders in the education. It also facilitates interdisciplinary research.

Many teachers, who are early innovators, state that the use of ICT is motivating for the students as well as for the teachers themselves. The use of ICT can improve performance, teaching, administration, and develop relevant skills in the disadvantaged communities. It also improves the quality of education by facilitating learning by doing, real time conversation, delayed time conversation, directed instruction, self-learning, problem-solving, information seeking and analysis, and critical thinking, as well as the ability to communicate, collaborate and learn.

ICTs also provide a platform for sharing information and knowledge, and for the betterment of programme delivery in terms of replication of best practices. It also helps researchers by provision of information, networking, online journals, libraries and data. The possibility of real time interaction in all the different aspects of the education system like teaching, collaboration, debates, etc., hold great promise for the future.

Investing in an ICT experience contributes mainly to increasing human and knowledge capital, which benefits the industry as well. In addition, investment in production of ICT is a more effective tool for development of the whole society as technology can support pedagogical, curricular, and assessment reforms, which intend to support the process of knowledge creation. Students and teachers plan their learning activities and build on each other's ideas to create new knowledge. It also facilitates monitoring of their progress in understanding and preparation for lifelong learning and participation in the information society. Besides being cost effective, ICT is most effective in tackling problems like expanding number of students in each class.

ICT-enabled distance education provides environmental benefits, as there is a major reduction in the amount of student travel. Economies of scale in utilisation of the campus site are generated and student housing is not needed which further saves costs. However, the cost of providing distance education depends on several factors, which include: geography and communities targeted, breadth of courses class size the technology used; amount of resources deployed in producing course materials as well as how frequently they are updated.

E-learning allows delivery, dialogue and feedback over the internet, and customisation in terms of content and exams. E-education can provide access to the best practices or knowledge available. It is possible to leverage the online environment to facilitate teaching techniques like role-play across time and distance, and development of scenarios, which can be rarely witnessed in practice. ICT can play a valuable role to monitor and log the progress of the students across time, place and varied activities.

ICT-based education can be expected to provide greater reliability, validity, and efficiency of data collection and greater ease of analysis, evaluation, and interpretation at any educational level. In absence of ICT, most of the responsibility of teaching and learning lies on the teachers. However, with the help of ICT one can transfer the responsibilities to the students so that they can self-manage. It helps to individualise the teaching or guidance method as per the student's need. It also boosts the confidence level and the self-esteem of the students who acquire the ICT skills through the process of being exposed to such kind of learning.

ICT-based registration, evaluation and administration help to link different levels of information and facilitate an overall view of the whole educational set-up, the evaluation and examination of the learning process, and results by the students and the parents in a flexible and convenient way. The globalisation process has also created a large market of offshore students. To reach them, information technology is the only convenient medium, which can offer education as a service. It increases education opportunities substantially and can contribute to mass education.

Emerging Issues

A number of issues have emerged from the uptake of technology whose impacts have yet to be fully explored. These include changes to the makeup of the teacher pool, changes to the profile of who are the learners in our courses and paramount in all of this, changes in the costing and economics of course delivery.

Expanding the Pool of Teachers and Students

In the past, the role of teacher in an educational institution was a role given to only highly qualified people. With technology-facilitated learning, there are now opportunities to extend the teaching pool beyond this specialist set to include many more people. The changing role of the teacher has seen increased opportunities for others to participate in the process including workplace trainers, mentors, specialists from the workplace and others. Through the affordances and capabilities of technology, today we have a much expanded pool of teachers with varying roles able to provide support for learners in a variety of flexible settings. This trend seems set to continue and to grow with new ICT developments and applications. And within this changed pool of teachers will come changed responsibilities and skill sets for future teaching involving high levels of ICT and the need for more facilitative than didactic teaching roles.

In the past, education has been a privilege and an opportunity that often was unavailable to many students whose situation did not fit the mainstream. Through the flexibilities provided by technology, many students who previously were unable to participate in educational activities are now finding opportunities to do so. The pool of students is changing and will continue to change as more and more people who have a need for education and training are able to take advantage of the increased opportunities. Interesting opportunities are now being observed among, for example, school students studying university courses to overcome limitations in their school programmes and workers undertaking courses from their desktops.

Cost of Education

Traditional thinking has always been that technology-facilitated learning would provide economies and efficiencies that would see significant reductions in the costs associated with the delivery of educational programmes. The costs would come from the ability to create courses with fixed establishment costs, for example technology-based courses, and for which there would be savings in delivery through large scale uptake. We have already seen a number of virtual universities built around technology delivery alone. The reality is that few institutions have been able to realise these aims for economy. There appear to have been many underestimated costs in such areas as course development and course delivery.

The costs associated with the development of high quality technology-facilitated learning materials are quite high. It has found to be more than a matter of repackaging existing materials and large scale reengineering has been found to be necessary with large scale costs. Likewise costs associated with delivery have not been found to diminish as expected. The main reason for this has been the need to maintain a relatively stable student to staff ratio and the expectation of students that they will have access to teachers in their courses and programmes. Compared to traditional forms of off-campus learning, technology-facilitated learning has proven to be quite expensive in all areas of consideration, infrastructure, course development and course delivery.

Influence on Stakeholders

While ICTs may not have had a large impact to date, their use will grow to play a significant role in many aspects of the design, development and delivery of educational programmes in the coming years. The various influences that have been discussed provide examples of an agent that has the capacity to influence education at all levels and hence to be an agent supporting and encouraging considerable change. When the future of education is considered in this way, it is interesting to speculate among the stakeholders, for whom the change will be the greatest. The stakeholders for whom technology would seem to proffer the most influence and change are the students. So while institutions are pondering how they will be influenced in years to come, whatever the outcomes, the beneficiaries of the activity and change will be the students.

References

Barron, A., "Designing Web-based training". *British Journal of Educational Technology, 29*(4), 355-371, 1998.

Berge, Z., "Guiding principles in Web-based instructional design". *Education Media International, 35*(2), 72-76, 1998.

Collis, B., "Information technologies for education and training". In Adelsberger, H., Collis, B, & Pawlowski, J. (eds.) *Handbook on Technologies for Information and Training*. Berlin: Springer Verlag, 2002.

Jonassen, D. & Reeves, T., "Learning with technology: Using computers as cognitive tools". In D. Jonassen (ed.), *Handbook of Research Educational on Educational Communications and Technology,* New York: Macmillan, 1996.

Moore, M. & Kearsley, G., *Distance Education: A Systems View*, Belmont, CA: Wadsworth, 1996.

3. FOUNDATION FOR EXCELLENCE IN HIGHER EDUCATION

Higher education in India is passing through a period of profound transformation, whether in terms of the place of the university in the life of the community or vis-a-vis the government or in terms of the networking between the university and its constituents. While higher education has made considerable strides in the country, each of its main objectives remain to be accomplished. Education was to be the medium through which equality of opportunity was to be made concrete yet it remains an endlessly deferred dream for many. Investment in education was meant to be a path of greater productivity and growth, yet its potential contribution to economy remains unrealised. Education was to be an aspiration for better experience of excellence in all fields. It was hoped that these aspirations would be linked together by founding of a just, productive and cultured society. There is a chasm here between what the educational systems is expected to achieve and what it is in fact accomplishing. New initiatives are needed if it is to accomplish its objectives. We believe that the proposed society will achieve these goals.

While comparing India with top universities abroad one finds the nature of gap and the extent of effort that will be required for Indian universities to reach world class standards. The comparisons also reveal the differences in the nature of linkages between the various stakeholders of the higher education systems in India and other countries.

Quality of Education

The economic and social well being of a society depends on the quality of its engineers, doctors, sociologists, economists and other human resources. According to UNESCO's WCHE declaration, higher education is should embrace all functions:

teaching and academic programmes, research and scholarship, staffing, students, infrastructure and the academic environment.

Research should be an ongoing process for advancement of knowledge. "Higher education institutions in all regions should be committed to transparent internal and external evaluation, conducted openly by independent specialists. However, due attention should be paid to specific institutional, national and regional diversity and to avoid uniformity. Curricula need to be recast so as to go beyond simple cognitive mastery of disciplines and include the acquisition of skills, competencies and abilities for communication, creative and critical analysis, independent thinking and team work in multicultural contexts."

There is a need for regular review and upgradation of curriculum. HEIs with greater autonomy have been successful in improving their curriculum on a regular basis and introducing courses in concurrence with the evolving market requirements. However, the same cannot be said of the overall university system. The state level universities and their affiliated colleges have not adequately responded to the market requirements due to the lengthy processes. For instance, curricula for a majority of colleges remain largely unchanged even after five-year periods.

As per the current evaluation standards, only 35 per cent marks are required to get a degree, that is, one-third of knowledge of the required syllabus. Moreover, in a typical university system, evaluation of subjects is do he by someone other than a teacher handling that subject. This poor testing and certification, in a way, transfer costs to the employers in terms of recruitment and training.

UGC has established an autonomous body, the National Accreditation Assessment Council, to assess the quality of HEIs on a regular basis. However, acquisition of accreditation is voluntary - and not compulsory, for HEIs. Thus, institutions that undergo accreditation voluntarily on a regular basis have been able to maintain a certain level of quality.

A majority of the HEIs that do not undergo accreditation continue to produce poor quality students. In contrast, the higher education system in the US follows a different institutional arrangement to ensure quality. The accreditation institutions themselves are evaluated by other agencies. Such a system tends to introduce greater transparency and faith among stakeholders—students, parents and others.

Two issues that need consideration are that the methodology and the criteria for evaluation of HEIs should be comprehensive to inform various stakeholders, students, faculty, industry, funding agencies and donors and these ratings need to compare institutions with international standards in order to reveal the differences in the quality of education among institutions. A thorough benchmarking of HEIs against the best in the world throw light on the nature of investments needed to bridge the gaps and pave the way for greater competition among HEIs.

Quality of Faculty

Attendance of adequate number of high quality faculty is critical for sustaining excellence in teaching and research. However, a serious concern has been a general decline in the number and quality of faculty in various Indian universities over the years. Many universities hire part-time faculty to run courses. Shortage of faculty has a direct bearing on the quality of teaching and attention to students.

The quality of faculty has also shown a downward trend, with the percentage of faculty with PhDs being low, especially in many affiliated colleges. The average citations over a 5-year period for a typical IIT is about two-three per faculty compared to 45 per faculty for MIT Engineering and 52 for Stanford Engineering. Further, much of the work lacks originality and is restricted to routine data collection or fitting somebody's data into somebody else's theory. The problem is likely to aggravate as several eminent faculty are slated for retirement over the next five- years.

Indian universities lack adequate autonomy and resources to develop high quality faculty or recruit eminent faculty with attractive incentives. UGC has initiated several programmes to promote excellence within the existing set-up. These include:

- Support to the permanent teachers of universities and colleges to conduct research through the schemes of Major and Minor Research Projects
- A scheme of UGC Research Award. The research scholar gets a grant for the research and his employer institution

is reimbursed with the full salary and allowances of the awardee.

- Travel grants to vice-chancellors and teachers of universities and colleges
- Assistance in the form of Emeritus Fellow and Visiting Professorship to enable the retired teachers to pursue active research in their field of specialisation and to use their services for innovative UGC programmes
- Cultural Exchange Programme—area studies and bilateral exchange programmes
- National education testing for entrants to the teaching profession.

However, a significant impact is yet to be felt as they have tended to focus on few individuals and failed to institutionalise the practice of excellence in a sustainable manner. Further, efforts at improving quality through such initiatives have also been unable to keep pace with the capacity expansion among the HEIs.

Teaching and Research Infrastructure

Absence of adequate infrastructure could restrict experimental demonstration of theoretical ideas, research activities and the ability of institutions to attract industry's support for financing R&D activities and generating revenues through consultancy services. At present, infrastructure in majority of HEIs is in need—of urgent upgradation. Many HEIs do not have adequate funds for renewal of physical infrastructure.

UGC's schemes such as Special Assistance Programme (SAP) and Strengthening of Infrastructure in Science and Technology (COST) have contributed to development of certain basic infrastructure but have suffered from administrative insensitivity and low quantum of resources. Their effectiveness also has been limited due to lack of long-term perspective within institutions and internal politics in HEIs in nominating departments for such schemes. Other programmes such as FIST (Funds for Improvement of S&T infrastructure in Universities and related Institutions) promoted by DST, are considered to have very good selection procedures but suffer from limitation of resources.

FINANCING

Government Financing

The Education Commission (1964-66) and the Majumdar Committee initiated by MHRD in 1999, advocated that allocating 6 per cent of GDP for education would be sufficient to finance universalisation of element and education and provide more resources for higher education. However, India currently spends about 3.2 per cent of its GNP on education and higher education receives a small share of this.

The Government had to curtail funding for many HEIs due to financial constraints and changing priorities. Further, rapid expansion in the number of HEIs meant that limited financial resources had to be spread among more HEIs. This forced HEIs to cut their outlay into teaching and research activities to offset the rise in operational costs.

Ironically, while government funding to HEIs has not grown in successive decades, the HEIs dependence on the government for funding has been increasing. This indicates either an increase in government control or a decline in initiative among HEIs to raise funds for self-sustenance or both.

Self Financing

Several financial reforms have been recommended for higher education based on two themes: (a) improving internal efficiency of HEIs and (b) mobilising resources from non-governmental sources.

Transparent costing mechanisms would assist HEIs in repricing their services to reflect the real costs incurred in the provision of such services. This could also help in bargaining for matching grants from the government. Further, a better understanding of costs could also help in reducing disparity in government's allocation of resources.

HEIs have been tying to improve their finances through enhanced fees, self-financing courses, consultancy, contract research and renting out facilities. The Swaminathan committee appointed by AICTE in 1994 to look into the possibilities of resource mobilisation in technical education, recommended (a) creation of corpus fund in institutions, (b) establishment of

Educational Development Bank of India (c) reducing the share of salaries in recurring expenditure from 80 per cent to 60 per cent and (d) enhancing fees to recover at least 20 per cent of the recurring expenditure.

In many colleges fees have increased over the last few years. However, they are still low in terms of share of total recurring expenditure as compared with earlier periods or other countries. To ensure success, increase in fees should be accompanied by improvement in quality and relevance of courses. One option to facilitate recovery through fees is to promote repayable loans for students which is increasingly gaining acceptance in the US. However, the practice has not gained acceptance in India due to the absence of well-established credit market for financing education. There is also a concern that loans (with their requirement of surety) may ultimately go to children from well-to-do families. HEIs have also been tying to generate revenues from services such as distance education programmes, consultancy and contract research.

Another source that HEIs in India are yet to tap on is the potentially large source of funding from alumni and donors. Most US universities have a history of successful campaigns for their fund raising through alumni. Private fund raising by both public and private institutions is increasingly becoming a mechanism for competitive advantage. Various schemes for gifting with related tax exemption benefits have been worked out and are widely publicised.

National Fund

In an effort to garner resources specifically for higher education, the Ministry of Human Resource Development (Government of India) has proposed a national fund, called Bharatiya Shiksha Khosh, into which donors can place their contributions. But however liberally such a fund may be operated, it will not satisfy donors for the managers of the fund can only be a few, while there will be thousands of donors.

So, most donors will be excluded, will have no sense of participation and will feel alienated. Also, for legal reasons, a centralised fund managed by the state cannot but have rigid rules. A centralised fund is also likely to be burdened with top-heavy administration, and will be slow to respond. This highlights the need for several decentralised funding mechanisms.

Institutional Autonomy and Arrangement

Most of the HEIs in the world are based on the European academic model which places faculty at the centre of university and emphasises autonomy. The primary focus of the model was on developing an elite group of people for the civil services. Several countries in the world have adopted this model, with subtle variations. For instance, in Germany under the leadership of Wilhelm von Humbolt, higher education was given significant resources by the government and entrusted with the responsibility for research aimed at national development and industrialisation and playing a key role in defining the ideology of the new German nation.

While Indian universities inherited the European academic model, they did not inherit its fundamental characteristic - autonomy. The British stress is on the authenticity and credibility of the individuals manning those bodies to give credibility to the institutions which Indian universities lack. For instance, there is a high degree of political influence in selection of vice chancellor of the university, especially state universities. The other innovations such as supporting national interest through R&D also developed in a manner that could make a difference.

One of the this may be because government has created separate institutions for research such as IARI, IICT, CLRI, and defence labs, and directed sponsored projects to those institutions. Indian universities also have not developed strong linkages with the market like the American universities since public funding brought with it greater government control over universities. Government funding has also meant adherence to several governmental procedures that are primarily designed to identify and punish deviance and the resultant delays.

As a result, HEIs lack institutional autonomy to respond quickly and effectively to changing scenarios and are yet to develop the spirit of competing for good students, faculty, and research funding that is a hallmark of American universities. Many Indian HEIs today are reduced to simple teaching shops with no clear mission or strategy towards their key stakeholders such as students, industry, funding agencies and society.

Capacity Expansion

Higher education costs, its public good characteristic and the concern to reduce inequity have encouraged governments at the centre and state to establish a number of universities and colleges.

With the expansion of the primary and secondary school education, the pressure on higher education system to expand is expected to continue in India. Governments have encouraged entry of private initiatives in education and also an increase in capacity in existing institutions. Inadequate regulations for maintaining quality has led to mushrooming of a large number of mediocre institutions in the private sector and also increased pressure on maintaining quality in existing institutions. It is obvious that Government is finding it difficult to combine mass education with excellence.

In order to reduce inequity in access to higher education arising out of income, social caste, geography and gender differentiation, governments in states and centre have been using reservation policies. As a result HEIs are forced to cope with diverse student quality which increases pressure on them to maintain uniformity in the quality of output. But, access is an issue that has to be dealt with in the national interest.

Government Initiatives

The investment in higher education needs to be consciously integrated with national development needs. Every effort must be made to operationalise this key concept which means that the socio-economic ministries are mandated to invest a certain percentage of allocation made to them in promoting higher education in disciplines relevant to their domain. The Tenth Plan should seek to set up inter-sectoral HRD committee with Secretary Education as its Chairman. This mechanism can be developed as one means of supporting the objective of integrating investments in development with investments in higher education.

There is an urgent need to increase the density of Ph.Ds in the country. This is one area that India has the best chance of bettering several developed countries. The potential in this respect is great. Government should encourage HEIs to become fountainheads of the emerging knowledge economy by directing sponsored research to competing universities—public or private. HEIs should be allowed to compete with established national research institutions for these resources. Unless university system is drawn into the fold of advancing strategic fields, the mission areas will not have adequate caliber human resources. Consequently, we will be witnesses to strategic departments being overloaded on the one hand and gross under-utilisation of university personnel on the other hand.

Greater autonomy to HEIs should be granted by government to facilitate their growth while maintaining quality. Increase in capacity of public universities should go with corresponding increase in resources to ensure that quality is maintained. It is clear that Government can support the existing universities only up to a certain minimum level of quality. While private sector should be encouraged to set up more number of institutions to meet increase in demand, government should continue to ensure quality and improve access.

Policy makers should recognise that a majority of stakeholders are likely to be more loyal to their personal interests than to the nation. They will ultimately choose the educational institution and the place of work that is most suited to them. Policy makers should be open to such views and focus on developing institutional mechanisms that are attractive to good talent.

For HEIs the financial constraint should be an opportunity for improving quality and moving to higher levels of excellence. This crisis is already encouraging dilution of government's control over academic institutions. HEIs must relate their request for public funding to specific missions and increase the proportion of non-governmental funds. That will pave way for increased autonomy thus triggering changes in academic and administrative freedom for institutions.

HEIs have to set clear mission statements, institutionalise good governance models to handle teaching and research functions, build efficiency and transparency, and become more accountable and responsive to their stakeholders - students, government, industry, donors, alumni and society. Addition of faculty to fill up vacancies can result in greater operating costs and bring down resources available for instruction or research.

HEIs have to devote time and effort to transform into a better system of operation. Lot of energy will be required to push the system into a higher orbit so that it produces high quality human resources on a sustainable basis.

One immediate initiative would be to set up a national foundation to improve the quality of existing institutions and catalyse their ability to attract of best talent, industry and funding agencies in a sustainable manner.

Academic Excellence and Marketplace Expectations

Higher education is a vital and indispensable sector within society, and those of us who work in colleges and universities have some of the most important jobs anywhere. The academy contributes in fundamental, pervasive, and lasting ways to the personal and professional lives of the more than thirteen million students enrolled annually in degree-granting programmes, and more generally to the cultural, intellectual, and economic vitality of our communities and our society. Higher education informs public understanding, cultivates public taste, and contributes to the nation's well-being as it nurtures and trains each new generation of architects, artists, authors, business leaders, engineers, farmers, lawyers, physicians, poets, scientists, social workers, and teachers as well as a steady succession of advocates, dreamers, doers, dropouts, parents, politicians, preachers, prophets, social reformers, visionaries, and volunteers who leaven, nudge, and shape the course of public life.

Our colleges and universities have always taken their academic role very seriously, and higher education institutions go to great lengths to document and evaluate their accomplishments. This is done in various ways, including accreditation reviews; disciplinary self-studies; and periodic peer evaluations of individuals, programmes, and institutions. Assessments focus on student qualifications, faculty teaching and scholarship, research-funding levels, instructional programmes, library holdings, computing facilities, and many other dimensions of quality. With regard to scholarship and academics, higher education institutions are the gold standard, the model to which other organisations throughout the world compare themselves and the ideal to which they aspire.

It would seem that the scholarly tradition has served society well in a great many ways. Yet for all that higher education contributes, its institutions, administrators, faculty, and staff often do not receive the level of recognition, support, and appreciation one would expect and hope for. There is a kind of dissonance between the purposes our society foresees for the university and the way the university sees itself. Increasingly, the image of the ivory tower—the protected sanctuary, disengaged from contemporary societal concerns, which has been the embodiment of the scholarly tradition—is increasingly under siege in many quarters. Also being challenged is the autonomy that has been a defining characteristic of the academy.

One response for some in the academy has been to ignore or dismiss the mounting criticism, and to point out that critique of higher education is to be expected. The academy, it is argued, has always been the subject of controversy, and it always will be. Colleges and universities are, after all, institutions whose mission it is to hold up a mirror to society and to challenge conventional ways of thinking. Such purposes are seldom achieved without arousing some discomfort and discontent. From this perspective, it follows that the task facing those of us in higher education today is to insulate ourselves from the influence of outside voices. They threaten our intellectual detachment and institutional self-determination, long regarded as essential to academic excellence.

There is nothing particularly new about the notion of competition between institutions for students, faculty, research support, funding, prestige, and athletic prominence. Nor is there anything novel about the need for change in higher education. Indeed, the academy has been evolving in a variety of ways since colleges and universities first opened their doors to students, and the literature reminds us that each era brings its own calls for innovation and change. Increasingly, however, colleges and universities are competing for scarce resources not only with one another but also with school education systems, for-profit educational and research providers, and even state prisons, transportation, and other publicly funded agencies. Many observers contend that the forces of change, the level of competition, and the economic pressures fuelling the competitiveness are intensifying more rapidly than ever before.

Ways to Attain the Expectations

To be successful in the increasingly complex, demanding, and competitive setting, the academy must recognise the leadership challenges it faces and devote increasing attention to expectations and concerns articulated by the external constituencies that provide the moral and financial support necessary to our functioning. The list of such groups is a long one: present and potential students, parents, alumni, members of advisory and oversight groups, employers, public officials, community groups, taxpayers, funding agencies, donors, and the general public. From this perspective, colleges and universities are viewed as providers of educational services. As with other service providers, changes in marketplace needs and expectations create intensifying demands and emerging opportunities. Organisations must adapt or risk obsolescence and atrophy.

For many in the academy—particularly some members of the faculty —discourse that positions higher education institutions in a marketplace or service context is not likely to be enthusiastically received. In essence, the concern is that these images and metaphors lead inevitably to corporate models for the academy. They are seen as promoting an inappropriate emphasis on marketing, consumerism, and corporate management approaches, all of which are regarded as fundamental threats to the traditions of academic excellence.

The development of more effective communication strategies to enhance stakeholder commitment to the academy's traditional values is another, and the negotiation of more appropriate and aligned expectations by all involved is a third. In each case, the gap between what is anticipated and what is actually encountered is diminished, and dissatisfaction is reduced or eliminated.

To attain academic excellence in higher education, the following points should be taken in consideration:

i) Broadening public appreciation for the work of the academy
ii) Increasing our understanding of the needs of workplaces
iii) Becoming more effective learning organisations
iv) Integrating assessment, planning, and improvement

v) Enhancing collaboration and community
vi) Recognising the importance of teaching
vii) Devoting more attention to leadership
viii) Framing the vision of excellence more broadly.

Broadening Public Appreciation for Academic Works

Beyond classroom teaching, the work of higher education is not well understood or fully appreciated by many of our publics. All too often, for instance, faculty members find themselves explaining what they do, that they don't really have summers "off," and why an answer to the question "How many hours are you teaching this semester?" isn't a full description of their work responsibilities. College and university administrators and staff find themselves not only explaining their own work and justifying the activities of the faculty but also describing the reasons many colleges and universities need to have bureaucracies as extensive as those of many towns or municipalities.

The work of higher education is not well understood, and constituents often have incomplete or incorrect impressions of our day-to-day responsibilities, our roles, our institutions, and the principles that guide the work of the academy. Many of the questions one often hears from those outside the academy are quite straightforward: Why don't colleges and universities focus their efforts exclusively on instruction and advising? In what ways are instruction, scholarship, and outreach complementary endeavours when they seem like distinct activities that compete against one another for resources? Why do faculty members in some institutions teach only one or two classes in a semester? How is it possible for some members of faculty to come to work only two days a week? Why aren't popular magazine rating systems necessarily a good way to judge the quality of a college? Why are there so many part-time instructors and foreign teaching assistants? Why are some departments understaffed and turning interested students away, while other departments have a large number of faculty and very little student demand?

There is ample evidence that many of us don't have answers to these questions, and where we do, the answers are often not the ones we wish they had. The problem is not that we are unable to address these issues at length, but rather that we often don't have concise, uncomplicated answers to give that respond to the fundamental concerns motivating them. Often, what is required are brief and compelling answers that can be shared in the two, three, or four sentences that most nonacademics are willing to invest in listening to us talk about such matters. We need answers that can be given during an elevator ride, or while exchanging pleasantries at a social or neighbourhood gathering with acquaintances or friends from business, health care, or government.

The responsibility for the communication failure, and the fix, falls squarely on the shoulders of all of us. It is tempting to look to people who are employed in university public affairs and public information offices to correct this problem; clearly, professionals in these departments have an important role to play. However, the nature and magnitude of the problem is such that it cannot be meaningfully addressed by a single department within an institution, or a series of brochures or public service advertisements on television, no matter how well-crafted and persuasive. Meaningfully addressing this challenge requires the collective and concerted effort of all who work in or value higher education.

To be effective ambassadors for the higher education community, we all need to be adept at translating our *own* understandings of our purposes and priorities into messages that speak more clearly and directly to the needs and concerns of our beneficiaries and the publics to whom we look for support. Given our values, our commitment, and our expertise in teaching-and-learning and research, there is no group better prepared than ours to excel in this kind of effort. Others expect higher educators to have these capabilities, and the expectation seems quite reasonable. This work is an important component of our teaching and public service, and we should seek out opportunities to engage in constructive dialogue with those who question, misunderstand, and criticise. In these efforts, as institutions and individuals, we must aspire to the same level of excellence that we do in other academic endeavours. The goal is a simple one: to foster mutually beneficial dialogue and enhanced understanding of the multiple perspectives of higher education, its purposes, and its priorities.

Increasing Understanding of the Needs of Workplaces

With the exception of community and career colleges, higher education generally does not devote a great deal of time or effort to thinking about the needs of the contemporary workplace. This is particularly true in the arts and humanities and other "nonprofessional" disciplines. This is often quite troubling to external constituencies, many of whom believe it is one of the most fundamental reasons for the existence of higher education. Researchers at one university found that 80 percent of entering students felt career preparation was a very important goal for attending college, yet only 20 percent of the faculty shared this view. Our inattention to these matters often confronts many of our stakeholders—students, parents, employers, and alumni in particular—as a particularly poignant demonstration of higher education's arrogance and self-preoccupation, and as confirmation of our lack of interest in the realities of the external world.

It does not seem unreasonable to expect that higher education would be vitally interested in the educational needs of contemporary workplaces. Since most students eventually work in one sector or another, an understanding of needed workplace capabilities would seem to be a priority among all disciplines, liberal arts as well as professional disciplines. This same logic suggests that college faculty and staff would be resolute in their efforts to determine whether graduates leave their institution with the disciplinary knowledge, skills, and competencies that are appropriate for workplace effectiveness and leadership. It would also seem that colleges and universities would want to know how well curricular and co-curricular programmes prepare students in these areas, and how the relevant teaching-and-learning processes could be enhanced. For reasons that are somewhat difficult to grasp—and nearly impossible to explain to our beneficiaries—we generally do very little systematic analysis of these topics.

The goal of a higher education is clearly not limited to vocational training. Still, most would agree that there should be an important connection between the knowledge and skills that are being cultivated in universities and the ability of graduates to make meaningful contributions through the various work-related activities in which they will engage over the course of their lifetimes. Even among those who do not regard workplace preparation as a primary goal of higher education, there is the possibility—perhaps the responsibility—of explaining this point of view, since it is not necessarily well understood or appreciated by our publics. There is a good deal being written on the topic of workplace competence in the popular and professional press.

The general conclusions of these writings, and inferences that can be drawn from them, are quite interesting and point to the value of further and more systematic attention to the subject. First, it is interesting to note that there is a reasonable level of agreement on many of the capabilities that are valued in the workplace. Second, many of the topics judged to be critical to success in the workplace—ethics, critical reasoning, leadership, written and oral communication, group and collaborative skills, cultural and cross-cultural understanding —are not domain-specific subjects but instead fall within the realm of the arts and humanities. Parenthetically, many of these same competencies that are identified as important in occupational settings are generally viewed as equally important in other interpersonal, group, and social contexts. Third, writings in the area point to the value of student life and co-curricular programmes as an important complement to traditional coursework.

In sum, there is a reasonably good level of agreement on many of the needed competencies, and many, if not most, of the workplace needs identified in the literature are consistent with the goals of university programmes—not only in professional schools but also in the humanities. Generally speaking, however, this compatibility and correspondence are often not well recognised by the academy or by external constituencies, because of differences in language, level of analysis, and publication venue. There is no question that more systematic research is needed on these topics. Equally important is increased dialogue on this topic among faculty, staff, students, parents, alumni, and employers. Such exchanges would clarify areas of difference, broaden the awareness of shared perspectives and goals, and encourage new collaboration in research.

Becoming More Effective Learning Organisations

Nothing is more basic to the purposes of the academy than the development of environments that value and support learning. A learning community need not be defined by the boundaries of a campus, nor limited to the years one is enrolled in classes. Rather, the values of learning that the academy endorses are lifelong pursuits, and the role colleges and universities are playing in support of these endeavours is increasingly expansive.

It should be a fundamental goal of the academy to ensure that the remarkable growth in demand for education throughout the lifetime of virtually every citizen can be satisfied and to demonstrate that we can meet this need at the highest level of quality imaginable, along with the greatest efficiency possible. Organisational learning requires clarity of goals, supportive facilities and work processes, effective evaluation, and most fundamentally openness and receptivity to a range of information and information sources.

Goal Clarification and Evaluation

The clarification of goals and evaluation of the impact of the academy's work is one of our most formidable and enduring challenges as a learning organisation. The importance of the task has increased with the introduction of new educational programmes and services and new educational technologies, serving increasingly varied constituencies.

The need to clearly articulate goals and develop corresponding measures to evaluate the extent to which they are being met is being given particular urgency by demands for greater accountability and performance measurement. In 1997, eighteen states were using performance-based assessments in funding or budgeting for higher education; in 2000, nearly three quarters had such a programme.

There is little argument about the importance of evaluating the work of colleges and universities. But given the complexity of the academy's mission and of the measurement issues involved, questions about what to evaluate and how to make these evaluations are matters of long-standing debate and controversy. Those within the academy understand better than others that many of the most important areas to assess in relation to research, instruction, and outreach are often the least amenable to straightforward quantitative analysis. It is considerably more difficult to discern the long-term significance and impact of one's work for academic peers or for society generally than it is to calculate the number of single and coauthored publications, dollar level of grant funding, and professional activities—as important as these indicators may be in their own right.

Supportive and Facilitative Processes

On campuses across the country, we find many striking examples of innovative facilities and processes that support learning. Among these are new and more flexible learning spaces, online information and library services, high-tech classrooms, widely accessible computing facilities, wired residence facilities, web page support and enhancement of classes, and an increasing array of distance learning and lifelong learning programmes and services. There are many other advances, such as the creation of increased opportunities for student involvement in faculty research activities, college-wide first-year courses, a renewed emphasis on undergraduate teaching, and new programmes to promote improvements in classroom instruction and to support student learning.

Receptivity to Arrange of Information

Learning organisations are characterised by active efforts to look beyond their own departmental, institutional, and sector boundaries in the quest for knowledge and insight to act with the benefit of knowing how others have addressed similar issues and opportunities. Certainly every academic and administrative department is unique in many respects, but there are also many commonalities across organisations, and these similarities provide the potential for learning directly and by analogy.

The use of comparisons and peer review has always been fundamental in evaluating education and improving scholarship. "Benchmarking," as it is often termed in the parlance of contemporary organisational studies—has also been useful in identifying and sharing effective practices in academic and student life areas. The approach can be equally useful as it relates to organisational practices. Even when there is agreement on the value of comparisons with other colleges and universities, there is often resistance to the idea that higher education can benefit from comparison with other sectors. The major barrier is the common perception that higher education is different from other organisations. But there are any number of areas where there are fundamental similarities, even if not obviously so.

Colleges and universities should be society's best examples of learning organisations, the standard of excellence when it comes to establishing clear goals, supportive work processes and facilities, and openness and receptivity to learning from any and all sources. Integrating assessment, planning, and improvement A fourth challenge is the integration of assessment, planning, and improvement activities. The issue is not that there is an absence of assessment, planning, or improvement activity within higher education. To the contrary, most universities have institutional research departments that collect and organise data to meet various reporting needs.

Assessment also occurs within academic units, where the quality of programmes, courses, faculty, and students is addressed in a variety of ways, among them disciplinary self-studies and accreditation review processes. Planning and improvement activities may also be a part of the work of many other administrative, student life, and service departments within an institution. The challenge here is that assessment, planning, and improvement are often not as well integrated as they might be, and typically episodic rather than continuous. Moreover, the focus of assessment, planning, and improvement is generally on individual faculty members, programmes, or services, rather than on organisations. It is often the case, also, that information and insights gained through assessment are not fully, effectively, or efficiently translated into improvements, and they may not be coordinated or aligned throughout the university. These concerns are not new to higher education; the frameworks adopted by the regional accrediting associations have evolved in recent years to address these issues more directly.

Enhancing Collaboration and Community

Another fundamental challenge facing the academy is the need to increase commitment to collaboration and community. The need exists *within* departments, but it is most pronounced *across* academic and administrative department lines. This is a complex and important topic, and one that has a number of facets. Faculty are socialised into a culture that positions them at the centre of the institution, linked directly to the instructional, research, and public service mission of the university; hence the rationale for the phrase "the faculty are the university." Unfortunately, this is a way of thinking and talking that can marginalise other university employees, foster resentment, contribute to a fundamental cultural divide, and undermine efforts to promote a shared sense of purpose and community.

There are certainly a number of examples in every institution in which faculty and staff members work together across cultural lines in pursuit of common purposes. Our challenge is to create many more boundary-spanning and community-building activities like these on our campuses—activities that reaffirm our common purposes, increase institutional cohesion, and call into question the patterns of thought and action that undermine it. In these collective endeavours, quality means that the *whole* must be something more than the simple sum of the distinguished parts.

Recognising the Importance of Teaching

Each day, at institutions of higher education all over the country, tens of thousands of faculty members enter classrooms to help discharge a key element in the mission of their institution: the sharing of knowledge. At every college and university in the country, there are also many more employees of the institution who are not faculty. So what in the world do all those nonfaculty people do? We know, of course, that they fulfil a variety of functions necessary to the operation of the institution and the support of its core mission, but in truth their roles are much more fundamental: they are teachers. Many students come to college or university at a time in their lives when they are first assuming responsibility for the management of their lives—living away from home, paying their own bills, overseeing their own health care, and in some cases living and interacting for the first time with people with whom they may have little in common. Clearly, they are gaining important knowledge inside the classroom. But they are also being taught poignant and enduring lessons outside the classroom as they watch how faculty and staff relate to them and to one another; strive to understand and adapt to institutional policies and procedures; and learn how a large, complex system functions. Together, faculty, administrators, and staff provide lessons for the next generation of teachers, government workers, corporate managers, and health care providers.

Perhaps one of our most fundamental tensions as it relates to teaching-and-learning is the fact that the instructional goals and intentions of the teachers on the one hand and the learning agenda, "goals," and learning outcomes of students on the other hand may not necessarily or automatically align particularly well. Improving our understanding of "teacher-learner" communication processes and beginning to explore the implications of the shared instructional role of administrators, faculty, and staff constitute an important challenge to be addressed in our efforts to reconcile competing perspectives on higher education, and to achieve the level of excellence that justifies our claim to leadership in this area.

Devoting more Attention to Leadership

Given the many pressing challenges facing the academy, perhaps no need is greater than for strong leadership at all levels of higher education: board members, presidents, senior administrators, deans, directors, chairs, faculty, and all members of the academic community who serve in a leadership capacity of one type or another. The tasks confronting leaders are daunting in many respects. The unique character of the academy presents unique opportunities, but also special challenges.

Well-developed leadership capacities are essential in any organisation. The recognition of the importance of leadership and of the scope of the requisite knowledge and skills has led business, health care, and government to invest substantial time and resources in this area. The leadership challenges in higher education are arguably more complex and difficult than in other sectors. In most private sector organisations leaders possess considerable authority. Typically, reporting lines are clear; the goals and measures of organisational success, the so-called bottom line, is well defined; and the people in leadership roles throughout an organisation have considerable resources, incentives, and sanctions available to motivate and encourage organisational innovation, advancement, and change.

In higher education, where independence is prized and shared governance is highly valued, the leadership challenge is enormous. It requires of individuals with insight and competence not simply to create and articulate vision, goals, and action plans but also to meaningfully engage one's colleagues throughout the institution—and sometimes external stakeholders—in the process of their formulation. For all the deliberations, delays, and difficulties that collaboration involves, failure to adopt this value sometimes leads to less useful ideas, and almost always to resisting implementation —even when the ideas are not particularly contentious. In higher education leadership, the maxim "pay now or pay later" truly applies.

Despite the incredible challenges associated with developing effective leaders in higher education, historically little attention has been devoted to this issue. It has generally been assumed that distinguished faculty or staff would quite naturally make equally distinguished leaders. The record demonstrates, however, that the knowledge and competencies needed for excellence in leadership are not capabilities that faculty or staff members naturally possess simply because they are outstanding teachers, scholars, or subject matter experts. The needed capabilities go well beyond the intellectual capability, subject matter expertise, and experience that come with mastery in one academic, technical, or occupational field. Also critical are knowledge and competencies in collaborative decision making, planning, process analysis, interpersonal and organisational communication, consensus building, conflict resolution, and various other organisational and people skills.

Framing the Vision of Excellence

Perhaps the most fundamental and pervasive challenge confronting higher education has to do with the way we conceive of excellence, and the vision to which we aspire as a consequence. How we think about excellence has fundamental implications for illuminating and reconciling differences in perspective and priority within the academy.

Colleges and universities have long been regarded as the gold standard when it comes to academics. The university is society's main repository of systematic knowledge and its main contributor to tomorrow's scientific and humanistic understanding. It is designed precisely for that mission. Other types of enterprises and institutions may therefore need to pay special attention to the university as the archetype of the organisation where discovery and transmission of knowledge are both the reasons for existence and the occasion for enduring satisfaction. Even with regard to academics, as we know, there are challenges that confront us in the pursuit of excellence. There are questions about mission balance and mission creep, the roles of tenure-track and part-time faculty, access and diversity, the appropriate extent of faculty participation in continuing education initiatives, the relationship between academic matters and student life issues, alignment between faculty incentives and institutional goals, the proper role of athletics, and any number of other issues. However, beyond issues related to academics and academic excellence—where the consensus is that higher education generally performs with distinction—there are at least two other dimensions of excellence where we fall considerably short of that standard. For lack of better labels, these can be termed service excellence and operational excellence.

The term service excellence can be used to refer to the complex set of communication processes through which we create and maintain relationships with those with whom we interact through our instruction, research, public outreach, and also through our administrative, student life, service, and other activities. Service is a way of talking about all forms of interaction between the academy and its many constituencies.

To clarify the concept of excellence in service, consider simple examples of situations where it is notable by its absence:

> A faculty member is in her office carefully preparing material for a class lecture. When a student arrives at her door during office hours with the hope of discussing a question from class, she reacts to the interruption abruptly and with annoyance. She tells the student that this is not a good time and to come back later. The professor here is hard at work maintaining higher education's reputation for academic excellence. Unfortunately, at the same time, she's making a less exemplary contribution to service excellence.

This situations illustrate the challenges of excellence in service, communication, and relationship development. Events like this help to explain why some of our beneficiaries fail to fully appreciate the work of higher education. When such situations occur—and most would agree that they occur much more often than we would like in many institutions—students and others who are touched by the event may be left with a tainted impression of their college or university experience, and too few kind thoughts about the institution, its faculty, and its staff. Unfortunately, many of the manifestations of academic excellence are deferred and intangible; deficiencies in the area of service are generally immediate and visible. In extreme cases, an accumulation of negative experiences can result in students concluding that graduating—and other positive outcomes they associate with their college experience—are things they did in spite of our efforts, rather than because of them.

It is important to point out that the fundamental issue is not one of treating students—or family members, visitors, or members of the public—in a particular way because they are customers, but rather because they are people. Casting the issue solely in marketplace terms is an all-too-convenient way of dismissing what are in actuality much more basic issues of human relationships, respect, and dignity—issues that should be basic to the work we do and the values we espouse.

A second dimension of relevance is operational excellence, matters having to do with the effectiveness and efficiency of how our institutions function. Operational issues affect external constituencies—students, parents, visitors, and others not employed by the institution—and they also affect internal users, such as faculty and staff.

References

KPMG, *Transforming Higher Education: At the Gateway of the Knowledge Economy,* KPMG LLP. 1999.

TFHE, *Higher Education in Developing Countries: Peril and Promise,* Task Force on Higher Education, The World Bank, 2000.

The Center, "Top American Research Universities", An Occasional Paper from the Lombardi Program on Measuring University Performance, University of Florida. 2000.

UNESCO, *Towards an agenda for higher education: Challenges and task for the twenty-frst centuly viewed in the light of the regional conference,* Paris, 1998.

World Bank, *Technical and scientific manpower development in India,* Draft, The World Bank, 2000.

4. CONCERNS AND DIRECTIONS OF HIGHER EDUCATION

The higher education system in India has grown in a remarkable way, particularly in the post-independence period, to become one of the largest system of its kind in the world. However, the system has many issues of concern at present, like financing and management including access, equity and relevance, reorientation of programmes by laying emphasis on health consciousness, values and ethics and quality of higher education together with the assessment of institutions and their accreditation. These issues are important for the country, as it is now engaged in the use of higher education as a powerful tool to build a knowledge-based information society of the 21st century.

The new challenge before the country at the beginning of the twenty first century is to become a developed society by the year 2020, which requires that not only a vibrant economy driven by knowledge has to be ushered in soon, but also a new society where justice and human values prevail has to be created. Moreover, challenges in higher education are no longer only nation centric. They have already attained global dimensions, particularly after trade in services has been brought under the purview of the WTO regime.

With the explosive growth of knowledge in the past century and with the development of handy tools of information and communication technologies as well as of other scientific innovations, competition has become a hallmark of growth all over the world. As a result, knowledge is not only going to be the driver of Indian economy, but also, it is going to permeate into all the strata of Indian society for a better quality of life and living conditions. Therefore, India has to rise to the occasion urgently and reorient its higher education system to be vibrant, competitive, meaningful and purposeful, Besides, there is absolutely no substitute to quality of higher education, although the country has been faced for a long time with the serious problem of meeting the quantity needs of our society. It is, therefore, essential that a careful balancing of the two is given priority to meet the twin requirements of the society in the foreseeable future.

Management of Higher Education

The Indian higher education system is one of the largest such systems in the world. It is estimated that during the X Five Year Plan period (2002-07), there will be a tremendous pressure of numbers on this system and a large number of additional students will be knocking at the doors of higher education institutions in the country. There are also new challenges of management and regulation being faced by these institutions, which require serious attention, both at the institutions in the public sector and also those in the private sector now growing at a fast pace. As a result, the old structures of management established in pre-independent India and working during most of the twentieth century are now required to undergo drastic changes. Besides, the demands of the society for equity and accommodation cannot be neglected any more.

The new regime under WTO where competence is the cardinal principle of success in international operations has made it abundantly clear that the country should exploit its excellent potential in higher education and training facilities and prepare itself to export the Indian brand of education to foreign countries. Policy planning and evolving strategies for this task are somewhat new for the country. But, this is an opportunity which cannot be missed by India, as it offers interesting possibilities for strengthening of the nation's talent and resourcefulness.

Public/Private Partnership

Indian higher education system has undergone massive expansion in post-independent India with a national resolve to establish several universities, technical institutes, research institutions and professional/non-professional colleges all over the country to generate and disseminate knowledge coupled with the noble intention of providing easy access to higher education to the common Indian. The public initiatives played a dominant and controlling role in this phase. Most of the universities were public institutions with powers to regulate academic activities on their campuses as well as in their areas of jurisdiction through the affiliating system. Even the private institutions enjoyed large-scale financial support in the form of grants from the public exchequer.

Private funds as well as individuals played key roles in the cause of higher education. With the public funding being no more in a position to take-up the challenging task of expansion and diversification of the higher education system in the country to meet the continuously growing demands at present, there is little option other than bringing in private initiatives in a massive way to meet the various challenges. The deregulating mechanism of controls started with the granting of "autonomous status" to identified colleges in the 1970s. Some of these colleges have graduated further to receive the "deemed to be university" status in later years. Now, the country is on the threshold of the establishment of private universities in different states.

Privatisation of higher education in India is gaining on a massive scale, not a result of changing ideological commitments of the momentum state, the judiciary or India's propertied classes but rather from a breakdown of the state system. As a result, the education system remains suspended between over-regulation by the state on the one hand, and a discretionary privatisation that is unable to mobilise private capital in productive ways. The result is a sub-optimal structuring of higher education.

Today India has more than 15,000 colleges and more than two-thirds of these colleges are classified by the University Grants Commission as "Arts, Science, Commerce and Oriental Learning Colleges". Recent growth is much greater in professional colleges as well as in private vocational courses catering especially to the IT sector. The fact that India has 1,253 medical colleges but just two in public indicates the priorities and interests that shape Indian higher education. India produces more lawyers than doctors, and nearly 0.7 million students were enrolled in engineering/technology.

There has been a rapid expansion in higher education, the growth being about two-and-half times the population growth rate. Enrolment ratios vary across Indian states, with the Southern and Western states faring better than their Eastern counterparts. Women now constitute about 40 per cent of all student enrolments, varying from a low of 24 per cent in Bihar to a high of 60 per cent in Kerala. The bulk of students (nearly two thirds) are enrolled in arts and science, with another 18 per cent in commerce/management. This is of some importance because most "private investment" in higher education is concentrated in engineering, medicine and management and consequently does little for the majority of students.

Although total expenditure on higher education has risen since independence spending per pupil in real terms declined for nearly two decades, before recovering modestly. Higher education occupies a low priority in public expenditures. Its share of GNP was nearly 1 per cent during the 1970s, just 0.35 per cent in the mid-1990s before increasing modestly to 0.6 by the end of the decade.

De Facto Privatisation

For Indians, higher education has been most vital for modern Indian power and opportunity. This realisation, coupled with the severe limitations of publicly funded higher education institutions and the greater purchasing power of the middle class, means that Indians are prepared to pay rather than be denied. According to NSS data, the government's share in overall education expenditure has been declining steadily. For states like Kerala, the decline is steep, from while for Madhya Pradesh it is lesser. Many students who formally enrol in publicly funded colleges and universities, barely attend classes there. Instead, they pay considerable sums to the burgeoning private sector vocational IT training firms such as NIIT and Aptech.

The most noteworthy transformation has been in the provision of professional education, especially engineering, medicine and business schools.

In the case of engineering colleges, the private sector, which accounted for just 15 per cent of the seats in 1960, now accounts for 86.4 per cent of seats (and 84 per cent of all engineering colleges). In the case of medical colleges, the private sector dominance is less stark, but the trend is unambiguous: the proportion of private seats has risen from 6.8 per cent in 1960 to 40.9 per cent in 2003. In the 1,000 odd business schools 90 per cent are private sector.

The BJP government passed the Private University Amendment Bill, 2004 under which proprietors of all private universities would have to deposit Rs 2 crore with the government and prove that they have 25 acres of land for their institutions. Belatedly, the UGC came up with the UGC Regulations 2003. Each private university would now require a separate State Act conforming to the relevant provisions of the UGC Act. A university set up under a State Act shall operate "ordinarily within the boundary of the State concerned," and can only open off-campus centres, offshore centres and study centres only after the development of main campus and after five years of coming into existence. Even then, it would require the prior permission of the UGC and the government of the host state, and such approval would be forthcoming "in exceptional circumstances" that are unspecified. The admission, fee structure and programmes of study of the private university will be have to conform to the norms and regulations prescribed by the UGC and other statutory bodies.

A major difficulty in the Indian case is whether most private institutions that claim tax-exempt status qualify as "philanthropic." By definition, all Indian universities and private colleges are "non-profit" organisations, but this does not distinguish between say, capitation fees colleges in the South and a regular college run out of trust funds that does not charge students. Technically, both are non-profit institutions, both qualify for tax exemptions. But there is a good deal of suspicion whether investment in private unaided colleges can be called "philanthropic" at all, even though they are formally not-for-profit.

The Shome Committee recommended that only such organisations that receive 90 per cent of their annual receipts through donations or grants be treated as organisations for a charitable purpose. However, the criterion presented by Shome Committee's definition of "philanthropic" or "charitable" would disqualify most existing organisations. Donations are an uncertain source of income for most organisations; free-rider incentives often keep the flow of funds to organisations below the socially optimal level; trusts run on donations are only part of the spectrum of philanthropic activity; and many NGO's are engaged in economic activities designed to generate incomes to make the poor self reliant. The Shome Committee wanted a criterion of charitable that was based on source of income rather than end purpose.

The extent of philanthropy in higher education in India depends upon whether or not one classifies a large number of private colleges as surrogate businesses or as genuinely philanthropic. This phenomenon is of some interest because it helps shed light on an apparent paradox. While the number of educational trusts is increasing, most of them are generating revenue by charging for services rather than through donations or endowments.

Contributions from alumni are beginning to creep up but have been most noticeable only in the case of IIT's, which have been able to tap into a large base of professionalised alumni amongst the Indian diaspora. Donors are making voluntary gifts because of emotional attachment or commitment to the institutes. They will not hand off money to a nameless bureaucrat or a feckless politician. The new UPA government has reversed this decision, allowing alumni to contribute directly to their alma matters. The lack of autonomy of educational institutions has been one of the biggest impediments in attracting diasporic philanthropy for higher education. Alumni who are prepared to give substantial resources also want to have a say in its use and an institutionalised mechanism to have their voice heard. However, the governance structures of most higher education institutions are so poor that such mechanisms are non-existent. Even in the case of the All India Institute of Medical Sciences, alumni have balked at contributing if they have little say in the governance of that organisation.

Policy Requirements

It is the primary responsibility of the State to provide the eligible with good quality higher education at reasonable cost. There shall be no withdrawal of the State from this responsibility. In fact, the investment in this area by the State shall be stepped-up to 3% of the GDP. This is essential for the intellectual strength of the State to address equity concerns.

A huge dedicated fund say, National Human Resource Development Fund, to the tune of at least one- percent of the GDP, may be created to tackle the equity problems. It shall be the accepted principle that no talented person shall be denied access to higher education opportunities on the grounds of economic and social backwardness. This fund may be dedicated to offer direct financial support in the form of scholarships, partial financial assistance and educational loans to students directly, based on the criteria of talent and financial and social backwardness. A well-designed mechanism to spot talents in different disciplines of knowledge is needed for this purpose. Further, foolproof criteria to determine financial or any other social backwardness is required.

Taxing the individuals, who had the benefit of the state resources in the past for their education, and the industries, which are likely to derive advantage from good human resources, are the options for creating such a fund. While it is difficult to arrive at an ideal solution to the equity problems, the absence of a credible and efficient method of addressing these problems will lead to lowering of the quality of human ware and large-scale discontent. The society may be the ultimate looser.

Industries may be encouraged to be partners with educational institutions directly for the development of human resources dedicated to their interests. This could happen in the areas of creating infrastructure, faculty sharing and direct support with funds. The UGC may set-up a High Power Committee to explore these possibilities and to workout the modalities for such a partnership.

The industries belonging to a specific discipline or related disciplines shall be encouraged to establish state of the art research and training centres to develop the necessary specialised man power. Automobile industry is a case point. Existing public and private institutions and possible new institutions may generate ample provisions for partnerships in this regard. The areas not capable of attracting private funds shall be supported sufficiently well from public funds. This, as indicated earlier, is essential for the balanced intellectual growth of the society.

Industries and individuals may be encouraged to channel a percentage of their profits to the higher education sector, with no strings attached to such contributions. Viable incentives may be offered for attracting such investments from the private resources. A committee may work out the modalities.

Strong quality control measures to assure performance above an acceptable benchmark is essential for the institutions. We are at the moment weak in this regard. The various rating agencies shall evolve scientific, transparent and consistent benchmarking techniques for this purpose. A regulatory system to ensure compliance to the set bench marking is needed with sufficient powers to close down non-complying institutions is a need of the hour. The higher education policy needs to incorporate such features in it in the interest of the nation.

It is important to realise that we live in a fast changing world, dictated by the developments in technology. Quick access to information has made knowledge creation fast, and the multiplier effect has made it even explosive. It is increasingly difficult to anticipate changes and respond to them with creative purpose. Designing courses with relevance to the future and developing the necessary manpower to deliver them is a challenging task. All this calls for a team of professionals in different areas to come together to develop proactive strategies for higher education to meet the future demands. A strategy planning body and an institution to design and develop futuristic courses for transferring them to the universities and colleges may be created.

Good faculty is a must for any higher education institution aspiring for quality. It is high time that an Indian higher educational service, along the lines of the IAS, is formed. This has the advantage of quality control of the teaching faculty for higher education. A new human resource development policy shall be evolved to facilitate this. This could assure that there is continuous infusion of young blood in to the teaching cadre; which is not happening at the moment. With some restrictions on faculty appointments, the present evil of inbreeding can be eliminated. The inbreeding has destroyed many departments at Indian universities.

Private universities are a reality now and, as such, strong regulatory mechanisms are to be put in place immediately to monitor and control their activities with the objective of ensuring quality and social accountability. Higher education is a public good and cannot be left to the market forces to control. Those who venture investment in this area shall be properly scrutinised. Those with commercial interests dominating over the interests and ethics of higher education shall be eliminated.

The present archaic administrative practices need a thorough reform. A healthy public/private partnership can do much in this regard by way of exchanging good practices. A management system, lean but professional, making use of modern communication and information technologies is required to facilitate quality higher education. According autonomous status to all performing institutions will facilitate rapid development of efficient and state of the art higher education institutions. There shall be a dominant role for genuine academics in the governing structure of higher education institutions. The proposed regulatory mechanism shall have instruments to ensure this.

Governance

Policy framework is carefully planned at the level of the Planning Commission, Ministry of Human Resource Development and University Grants Commission. However, the policies are not fully implemented mostly because of faulty management of the institutions of higher education. The administrative structure of the Universities, which was devised in the pre-independence period seems to be still continuing. The new challenges facing the system of higher education in the country cannot be met without a total overhaul of the structure of management of higher education institutions. This has become all the more necessary because of globalisation, which requires talent, competence, drive, initiative and innovation at several levels. This cannot be achieved without overhauling the administrative set up of universities/institutions.

The governmental control in the universities must be reduced, so that the university autonomy and accountability are strengthened and academic decisions are taken on merit. New methods and procedures of financial regulations should be devised and direct interference of the finance department in the financial management of universities, which is counter productive should be stopped.

As the colleges are the feeding sources of the universities, a better coordination in their working and activities is very much required. The participation of the teaching faculty in through a democratic process should be ensured. Complete transparency should be maintained in the working of executive/academic bodies and other governing councils of the universities. There is an urgency to review the university acts in different states and revise the same in the light of the new requirements and the challenges being faced by the universities. New technologies of information and communication should be utilised for obtaining administrative efficiency.

Access and Equity

Today the world economy is experiencing an unprecedented change. New developments in science and technology, media revaluation and internationalisation of education and the ever expanding competitive environment are revolutionising the education scene. A paradigm shift has been noticed in higher education now a days, from 'national education' to 'global education', from 'one time education for a few' to 'life long education for all', from 'teacher- centric education' to 'learner centric education'. These changes make new demands and pose fresh challenges to the established education systems and practices in the country. Because of interdependence and integration of world economy in recent years, the Indian higher education system has a new role and a challenge to provide to the nation and the world at large, skilled human power at all levels, having breadth of knowledge and confidence to effectively confront the social and economic realities.

It is worth noting that while India has the second largest system of higher education, next only to USA, the total number of students hardly represent 6 percent of the relevant age group, i.e., 18-23, which is much below the average of developed countries, which is about 47 per cent. Thus, access, equity, accountability and quality should form the four guiding principles, while planning for higher education development in India in the twenty-first century.

It is true that enhancing social access to higher education is still important in the country. But, the major challenge before the

Indian higher education system is to bring equity in quality of education across the length and breadth of the country. This is more close to the heart of students in rural, semi urban and urban areas, because they also wish to be able to participate in the new economic revolution.

Several social, economic and political reasons seem to act as constraints to access and equity in higher education in India. Poverty leads to high drop-out rates even at primary, middle and secondary school levels. Lower status of women, lack of easy access, lack of implementation of existing programmes, inadequate utilisation of resources, absence of political will and inadequacies in coordinated actions across all equity fronts within institutions seem to be the other reason. Financial constrains also often form a significant factor in advancing equity.

Strategies for higher education should be set within an educational chain extending from early childhood to post-graduate education to career advancement. Improving the interrelationship of all stages and levels of education should be a long-term policy goal. Rural, urban and gender disparities must be kept in mind by policy makers in planning and implementing the higher education system.

While quantity is important, say achieving, double digit percentage for higher education, quality is paramount. Higher education should continue to be subsidised by the government in an adequate manner. For improving the quality in education the role of public sector should be enhanced. While the Western models of higher education should be suitably adopted, the education planners/implementers and the institutions should devise and develop indigenous ones.

Policies of higher education should be designed to strengthen indigenous research agenda. One reform that is urgently needed is the right to information in the institutions of higher learning. Transparency in the functioning at all levels is required so that those committing wrong are deterred. Increasing reliance on the generation of internal revenues through consultancy and interaction with industry may produce imbalances in the universities across various disciplines of study. So, efforts for the mobilisation of resources have to be made extremely cautiously. Keeping in view our concerns of equity, efficiency and excellence in university education. Hence, the best method of financing of the universities may still be by the state.

Export of Higher Education

Increasing economic integration across the World over the past decade has cast tumultuous impact on all the areas supporting human life in the developing countries, which constitutes about 80% of the work force. The so-called structural adjustments in national policies and the new international economic order have brought about severe stresses never perceived before. There are exhortations to the policy planners of higher education emanating from GATT regulations made under WTO formulation e.g. withdrawal of subsidies, reduced control of the state, larger privatisation and access to corporate players, designing of courses to meet the human resource needs of the markets in the changed scenario, and reliance on self-financing type management. There are also obligations to allow free import of higher education as a service commodity from developed nations in the form of cross-border supply, consumption abroad etc. The cumulative effect of all these factors and the prevailing competitive environment have hustled the morale, confidence and commitment of the university community in general, even inducing trepidation.

Improving the low level of enrolment ratio, ensuring better equity, access, sound and realistic man-power planning, faster growth of skilled human resource for a self-reliant course of economic development and universalisation of basic education are the other major challenges. In such a skewed and gruelling perspective, the university academics and administrators, are confronted with so many challenges calling for knee-jerk response and pro-active approaches to management of institutions of higher education with a high level of professionalism, competence and quality assurance. They are duty bound to tide over the challenges facing the institutions and deliver quality goods and services to the customers and users without any opacity, obsession or prejudice. Outline of the strategies, the imperative scope of expansion, dimensions of diversification, potentials for both short- and long-term planning and modalities of placid administrative processes warranted in the contemporary ambience, but in the changed context, have been discussed by experts and researchers.

There was a consensus that without compromising the national ethos of equity and access to higher education to all the intending learners at reasonable cost and to the socially disadvantaged ones at subsidised levels, higher education institutions in India must boost their activities to provide diversified academic products and services of high quality and with a strong market orientation.

The central and state governments should introduce a range of programmes and incentives designed specially to improve the links between universities and industry. The universities and national institutes of higher learning should design their courses in collaboration with industry and such courses be updated regularly, e.g., every year, according to need. There should be uniformity, as far as possible, in the standards of the courses, academic calendar and the examination system of universities.

Working facilities and workload of teachers should be as per the international norms. Teachers should be encouraged to attend various conventions, conferences, seminars, workshops in their disciplines to update their subject know how. As per need, hostel facilities should be developed for foreign students in the universities. And a foreign students' advisor's office should be created to look after the foreign students in a proper way.

There should be regular monitoring and evaluation of teaching and research in the universities and other institutions of higher learning. A monitoring and evaluation unit should be set-up at state level preferably attached to chancellor's office; and for its effective functioning, a statistical cell should be set-up in each university in the state, under the over all supervision of the unit. Necessary steps should be taken to attract bright students after graduation/post graduation to the teaching profession.

Campuses of top Indian universities and other premier institutions should be established in the target countries with the permission of the concerned governments. A tie-up with a foreign institution of higher education could also be a possible way by which the Indian institutions of higher education can make entry into the target markets.Franchising was also suggested by the speakers as one of the modes of entry into foreign countries. The Indian institution could offer our educational system and the operational details to a foreign institution, allowing the use of its name in exchange of an agreed fee. But, this requires careful monitoring and follow up. E-learning appears to be a fast emerging mode of global entry at the present time. The universities and other institutions of higher education can design their web sites for offering online education worldwide.

Deputing teachers of Indian institutions to different universities abroad on contractual basis with the built-in condition of introducing and operating the Indian higher education system there, is also a likely mode of entry into the foreign market. This should be given due consideration. Other desirable initiatives for export of higher education include:

i) Developing educational products of new models based on flexibility and learner's choice;
ii) Preparing students for the knowledge society;
iii) Providing methods and styles of working for lifelong learning;
iv) Arranging facilities for e-learning and distance learning;
v) Ensuring total quality management in the higher education system;
vi) Catering to the changing market demands and churn out adaptable work force, instead of providing them scope for narrow specialisation.

Economics of Higher Education

Access to higher education needs to be widened in the country, both within the formal system and through other effective innovative measures, such as a truly open system and networking of universities. It is now imperative on the part of Indian universities to generate their own resources to a large extent. This could be done through several methods, like raising tuition fee and collecting capitation fee, both of which having severe limitations; and others like, launching courses for foreign students, obtaining donations from philanthropists, etc., which have a good potential.

In the globalised world, the state-protected educational system cannot withstand the pressure without making itself competitive. There seem to be four reasons why new policy initiatives should be taken by the government in this connection. They are:

i) that the economic returns of primary education far exceed the returns of higher education;

ii) that the private returns on higher education far exceed the social returns;

iii) that the state funding for higher education is insufficient in countries like India; and

iv) that since private sector benefits the most from higher education, it is only just that it should make a decisive contribution.

Whether or not one accepts the government's rationale, new strategies need to be developed for the survival and well being of the higher education system in the present scenario. An organised structure for higher-educational fund raising and creating a culture of giving are the only possible solutions.

Reorientation of Higher Education

In the emerging new globally competitive environment in the country, the Indian student is required to develop a multifaceted personality to cope up with the rapid changes in the world at large. This calls for the development of body, mind and spirit, through the educational processes in the institutions of higher education.

Health consciousness and physical fitness for a healthy body should be an essential part of the university culture. But, a healthy body alone cannot be attained and maintained without a healthy mind. Therefore value education becomes a desirable moral necessity for meeting the challenges of the contemporary world. Professional competence is of little value if professional ethics are forgotten.

Similarly, brilliance is of no use if it is employed for anti social activities. In order to achieve all these ends effectively one has to see that the processes of education are properly regulated in terms of assessment and evaluation of learning. A close interaction between the teachers and the students in the evaluation of the progress of learning is desirable, so that teaching-learning process is not superficial.

Health Consciousness and Physical Fitness

Physical fitness and sports are two sides of the same coin and are mutually dependent on each other. As the famous dictum goes, mind is the key to man and eyes cannot see what mind cannot perceive. The relationship between mind and body has been acknowledged scientifically. It is generally believed that a healthy body has a healthy mind; but it could be the other way around also i.e. a healthy mind has a healthy body. However, this requires appropriate training.

Present day education is largely academic. Realistically, this orientation needs to be changed for a balanced development through inculcating health conscious amongst students. This includes the development at physical, mental and social levels. With the increasing emphasis on academics in the world of employment and elsewhere and the rapid advances in science and technology all over the world, parental pressure has been driving academic training at the cost of health and physical fitness of the youth. It is in this context that there is now an urgency to lay a strong foundation and strengthen physical education and sports programmes in the higher education institutions. This calls for the integration of physical education, sports, yoga and recreation activities in the higher education system for the overall good of the younger generation.

At present physical education is the only course taught at schools and colleges. It is important new subjects like, health management, fitness management and sports marketing are included in the curriculum, preferably as core/specialisation subjects at professional preparation courses.

Olympics education may be included from the elementary/ secondary level to higher secondary level of education to develop sports awareness among the children. Raising the standard of professional preparation courses in physical education and sports sciences is an urgent requirement in order to produce competent physical education teachers. This calls for institutions offering physical education courses to take effective measures in attracting students with sports background and achievements. There is need for counselling centres for providing guidance to the students aspiring to take up physical education as a career.

Standardised physical fitness testing procedures should be applied on a uniform basis at the professional colleges at the entry level. Besides, there is a need for restructuring professional programmes to update the courses in the field of physical education and sports so as to provide opportunities for the physical educators to adopt the emerging trends. Physical education programmes should also include yoga and meditation in order to create a positive attitude among the students so as to achieve success in life and make physical education more meaningful and relevant in terms of education for life. All the universities may be encouraged to establish facilities for education/training in yoga and meditation.

The development of fitness culture among university youth has to be given due priority. In this direction, physical fitness centres need be established at all the universities to provide fitness programmes for university teachers, students, and employees. These centres may also conduct special fitness programmes at various levels during holidays and vacations. Necessary financial allocation may be provided in the University budget and UGC may also consider suitable grants in this regard.

Professional Ethics and Value Education

The rapid developments in science and technology and the challenges of globalisation are posing additional challenges to the education system in the country. This is also the time when parental care to the children is on the wane. The adverse effects of the media on the mental development and moral values of the younger generation are being felt increasingly in all spheres of life. Gross consumerism has distorted the outlook of persons into one of equating possessions with richness. Exploitation of natural resources is proceeding without reference to sustainability. The hiatus between the rich and the poor is getting wider. While the education system needs to keep pace with the scientific and technological developments in terms of building the skills and knowledge, it also needs to address the more fundamental issues of the social and moral consequences of such unregulated activities. In this context, there is now a growing demand to lay greater emphasis on education to inculcate, nurture and develop values, particularly among the youth of the country.

The need of the hour is to inculcate human values in the University students, like quest for peace, adherence to truth and right conduct, non-violence, compassion, tolerance, love for all living beings, respect for the motherland and the glory of its culture and traditions, in order to promote societal concern and responsible citizenship; so that such an effort is in the interest of the students, society and the nation. It is entirely feasible to inculcate 'values' in the students at the tertiary level, and there are several institutions in the country where such value-based education is imparted with impressive results. Nowever, it requires sustained efforts to practice, absorb, and assimilate values. It is desirable that human values should permeate and form part of the teaching in all disciplines and subjects.

The UGC may work towards evolving a syllabus for a compulsory paper of appropriate credits at the undergraduate level of all disciplines, to stress human values and the duties laid down in the constitution, and the same may be suitably supported by the methodology and examination/evaluation criteria facilitating a learner-centric approach. Recognising the special role of teachers in this effort, it would be desirable to impart them the necessary skills and insights into value education by devising suitable orientation courses and extending support to institutions for imparting such training. This may be given due consideration by the UGC and effective steps taken to introduce these courses at identified Academic Staff Colleges.

Human values should be the guiding parameters for governance processes at higher education institutions. The university system may take note of this. The UGC may consider taking suitable measures for disseminating this information in the higher education system. Due recognition should be given to the expanding socially relevant role of open education and to explore the methods of communicating and internalising 'human values' among the students. Special attention should also be given to develop appropriate study material for this on a priority basis through proper supportive measures.

Evaluation and Assessment Systems

During the last 50 years, higher education in India has made great strides leading to the Indian higher education system becoming one of the largest systems in the world. Unfortunately, it is the Indian experience that this expansion in quantity has overshadowed the quality of higher education. Lately, a chorus of criticism is heard from various well-meaning quarters about the deteriorating quality of higher education. It is well known that one of the important components of higher education is the manner in which students' academic performance is evaluated. A concerted debate has been going on to determine the best system of assessment to be followed by the universities in the twenty first century. A great degree of diversity has been observed in terms of assessment and grading of the students in the university system at present. It is desirable that a certain optimum degree of standardisation in the examination system and in the assessment of students is put in place before grades are awarded to them.

Continuous internal assessment should be given the attention it merits in the students' academic programmes at the universities. The grading system with a linear 10-point scale and its equivalence in terms of percentage of marks should be followed uniformly across universities and disciplines. However, the evaluation methodology may vary across disciplines/institutions. Pre-and post-processes of examinations should be made transparent. i.e. the pattern of papers, evaluation methodology, disciplinary rules etc. should be properly documented and communicated to students well in advance.

Appropriate and effective feedback mechanism (e.g. returning corrected answer books to students, responding to students' queries on the evaluation procedure, etc.) should be established at all institutions. Examination should be designed in such a way that at least some portion of it evaluations the students' insight into the subject, In the continuous evaluation based on objective-type questions, measuring the higher mental ability of students should be adopted and ICT may be effectively used to set and evaluate such papers. Serious efforts should be made in developing question banks by following rigorous scientific procedures across disciplines. If need be, regional level workshops may be organised for the purpose. Computerised database may be created in each discipline.

Proper orientation on assessment methods should be given to all the teachers, particularly to the newly appointed teachers. The

Academic Staff Colleges set up by the UGC at different universities may be assigned this task A proper structure for examination reforms units for the universities should be evolved, supported by UGC to keep the nationwide evaluation processes at universities under continuous scrutiny. Research on the desirability and relevance of existing examination patterns and improvements there on in any given institution should be encouraged and facilitated. Innovative practices related to examination reforms should be empirically tested and institutionalised.

Quality Assurance

In an environment of global competitiveness it is important that Indian products of the higher education institutions are as competent as graduates of any other country, not only in their scholastic attainments, but also in terms of the value system and richness of their personality. Unless the quality and standard of Indian higher education institutions is enhanced sealously and sustained at a high level through innovation, creativity and regular monitoring, it seems to be difficult for the Indian academics/professionals to compete in the world scene. This calls for suitable assessment and accreditation mechanisms to be available in the country to ensure the quality and standard of the academic/training programmes at higher educational institutions. The assessment has to be continuous and the process has to be transparent to gain the acceptance of the society at large.

Sustaining Quality

Quality has both absolute and relative connotations. The concept of absoluteness in quality props up the morale of the higher education system at the delivery end i.e. institutional, and at the receiving end i.e. students. Quality dimensions seem to have two implications, i.e., functionality of the output and meeting the basic standards. Hence, the quality of a higher education system may be seen from the point of view of norms and standards, which may evolve depending on the need of the hour. In the 21st century, it is crucial to identify the relative norms for different components of a higher education system. The alternative dynamics for teacher preparation and the sustaining quality in teacher input, like:

Curriculum design and development; Curricular practices *vis-a-vis* emerging principles of pedagogy; evaluation of learners performance and progress *vis-a-vis* curriculum evaluation; and, quality management practices become crucial. The quality of these components may also differ from institution to institution. Therefore, sharing of the experiences among institutions on quality issues may generate ideas for evolving norms and strategies for their quality assurance of management processes, curricular inputs and practices and the evaluation system as well.

Of late, various developments have been witnessed relating to quality assurance mainly through the intervention of information and communications technologies (ICT) in education, like networking of the open learning system with traditional universities, interdisciplinary interactions at intra-institutional and inter-institutional levels, networking of institutions globally, data based management of higher education, changing the orientation of institutions by incorporating self financing in their financial management, assessment and accreditation of higher education institutions and creation of different statutory and regulatory bodies at the national level.

Integrated approach by involving experts from different fields with major focus on sharing of experiences in a holistic framework and having dialogues at different levels such as: at core committee level and at sub committee level. Multidisciplinary curriculum must be developed with a view to cater to the needs and fulfilment of expectations of learners, teachers parents, employers and society in general.

Every university must have its own curriculum. There should not be any mechanism for central curriculum framework at higher education level. Context, specificity and inquiry oriented experience must be reflected in the curriculum. Learners' participation in the generation of knowledge must be the focus of constructiveist curriculum. Problem solving abilities must be developed through experimentation life-like situations.

Assessment and Accreditation

The fact of the matter is that the Indian elite and middle classes have not cared for making education, what to say of higher education, accessible to the other sections of society. It is ironic that the beneficiaries of privileged access to institutions of higher learning are ever ready to persuade others to believe that the Indian education system has expanded beyond reasonable limits. The fact of the matter is that the system needs to be expanded to a much greater scale to serve the needs of the Indian youth. Many institutions of higher education in the country are excellent in the sense that their infrastructure, resources, faculty, programmes of teaching and research are almost as good as the best in the advanced countries. But, the same cannot be said of the average institutions of higher education in the country. They do not come anywhere near the level of average institutions of higher education in the advanced countries. This vast gap in standards and facilities has been a cause of constant anxiety and concern to the policy planners of higher education in India.

The issue of accessibility to quality higher education needs to be addressed in the light of the vast economic and social disparities, cultural and linguistic diversities, and extremely uneven opportunities of learning at the school level together with the aspirations and capacities of the potential students. Therefore, the question of access to higher education needs to be addressed at the local, regional, national and international levels from transdisciplinary, interdisciplinary and discipline-specific perspectives. The issue of accessibility of quality higher education arises in the context of the transition in the country from elitist to mass education in the post-independence period. The issue has significant implications in the sense that it demands a redefinition of the aims of higher education. Accessibility and quality upgradation are inseparable dimensions of higher education. Overemphasis on one at the cost of the other would be counterproductive.

India being a country of the sub-continental size with a population above 1 billion, the quantitative expansion of education (i.e. accessibility dimension) is of paramount importance to mitigate disparities across regions, gender and social strata in the field of education. This should be given due consideration. Along with the necessary and inevitable quantitative expansion of higher education, it is equally important to improve the quality of higher education. Institutions of higher education would find it difficult to meet the challenges of globalisation of higher education if one fails on this front. Emphasis on quality parameters becomes all the more necessary in the light of mushrooming of private institutions with the opening up of the Indian economy.

Quality upgradation is not a one time phenomenon. Quest for excellence is a continuous and perennial pursuit. In view of this, post- accreditation complacency must be arrested by evolving quality assurance mechanism for self-regulation. The setting up of an Internal Quality Assurance Cell (IQAC), is one such mechanism. The IQAC comprising the chief executive, senior academics and officers of the institution should work as a steering group. The cell may constitute two quality groups, one for academic excellence and another for administrative efficiency. These groups may design strategies for quality enhancement for consideration and implementation by IQAC.

Effectiveness of quality upgradation initiatives in higher education largely depend on the quality of primary and secondary education. Institutional mechanisms on the pattern of NAAC, may be set up for upgrading the quality of education at these levels to further enhance the outcome of NAAC efforts. Periodic assessment exercises in the future should be undertaken by IQAC as part of post assessment and accreditation exercises. These could be conducted in collaboration with NAAC.

With a view to ensure maximum participation of college teachers in workshops/seminars/conferences and orientation/ refresher courses, it is suggested that these events be organised during lean periods in institutional academic work. This would help the teachers to participate in these activities without upsetting the teaching schedule. Assessment and accreditation bodies like NAAC should take into account these implications while reviewing the quality parameters. The NAAC could also inform the institutions as to where they stand in terms of the standards of excellence from a global perspective.

References

Carnoy, M., *Globalisation and Educational Reform: What Planners Need to Know*, Report No.63, International Institute of Educational Planning, Paris, 1999.

Government of India, *Programme of Action on the National Education Policy*, Ministry of Human Resource Development, New Delhi, 1992.

Salmi, J., "Perspectives on the Financing of Higher Education", *Higher Education Policy*, Vol.5, No. 2, pp.13-19, 1992.

Stewart, F., "Globalisation and Education", *International Journal of Educational Development*, Vol.16, No.2, pp. 327-33, 1996.

UNESCO, Higher education in the Twenty-first Century: Vision and Action, Final Report, World Conference on Higher Education, UNESCO, Paris,5-9, October, 1998

UNESCO, *Higher Education in Developing Countries: Peril and Promise*, The Task Force on Higher Education and Society, World Bank, Washington, D.C., 2000.

World Bank, *Higher Education: Lessons from Experience*, Washington, D.C., 1994.

World Bank, *Constructing Knowledge Societies: New Challenges for Tertiary Education*, Washington, D.C., 2002.

Ziderman, A. and D.Albrecht, *Financing Universities in Developing Countries*, The Stanford Series on Education and Public Policy, The Falmer Press, Washington, D.C., 1995.

5. INTERNATIONALISATION OF HIGHER EDUCATION

Today is an era of globalisation students are migrating to other countries to obtain higher education and today they continue to do so in increasing numbers. Increasingly, institutions of higher education are building partnerships with universities in other countries, delivering education using online and other technologies, and setting up branch campuses abroad that are changing the structure and relationships that traditionally existed in higher education. With such trends continuing, growing numbers of students seeking higher education in the years ahead will be able to obtain quality education in their homelands or neighbouring countries rather than having to travel to other regions to do so.

The results of globalisation show the integration of research, the use of English as the lingua franca for scientific communication, the growing international labour market for scholars and scientists, the growth of communications firms and of multinational and technology publishing, and the use of information technology (IT). IT's communication, efficient storage, selection, and dissemination of knowledge allows providers to offer academic programmes through e-learning.

The international activities of universities range from traditional study abroad programmes allowing students to learn about other cultures, providing access to higher education in countries where local institutions cannot meet the demand to upgrading the international perspectives and skills of students, enhancing foreign language programmes, and providing cross-cultural understanding.

Global capital has, for the first time, invested heavily in knowledge industries worldwide, including higher education and advanced training. This investment indicates the emergence of the "knowledge society", the rise of the service sector, and the dependence of many societies on knowledge products and highly educated personnel for economic growth. These elements of globalisation underlie our analysis.

Internationalisation vs. Globalisation

The focus here is on academic programmes, institutions, innovations, and practices created to cope with globalisation, and to reap its benefits. Globalisation may not be alterable, but internationalisation involves many choices. Globalisation concentrates on wealth, knowledge, and power in those already possessing these elements. International academic mobility similarly favours well-developed education systems and institutions, thereby compounding existing inequalities. Initiatives and programmes, coming largely from the North, are concentrates in the South. Northern institutions and corporations own most knowledge, knowledge products, and IT infrastructure, though South-to-South activities are increasing, especially in Asia and Africa. Internationalisation is a two-way process—students move largely from South to North, for example—and meets important needs of the developing world. But the North largely controls the process. Cross-border of students and of higher education programmes and institutions—big businesses for universities and other providers—the growing international market for academic and scientific personnel, curricular internationalisation, and the commercialisation of international higher education, especially the growing influence of the for-profit higher education sector all come under the purview of internationalisation.

The role of interactions between systems of higher education has increased as the interactions between individuals, institutions, and countries around the world have accelerated. This includes the inter-connectedness of economies, environments, technologies, political, and other systems. These interactions around the world require a look at education systems beyond an individual nation-state and from the perspective of the nation-state of those forces beyond its borders. Knight and DeWit define global and international education as follows:

> "Globalisation is the flow of technology, economy, knowledge, people, values, ideas...across borders. Globalisation affects each country in a different way due to a nation's individual history, traditions, culture and priorities.
> Inter-nationalisation of higher education is one of the ways a country responds to the impact of globalisation yet, at the same time respects the individuality of the nation.".

Twenty-first century forces require that countries look at the impact of the global on their higher education systems (mission, administration, faculty, students, community, teaching, research, and community service) as they provide education to support individual country, regional and world educational needs for the future. Whether policy-makers decide to provide policy that will increase collaboration or decrease interactions across borders, this policy should be developed from a framework, which looks at the global and international forces in place. Altbach and Teichler, elaborate on some of these forces:

i) Common academic model worldwide

ii) Increasingly global academic marketplace: students and staff

iii) Use of English internationally for research and teaching

iv) Use of distance education and internet for research and teaching

v) Trend of institutional partnering with other country institutions

vi) Creation of off-shore campuses

vii) Franchising of educational programmes and degrees

vii) Harmonisation of degree structures, courses, credits, related mechanisms of evaluation, and measurement of academic progress.

Institutions should take into account the various levels at which these forces provide impact upon their constituents. Following is a list of ten levels of these forces to help provide a framework. Below each level, a sample of relevant institutions or programmes that make up the organisations at each level is listed. Many more institutions could be added at each level as institutional leaders consider the impact of the individuals and institutions that will impact them in providing for educational policy:

i) *Worldwide (Global/Multinational) Government Level*
   - a) United Nations
   - b) World Bank

ii) *Regional Government Level*
   - a) European Union
   - b) North American Free Trade Agreement (NAFTA)

iii) *National Government Level*
   - a) Fulbright: US Department of State
   - b) FIPSE: US Department of Education

iv) *State/Province Government Level*
   - a) Illinois International Education Association
   - b) K-12/Higher Education: State Department of Education

v) *Local Institution Level*
   - a) University System Realities
   - b) Individual University Realities

vi) *Cultural Group Level*
   - a) Religion/Missionary
   - b) Heritage Student Programmes

vii) *Personal Level*
   - a) Travel, Study, Work, Job Training Abroad
   - b) Language Learning/Cultural Learning

viii) Technological Level
   - a) World Wide Web/E-Mail
   - b) Distance Learning

xi) Agency Level
   - a) American Council on Education
   - b) Institute of International Education, NAFSA: Association of International Educators

x) Corporate Level
   - a) Motorola
   - b) Siemens

Meaning and Nature of Internationalisation

The term "internationalisation" covers different things, and includes different dimensions, with varied stresses at different levels of higher education. The definition of internationalisation of higher education varies and depends on the stakeholder groups, government, private sector, institution, faculty member, academic discipline, and student. These differing perspectives result in several reasons for many program approaches to internationalisation of higher education. A commonly accepted definition in this study is Knight's definition.

> Internationalisation of higher education is the process of integrating an international/intercultural dimension into the teaching, research and service elements of an institution

This definition is accepted, given its emphasis on process and the three important functional dimensions of universities: teaching, research and service. There are also three key concepts in this definition. The idea of internationalisation is that it is a dynamic process and not a set of isolated activities. Integration and infusion are also the keys in this definition to ensure that the international dimension is a central part of programmes, policies, and procedures, not marginal, yet an easily expandable element. Both an international and intercultural dimension are included in this definition to emphasise the fact that internationalisation is not only oriented to countries or national states but also includes different cultural/ethnic groups within a country.

Knight in her later work has refined her definition to include what she refers to as both a bottom-up and top-down approach, where she considers the important influence of the national/sectoral level on the international dimension of higher education through policy, funding, programmes and regulatory frameworks. Internationalisation at the national/sectoral/institutional levels is defined as: The process of integrating an international, intercultural or global dimension into the purpose, functions or delivery of post secondary education. She has proposed a more generic definition that is generalisable to different national educational contexts—one that does not specify the reasons, benefits, outcomes, actors, activities and stakeholders of internationalisation.

In the second half of this century, education has become more international. In this period, governments emphasise on internationalisation of higher education through international co-operation and exchange. Institutions and universities develop their own strategies to internationalise their researches and their teaching. Why is this happening? What are the reasons behind this revival? Is internationalisation the solution to all the present problems of a multicultural and international society? Finally, why does a country or a higher education institution believe that internationalisation is fundamental? What determines the nature and extent of its support and action in favour of internationalisation? These important questions are related to the importance of internationalisation of higher education, which should be answered in the following. There is not one single answer to those questions, as often thought. There are several and different reasons for internationalisation of higher education. Such reasons are changing and closely linked to each other; they are either complementary or contradictory, especially when they vary based upon the interests of diverse stakeholder groups. Furthermore, reasons for the internationalisation of higher education vary between and within countries.

An examination on the motivation for internationalising the higher education sector is a fascinating and complex task, but for brevity's sake, the reasons for internationalisation can be categorised into four groups: political, economic, academic, and social-cultural. The political reason is often considered more important at the national than at the institutional level. The economic reason has increasing importance and relevance in developed countries around the world. An effective way to improve and maintain a competitive edge is to develop a highly skilled and knowledgeable work force and to invest in applied research. The academic reason is linked directly with enhancing the teaching and learning process and achieving excellence in research and scholarly activities. The social-cultural reason for internationalisation is changing in light of the potential impact of globalisation. Higher education has traditionally been a part of cultural agreements and exchanges. Today's globalised economy, information and communication system suggest another aspect of the social-cultural reason.

These four types of reasons are not entirely distinct or exclusive. An individual's, an institution's, or a country's motivation is a complex and multileveled set of reasons evolving over time and in response to changing needs and priorities. Knight has listed other reasons for internationalisation, which are human resources development, strategic alliances, commercial trade, nation building and socio/cultural development, cultural identity, citizenship development, national security, technical assistance, peace and mutual understanding, and economic growth and competitiveness.

Prerequisites

Globalisation is a basic element to qualify and internationalise higher education. There is a close relationship between internationalisation, globalisation and qualification of higher education. The prerequisites of internationalisation and qualification of higher education are not much different. The prerequisites of quality education are mission, vision, core values, smart objectives, admissions, libraries, laboratories, sports, disabilities, staff, and counselling. Therefore, the prerequisites of internationalisation of higher education can be categorised as mission and vision statements, core values, smart objectives and services provided by a university. Mission, vision, core values and smart objectives are elaborated with hypothetical statements as below:

i) *Mission statement*: The purpose of university is to provide quality education in the arts, and sciences, at both the undergraduate and graduate levels.

ii) *Vision statement*: The vision statements may produce discoveries that make the world a better place, open the world to students, provide career-oriented and graduate innovative programmes, achieve a higher quality of education and research, learning and teaching excellence, effective engagement with community, enterprise multiculturalism, currency and relevance, increased access to innovative pedagogy, creative use of technology.

iii) *Core values*: The core values in internationalisation of higher education are integrity and respect, honesty and accountability, and intellectual rigor.

iv) *Smart objectives*: The objectives of internationalisation of higher education should be specific,measurable, achievable, and realistic in nature to be achieved within a fixed time frame.

v) *Services*: The features of universities are the services they provide.

Internationalisation of higher education requires tolerance and international cooperation in educational activities and plans in order to generate science. In spite of today's issues, it also requires communication skills, rationality, creative thinking, active participation, collective action, tolerance of each other, acceptance of criticisms, and scientific approach for internationalisation of higher education. Based on this, pre-requisites of internationalisation of higher education are as follows:

i) In spite of culture, geography and regional policies, we should pay attention to that: we are human;

ii) Encourage the knowledge and realisation of cultures and affirming on the bilateral respect;

iii) Achievement of necessary skills, tolerance and learning from others;

iv) Affirmation and realisation of world challenges accompanying the needs;

v) Flexibility in facing cultural affairs;

vi) The necessity of the constructive approach to solve international problems;

vii) Acceptance of responsibility in and effective execution of regional and international projects.

Universities should construct themselves by international cooperation to prepare for the possibility of bilateral knowledge for a better future.

Context of Internationalisation

There has been a great flow of students for decades to other countries for higher education, and teachers and researchers of high-income countries have been awarded grants and travel assistance to enable them to collaborate with scholars and institutions in other countries. Cross-border mobility of students, teachers and researchers has increased in recent decades and international flows of academic personnel now crisscross the globe in all directions. As a consequence there are growing numbers of people from diverse cultures into exchange with each other in a neutral environment focused on learning and intellectual exchange. Students who crossed international borders for higher education purposes used to originate mainly in countries in the South and flowed to countries in North America or Western Europe to continue their advanced studies. Today, in contrast, significant south-to-south and north-to-south flows are occurring as well, and flows in all directions are growing rapidly.

Earlier there was international research collaboration mainly comprising individual faculty members from developed countries travelling to another developed country or to a developing one for research collaboration. On those trips, they gave delivered lectures or participated in seminars at the host institution but their main purpose was to collaborate with research colleagues in another country. Graduate students often accompanied their professors abroad and visiting faculty took advantage of their travel to recruit prospective graduate students for study at their universities. Individual research collaborations between academic professionals from different countries remain important today. However, formal collaborations between universities that involve curriculum and programme development are growing and likely to expand in the years ahead.

With the increased international mobility of students and academic personnel, universities have taken steps in recent decades to enhance the international content of their programmes and course offerings and to require students to learn foreign languages so that they will be well equipped to work in corporations, government agencies and other institutions that have transnational operations. To equip their students for work in the global economy, leading universities encourage students to participate in study abroad programmes and to pursue such programmes that include international curricula. In addition, business schools are developing international MBA programmes, law schools are expanding their course offerings in international law and regulation, and medical schools are collaborating with health programmes abroad to make their students aware of tropical and other diseases that travel rapidly from one country to another as international flow of people increase.

Closure of Private Foundations and Bilateral Agencies

Multilateral and bilateral agencies and private foundations have acknowledged for decades that to advance economic and social development, the supply of human capital in emergent economies needed expansion and higher education capacity needed to strengthening. To meet this perceived need, in the 1960s, private foundations and bilateral agencies developed scholarship programmes that enabled students from developing country to obtain higher education in North America or Europe. However, sending students to another country for higher education was costly and fell out of favour in the 1980s as evidence accumulated that scholarship programmes led to a "brain drain" for most sending countries and a "brain gain" for countries where foreign students went. In response, funding agencies phased out their scholarship programmes in the 1980s. A few private foundations continued to provide scholarships for foreign students in selected fields such as agriculture and population studies, but most of those programmes too were eventually phased out in the 1990s.

Deterioration in Higher Education

Focus on study abroad and capacity building at home shifted in the 1980s to primary and secondary education which was a more equitable and efficient means of improving health and other social indicators. Experts argued that before investing further in elite higher education, countries should invest in elementary and secondary education and seek to achieve universal education at those levels. In addition, countries were encouraged to provide short-course training to extension agents and others who need specialised skills to deliver health, agriculture and community-delivery services. "Funds were cut back for universities at the same time that tertiary enrolments started to increase rapidly as a result of economic and population growth. As a result, education quality suffered at many third-world universities. Further deterioration in higher education capacity occurred in countries where governments passed laws that required universities to admit all qualified students but restrained them from raising student fees to cover the costs of growing student bodies. As a result, many faculty members associated with universities in Africa, Latin America and Asia left them to work in the private sector or fled their countries to work with international agencies or NGOs that sought to internationalise their staffs. Those developments led to further deterioration in higher education institutions in the developing world and exacerbated the brain drain.

Indian Context

It is important to look at ways that globalisation in education can have negative, as well as positive consequences. Today, trends such as the rise of the Internet and the globalisation of knowledge have the potential for creating severe problems for academic institutions and systems in smaller or poorer nations. In a world divided into centres and peripheries, the centres grow stronger and more dominant and the peripheries become increasingly marginalised. Inequalities grow more pronounced. There is little leeway for academic systems or individual universities to independently develop in the increasingly competitive and fast moving global higher education scene dominated by the world-class universities in the industrialised countries. The traditional academic centre becomes ever stronger and more dominant-mainly in the English-speaking countries of the North (the United States, the United Kingdom, Canada) and in Australia, and in the larger countries of the European Union (Germany, France, and to some extent Italy and Spain).

The norms, values, language, scientific innovations, and knowledge products of countries in the centre crowd out other ideas and practices. These countries are home not only to the dominant universities and research facilities but also to the multinational corporations so powerful in the global knowledge system. Information technology companies such as Microsoft and IBM, biotechnology and pharmaceutical firms, multinational publishers like Elsevier or Bertlesmann, among others, dominate the new international commerce in knowledge, knowledge-based products, and information technology. Smaller and poorer countries have little autonomy or competitive potential in the globalised world. Globalisation in higher education exacerbates dramatic inequalities among the world's universities.

The Indian universities have not been able to take advantage of the possibilities that internationalisation offers for improving the quality of education, promoting Indian culture in different countries, and deriving political or economic benefits. In the context of recent national and international developments, in all major areas—it is imperative that we take up the task of internationalisation of our higher education seriously.

After all, globalisation has permeated into practically all areas of India's social, cultural, political, and economic activities. The opportunities consequently available to the youth, in the national and global employment market, cannot be disregarded. These require that students be not only well versed with national issues, but also be conversant and informed about the global scene. In the coming years, international experience will be an added value, and perhaps a necessary requirement, in the student's portfolio. At the same time, there are concerns for the quality of programmes that are in place for Indian students. This concern reflects programmes available from international educational institutions in India and those available for Indian students around the world.

In order to promote quality education, it would be worthwhile to promote genuine institutional links that are based on equal participation and have adequate controls related to quality and financial arrangements. As a step in this direction the Association of Indian Universities (AIU), in 1999, formulated guidelines to enable the grant of equivalence to degrees offered in India by foreign universities. The main conditions laid down are:

i) The Indian institution (partner) has adequate infrastructure and facilities as substantiated by a report of a review committee of the AIU.

ii) The programme is implemented jointly by the foreign and Indian universities, or academic institutions affiliated to them, with both contributing to the academic programme in approximately equal measure.

iii) The foreign university gives and undertaking, in the form of a certificate, that the degree/diploma awarded to the student in India would be considered as equivalent to the corresponding degree/ diploma awarded by the University at home, and that it would be recognised in that country as being equivalent to the corresponding degree/diploma of the awarding university".

As the primary context for education continues to be inside the nation-state, it is important that governments look closely at the impact which international education can have on its system of education. In India, when thinking about internationalisation in education:

i) One would need to have set reasons/goals for internationalisation.

ii) Priorities may be fixed on the aspects of the internationalisation.

iii) The internationalisation should not be at the cost of country's own identity or its basic higher education or values.

iv) The educational knowledge created should be quality orientated.

v) The inter-cultural aspects should not pose a challenge to our own culture.

vi) Economic gains should not be the main consideration.

vii) The existing systems should be strengthened to meet the challenge.

viii) Proper ways and means should be worked out to implement the process.

ix) The model to be adopted should be a tested one, and must fit in to the country's environment.

x) The significance of internationalisation of higher education should be taken as development of the existing system, rather than something new or imported.

Free-Trade Context

The contemporary emphasis on free trade stimulates international academic mobility. The perception today is that international higher education is a commodity to be traded freely and sees higher education as a private good, not a public responsibility. Commercial forces therefore have a legitimate or even a dominant place in higher education, which comes under the domain of the market. The World Trade Organisation (WTO) will provide a regulatory framework to encourage international trade in education and service-related industries as part of negotiating the General Agreement on Trade in Services (GATS). GATS remains under negotiation, and individual countries may agree to some or all of its provisions. But GATS will, when WTO member countries implement the agreement, focus on facilitating academic mobility via:

- *Cross-border supply.* This mode may include distance education (e-learning), and franchising courses or degrees. It does not necessarily require the physical movement of the consumer or provider.
- *Consumption abroad.* The consumer moves to the country of the provider. This mode includes traditional student mobility.
- *Commercial presence.* The service provider establishes facilities in another country including branch campuses and joint ventures with local institutions.
- *Presence of natural persons.* This mode includes persons, including professors and researchers, who travel temporarily to another country to provide educational services.

Motivations and Sources

The most important stimuli for academic internationalisation has to be considered as a prerequisite for our analysis.

The for-profit higher education providers—such as Laureate (formerly Sylvan Learning Systems), and the Apollo Group (the present company of the University of Phoenix, now the largest private university in the US)—stormed the international market by establishing new institutions, purchasing existing institutions, and partnering with firms or educational institutions in other countries. Many countries also encourage and have new private universities with overseas links, some in the for-profit sector. Many universities use American, British, German or other foreign curricula; many teach in English, and some are accredited in other countries.

Traditional non-profit universities also have entered the international market. Their main motivations for internationalisation are to enhance research and knowledge capacity and to increase cultural understanding. Many universities are located in countries where governments cut public funding and encouraged international ventures—Australia and the United Kingdom, for example. Most initiatives including branch campuses, franchised degree programmes, and partnerships with local institutions—are focused on developing and middle-income countries.

Many countries, including Australia, Canada, the United Kingdom, and the US recruit international students to earn profits by charging high fees International graduate students also provide research and teaching services for modest compensation. They also spend significant amounts of money in the host countries. The sums are large since knowledge industries—especially higher education —often form a substantial part of the total economy.

Access Provision and Demand Absorption

The number of young people demanding and obtaining access worldwide increased dramatically with the advent of mass higher education. Demand is increasing rapidly even in countries still enrolling under 20 per cent of the age group, such as India, China, and much of Africa. Many international higher education services—focused on profits—provide access to students in countries lacking the domestic capacity to meet the demand. Access can take many forms: branch campuses, franchised foreign academic programmes or degrees, or independent institutions based on foreign academic models.

Traditional Internationalisation

Campus-based internationalisation initiatives include study abroad experiences, curriculum enrichment via international studies majors or area studies, strengthened foreign-language instruction, and sponsorship of foreign students to study on campus. Traditional internationalisation is rarely a profit-making activity, though it may enhance the competitiveness, prestige, and strategic alliances of the college.

Developing-country Internationalisation

Developing countries enter to a significant number of international students, though they produce a small minority of the worldwide student flow. Such countries seek to attract foreign students to their universities to improve the quality and cultural composition of the student body, gain prestige, and earn income. India and the Philippines, for example, are significant host countries for students from other developing countries. India hosts more than 8,000 students from abroad, 95 per cent from developing countries. China, Malaysia and India are developing strategies to attract students and to export educational programmes and institutions.

Individual Internationalisation

Students, constrained by immigration regulations, have the option either to return home following their academic work or stay at home and enrol in the programmes offered by foreign education providers. Most of the world's more than two million international students pay for their own academic work. They are therefore the largest source of funds for international education—not governments, academic institutions, or philanthropies.

Cross-border Higher Education

International higher education initiatives exist in almost every country. But the developed countries—especially the large English-speaking nations and, to a lesser extent, the larger EU countries—provide most services. By any measure—such as flows of international students, franchisers of academic programmes to foreign providers, international accreditors or quality guarantors, or controlling partners in mutual arrangements—reap the main financial benefits and control most programmes.

The "buying" countries are Asian and Latin American middle-income countries and, to a lesser extent, the poorer nations of the developing world that lack capacity to meet growing demand. The largest markets are therefore for "demand absorbing" programmes that provide access to students who could not otherwise attend a post-secondary institution. Government policies favouring particular ethnic groups over others may also influence demand in a few cases, such as

Malaysia. Foreign providers—almost always aiming to earn a profit—may link up with local entrepreneurs or public or private academic institutions, or may establish their own branch campuses.

Many prestigious European and American institutions have opened branch campuses in Singapore and Qatar, and the University of Chicago has established a business school in Spain. Their degree programmes may include study at the home campus, or entirely offshore studies. The market for international higher education initiatives thus ranges from students who cannot obtain access at home and seek almost any means to study to carefully targeted elite students in small high-quality programmes.

In by gone days, the cross-border flows in higher education was for students to migrate from one country to another to advance their studies. Lately several economic and social factors are encouraging international student mobility and competition between countries for foreign students. Students themselves are eager to advance their education and, if opportunity and resources permit, they are willing to do so by leaving their homelands and migrating to another country. In addition, universities in North America and Europe have been eager to receive foreign students for a host of reasons. Foreign students were welcomed traditionally because they brought cross-cultural and international diversity to universities. Universities in North American and Europe still value foreign students for that reason but also acknowledge that foreign students can help stabilise their student bodies and revenues. As the tertiary school-age population declines in countries with aging populations, a trend already underway, foreign students become substitutes for domestic students and can allow universities to stabilise their enrolments.

Governments of countries that send or receive foreign students usually view this type of cross-border flow favourably. Many receiving countries even recruit and provide scholarships to foreign students as a means of enhancing their international status and relations with other countries. As most foreign students subsidise their own living costs and fees, governments recognise that they bring in foreign exchange for expenditure in the cities and regions where education institutions are located, thereby stimulating local economies. This is seen as a means of advancing development. To achieve that end, governments and private foundations started scholarship programmes in the 1960s and 1970s as a means of building human capacity in Asia, South America and Africa. However today, sending countries are more likely than receiving ones to provide scholarship support, particularly in science and technology fields, but receiving countries continue to subsidise foreign students in other ways.

Importance of CBHE

In the olden days, most students went to the United States or Europe to do higher studies and that continues to be the trend today. However, even as the overall volume of international students increased in recent decades, the composition of flows to different destinations has changed. Moreover, further change may be on the horizon as cross-border education activities grow. The governments are becoming aware of the opportunities and challenges presented by cross-border higher education (CBHE) which has enormous potential for expanding the pool of human capital available to low- and middle-income countries which, in turn, could advance their economic and social development. Therefore, it is necessary to document the type of CBHE activities emerging to ensure that countries wishing to strengthen their higher education capacity and increase their pool of skilled workers can take advantage of new opportunities. It is equally vital to document how international student mobility is changing and identify trends that may emerge in the future as CBHE grows. The main objective is to start this documentation effort by reviewing trends in CBHE and international student mobility.

Strategies

Different elements have different roles in the internationalisation of higher education. These elements have been defined in various ways such as mechanisms, facilitators, activities, challenges, factors and strategies. The strategies are applied to describe the activities done by a university to integrate a global aspect into research, teaching, service functions, management policies and systems. Thus, internationalisation needs a suitable and operational strategy. The University of Tokyo specified five strategies for the internalisation of higher education. These strategies are global in nature, and may be operational to other universities to complete their plans. In these strategies, individuals at all levels must effectively play their roles and duties. In sum, the five strategies are:

i) Provision of an internationally high standard of education;
ii) Enhancement of research activities through strengthening international research networks;
iii) Promoting cooperation with international society;
iv) Improvement of infrastructure to promote internal internationalisation;
v) Formulation of a long-term internationalisation plan.

In addition to these strategies, internationalisation of higher education emphasises on active participation in educational programmes, research activities, educational reforms, challenges, opportunities and consequences of international and national changes in higher education. It seems that the most important point of view in internationalisation of higher education is the participation in the different educational and research programmes. Internationalisation with this important specification basically prevents from unification and omission of experiences and regional favours. Internationalisation also emphasises on cooperation, instead of unification. A realisation of this important viewpoint is necessary to plan and implement essential programmes for internationalisation. So, the most important strategies of internationalisation of higher education originated from global experience are as follows:

i) Revision of textbooks and representation of courses which correspond to the content of global community knowledge and international problems;
ii) Development of humanistic resources for the realisation of social, economic, cultural consequences of universities internationalisation;
iii) Scientific and cultural cooperation by the students unions and scientific boards of universities;
iv) Use of the comparative studies to present the content of existing educational programmes;
v) Emphasis on inter-cultural skills for planning in higher education;

vi) Acquaint students with abilities and skills in the international arena;
vii) The planning of special textbooks for foreign students;
viii) Exchange experiences among universities;
ix) The cause the effective and more international scientific cooperation among the universities;
x) Enrichment of university environments for educational and research activities according to the global standards;
xi) The planning of educational programmes according to the time needed through regional and international cooperation among universities;
xii) The acceptance of more numbers of scientific boards and foreign students in universities;
xiii) The protection of researchers, scientific boards and young managers in higher education;
xiv) The effective cooperation in planning, executing, accessing of the international research projects;
xv) Preparation of facilities for scientific boards to use new technologies;
xvi) Exercise of scientific cooperation through cooperation at international and regional levels;
xvii) Preparation of public information to save time and spend the existing capitals in other sectors in higher education;
xviii) Necessary preparation at the managerial level to develop an international higher education;
xix) Necessary preparation at the managerial level to face the challenges of higher education;
xx) Development of international and regional cooperation to promote the quality of educational programmes

Duties of Universities

Today, education in universities and higher education institutions have some aspects in common, i.e. communication information, the combinational approach and internationalisation and inter-cultural dialogue. The process of globalisation renews roles and responsibilities of a university. As a result, universities should revise their duties. They should then pass the internationalisation of international scientific cooperation at different educational and research levels using practical and possible programmes. Otherwise, the process of globalisation will bring problems for universities by serving communicative and informatics technologies.

The universities should pay attention on their roles and duties, such as training experts in international relations, increasing the number of international students, and emphasising cultural identity through a variety of educational programmes to prevent predictable crisis and solve existing difficulties. The main duties and roles of universities in the internationalisation of higher education process consist of:

i) The presence at the regional and international arena to internationalise the higher education;

ii) Development of higher education through a number of volunteers;

iii) The improvement of higher education quality by effective inter-university cooperation;

iv) The economisation of higher education institutions and universities' scientific cooperation;

v) The emphasis on community participation for using and generating science and knowledge;

vi) The realisation of serious vulnerabilities of the economic approaches in higher education, and attention to the humanistic values especially on the internationalisation of universities;

vii) An change in the attitude of the scientific boards in using new technologies.

The informatics and communication technologies have more effects on the performances and roles of universities and higher education institutions. They help the universities in textbooks planning, content, management and structure for coordinating the time upheavals. In spite of the preparation of more volunteers to enter the universities and institutions of higher education, these technologies and new tools of education have great effects on the necessity of continuous learning.

International Education Arrangements

International research and programme collaborations between universities in two or more countries are growing rapidly and have implications for international student mobility. Universities, governments and other institutions are setting up collaborative programmes that usually involve the delivery of higher education itself in a different country than the one where the host institution is located.

GATS framework classifies education services into four categories: cross-border supply of education services from one country to another; the supply of education services in one's territory to a national of another country; the supply of education services by an institution from a foreign country; and the supply of the education service by a provider from another country. Under this typology, foreign students would be a consumption abroad service while movement of natural persons would involve the international mobility of the supplying institution's teachers or managers.

Study abroad programmes can be set up in universities in several ways but typically they do so by collaborating directly with universities in another country; by setting up an office in another country and delivering the service themselves; or by contracting with education agents who deliver the service to their students. The Erasmus Programme in Europe, the largest study abroad programme. One set up in 1987 under the auspices of the Socrates programme, permits European nationals to spend 3-12 months of study in another European country—31 European countries currently participate in the Erasmus programme.

The United Kingdom is the biggest net importer of Erasmus funded students followed by Ireland, Sweden, and the Netherlands. In 2003, the European Parliament and Council allowed students from third-world countries to study in Europe. Under this extended programme, students from the Third-World will receive up to 5,000 scholarships annually and European Union graduate students can compete for 4,000 scholarships for study in Third-World countries.

Programme Partnerships and Branch or Offshore Campuses

Programme partnerships and branch or offshore campuses are

difficult to differentiate because both involve some form of collaboration between institutions located in two or more countries. The distinction between these two types of institutional collaborations depends upon whether students receive a degree for their study as well as course credit and, if a degree is awarded, which institution awards the degree. Programme partnerships are defined as international institutional collaborations under which each of the participating partners awards course credit. While some of these may require study abroad participation as part of the degree, as long as the degree is awarded by a single institution to students enrolled in the study programme in the university's home country, it can remain outside of a country's regulatory framework. Thus, according to this definition, programme partnerships are "informal" and mainly involve collaboration on programme "content" rather than formal accreditation.

Branch or offshore campuses are formal cross-border higher education initiatives (CBHE) with the intent of awarding participating students with a joint degree in the name of the participating partners or under the brand name of the foreign participating university even though none of the education may have taken place in the university's origin country. It is becoming common under branch campus arrangements for students to receive a degree from the foreign university that set up that campus even though it is not located in the country where the higher education took place. This may lead to "quality" being compromised. If a prestigious international university allows its name to be used on the degree, this sends a strong signal to prospective students and their future employers that quality standards were high.

It is more viable for universities to establish programme partnerships than branch campuses in another country because they are informal collaborations and thus less likely to be restricted by a country's regulatory framework. Since Programme Partnerships can usually be set up by two or more universities in different countries, they are more common than branch campuses. In most countries, from a juridical standpoint, as long as the foreign university is not setting up a branch campus in its own name but only collaborating with an established higher education institution in that country, it does not have to obtain government approval. Thus, establishing a programme partnership between two or more universities incorporated in different countries is an easier way for foreign universities to deliver higher education services in another country since no accreditation issues are involved. For foreign universities, however, the branch campus is a better option arrangement because that enables them to retain greater control over the curriculum and expand their revenue base.

Increasing numbers of universities are teaming up with universities in other countries to develop joint study programmes or programme partnerships. Students at participating universities may spend up to a year at the partner institution(s) as a study abroad student. Programme partnerships are similar to study abroad programmes as each participating institution awards students credit for study carried out at the participating foreign university but they differ in that all or most of the content of the foreign study programme is developed jointly by the programme partners. Moreover, students enrolled in the study programme are required to follow the joint curriculum and usually have to do part of their training at the foreign participating institutions.

The Trium Global Executive MBA programme offered jointly by the London School of Economics and Political Science, the New York University Stern School of Business, and the HEC School of Management, Paris, starting in 2000 is a fine example of programme partnership. Each collaborating partner delivers one module and students do another module at Shanghai University and the final one focuses on emerging markets and its location will vary annually. The Trium MBA is awarded separately by each partner.

In contrast, Branch or Offshore Campuses can be set up by a foreign university in another country or can be set up as collaboration between universities located in two or more countries. The regulatory framework of the country where the campus is developed has to allow foreign education providers to deliver higher education within their borders. Students receive a degree either in the name of the foreign university or jointly in the name of both partner universities. Since most countries have restrictive laws regarding the delivery and certification of education services within their borders, branch campuses are relatively rare. Generally, branch campuses can only be set up in countries that have legal frameworks that enable and permit foreign institutions to provide higher education services and degrees. While some may allow foreign institutions to set up and deliver whatever type of programme they wish, others may require that the foreign provider can only develop programmes with established universities in the host country.

The number of branch campus partnerships operating globally is not established because there is no comprehensive listing of universities that supply higher educational services in another country. Therefore, information is mainly from internet sources set up by universities, governments, education agents, and for-profit institutions that engage in the delivery of crossborder education services. The countries of origin covered by the foreign universities include there initiated by the three most active countries in CBHE activities – Australia, the United Kingdom, and the United States –as well as by universities in India, China, Singapore and Thailand. Most of the foreign partnership universities, in turn, are located in a few countries in Asia or the Middle East and all but three of the partnerships were set up in the twenty-first century.

Several Australian universities have set up Programme partnerships and branch campuses in Asian countries. In 2001, 26.5 percent of Australia's international students were enrolled in Australian institutions of higher education offshore but by 2003, that percentage had risen to 40.5 percent. The Australian universities with the largest offshore tertiary enrollments in 2003 were the University of South Australia, Curtin University of Technology, Royal Melbourne Institute of Technology, Charles Sturt University, and the University of Western Sydney. In 2003, 34 Australian universities had foreign students enrolled offshore. Malaysia and Singapore had the largest numbers of Australian offshore students.

Branch Campus in Qatar

Many CBHE initiatives develop with support or encouragement from the host country. Qatar Foundation, for instance, a private foundation founded and endowed in 1995 by the Emir of Qatar, built a physical campus, Education City, in Doha, Qatar, and recruited five prestigious US universities to set up Branch Campuses at the City to deliver higher education services to Qatar nationals and foreign students from the region and elsewhere. Training is provided in specific fields that follow the same curriculum they offer to students enrolled in that study programme in the United States. Carnegie Mellon University offers undergraduate degrees in business and computer science. Cornell University has developed Weil Cornell Medical College in Qatar and offers a two-year pre-med programme followed by a four-year Medical Programme. Georgetown University School of Foreign Service educates undergraduates in foreign affairs and for work in diplomatic services.

Texas A&M has developed an undergraduate degree programmes in chemical, electrical, mechanical and petroleum engineering and offers graduate degrees in those fields. Virginia Commonwealth University awards a Bachelor of Fine Arts degree in communication design, fashion design or interior design. Each foreign university partner awards the degree under its own brand name but may give the degree itself a new name to indicate where the study occurred. Students who successfully complete the Cornell University Medical Programme, for instance, will receive their Medical Degree from Cornell University under the designation Weill Cornell Medical College in Qatar.

Branch Campus in Dubai

Dubai of the United Arab Emirates adopted a similar approach to strengthen its higher education system. The government funded Dubai Knowledge Village (DKV) and invited foreign universities to establish Branch Campuses at the Village and award tertiary degrees under their brand name. Since it opened in 2003, 13 universities from seven countries have set up higher education programmes. Several British universities and other foreign partners come from Australia, Belgium, India, Iran, Ireland, and Pakistan participate in the programme.

A variant of the Branch Campus occurred in the case of three British universities that opened up programmes at DKV. The three universities – Edinburgh, Birmingham and Manchester – agreed in 2004 to set up research-based, postgraduate education programmes in different fields at DKV under the name of a new university, British University of Dubai. Subsequently, the University of Cardiff and the Sir John Cass Business School, City University, joined the British University partnership. However, rather than awarding degrees under their separate brand names, the participating British universities will award the degrees under the name of a new university, British University of Dubai.

Distance Learning

Distance Learning services are becoming popular because they allow students to do all or at least a significant part of their study programme at home. Improvements in ICT make it easier for universities to deliver study programmes using new technologies that allow enrolled students to carry forward their higher education in their homelands.

New technologies that facilitate Distance Learning include the Internet, videoconferencing, videocassettes, and CD-ROM. E-mail communications enable enrolled students to receive rapid feedback from faculty members and administrators who monitor their course work. Most universities delivering distance learning are for-profit institutions and limited to applied fields such as business, ICT, education, and healthcare. One online provider—American Inter-Continental University (AIU)—offers online education but also has campuses in the United States, London, and Dubai where students can finish their studies after starting it online.

Universitas 21 Global based in Singapore collaborates with universities in North America, Europe, Asia-Pacific, and Oceania to provide distance learning services to students worldwide. Set up jointly by Universitas 21, a British firm, and Thomson, a multinational corporation, it provides information, software applications and services to business and professional markets. Thomson Learning, an affiliate of Thomson, focuses on the higher education marketplace. Distance Learning providers are marketing their services as a cost-effective way for students to obtain a higher education degree. It is interesting to note that established universities are joining commercial online providers to attract students wishing to do part of their studies through distance learning and another part at a regular university campus.

Corporate Collaborations with Universities

Corporations now provide worker training in collaboration with universities or by drawing on the services of corporations like Thomson that cater to that market. E-Cornell, for instance, the profitable wing of Cornell University, has signed contracts with corporations in recent years to provide professional and executive development training. e-Cornell has developed a speciality niche in hospitality management and signed agreements with several hotel chains to train their employees drawing on distance learning and face-to-face training. With Microsoft spreading its computer operations globally, it has set up 1,700 Certified Technical Education Centres at which Microsoft certified personnel train locals using a curriculum developed by Microsoft. IBM teamed up with the University of the State of Puebla, Mexico, to provide students training in IT technology. There are countless other examples of corporate collaborations with universities in developing countries.

Outward Bound Programmes

Some universities in emerging economies have set up programmes to train nationals and foreign students for a niche market in another country. These programmes, dubbed Outward-Bound programmes here, are relatively rare. Generally, the host countries where these programmes are located have encouraged their universities to develop them with recognition that graduating students will practise in the US market or work in another high-income country and generate foreign exchange or remittances. These specialised training programmes have arisen mainly in the medical field and respond to shortages of medical personnel in advanced economies. Many of the students enrolled in offshore training programmes are US nationals that were not accepted at a US medical school because of limited training slots. Others are foreign nationals seeking to immigrate to the United States following completion of their medical studies. Since medical personnel immigrating to the United States or other advanced economies have to be certified, the Outward Bound training programmes generally use the curricula that US universities do.

St. George School of Medicine, Grenada, is an example of an Outward Bound training programme. It was set up in 1977 to train medical doctors for the US medical market but today it trains medical personnel for the United Kingdom as well. Other examples of Outward Bound programmes include the training of nurses in the Philippines and medical doctors in India.

The current and projected numbers of students in the 20-24 age group is used as the tertiary education referent population by UNESCO and other agencies to calculate tertiary gross enrolment ratio (TGER) and compare trends across countries. While UNESCO asks countries to report their numbers of students enrolled in higher education, it does not ask them to give the age distribution of those students, and thus it is not possible to calculate refined enrolment rates for different countries by age.

Future global demand for higher education will depend on age structure changes and changes in enrolments. However, trends in these two factors will differ for OECD and non-OECD countries. The TGER gap between OECD and non-OECD countries should narrow in the years ahead since demand for higher education is rising rapidly in the latter and TGERs have levelled off in the former. However, non-OECD countries will also face increased demand due to expected growth in the size of their 20-24 age populations.

It will be a herculean task for developing countries to build sufficient higher education capacity to meet projected growing demand in the years ahead. At the same time, declining enrolments due to demographic changes in developed countries mean that many tertiary institutions in Europe, North America and Oceania will have surplus capacity that will not be used unless enrollment rates of domestic students increase. Foreign students, on the other hand, are potential substitutes for domestic students, and will be sought after by both the traditional host countries and new countries that seek to recruit foreign students.

Student Mobility Issues

When developing study abroad and student exchange programmes, it is important to look at the change in the outcomes expected and ways that these expectations have changed over time. There has been a change in emphasis from an 'exchange paradigm' to a 'competency paradigm'. The 'exchange paradigm' looks at exchange as a value in itself, long term benefits (hard to measure), the virtue of reciprocity, mutual trust, transparency, improvement through cooperation, joint efforts to reduce costs, and learning through mutual understanding. They contrast this with the current 'competency paradigm' which, includes the following features: lack of concern for equality of opportunity, a neglect of features of learning that don't produce results, the exploitation of foreign students (financially or through poor programmes), an overemphasis on easily marketable products, selling of knowledge products to foreigners (not emphasising internationalisation and mutual understanding), the growth of for-profit enterprises (delivering easily marketable programmes, some with little regard for standards or quality.

Finding Foreign Partners

Finding appropriate college or university partners from foreign countries can be a challenge. With over three thousand higher education institutions, it is not easy to determine which institutions would be appropriate exchange partners. There is no single source which evaluates the quality of higher education programmes. One can narrow down the field a bit by ensuring that their college or university partner is an accredited institution, but that only confirms that the institution meets a minimum standard, which has been confirmed by a regional accrediting agency. The process of approval follows a self-study process, which includes an institutional self-study report, a peer site review of the report and a site visit. The self-study and report of the peer review team will generally both include institutional strengths and weaknesses and suggestions for ways to improve the quality of teaching, research, and community service, where relevant. Even this review does not provide a clear understanding for foreign institution partners of what "level of quality standards" has been met. Institutions, for the most part, are either accredited, or not. Some individual academic departments are also reviewed for accreditation in a separate process (faculties of law, medicine, education, business, engineering, etc.). Those programmes which do undergo a review for accreditation have only limited, if any, review of the types of special programmes which are offered for study abroad or international students.

The US News and World Report magazine annual rankings of US colleges and universities at the undergraduate and graduate levels are generally controversial, in terms of their validity or importance, from the perspective of US colleges and universities. However, they do provide some feedback about US higher education institutions, both at an institution-wide level and with reviews of specific academic departments. Their annual survey also rank institutions within categories, based on types of higher education institutions. The GATE review process has been discussed as a possible help in this area for the future. However, at this time, each international partner and each international student has a significant challenge in trying to identify an appropriate partner in the US. Some of these challenges include:

i) Education as responsibility of each of 50 states
ii) Independence of over 3,000 us colleges and universities
iii) Differences in each academic unit/programme
iv) Differences in institutional locations: urban/rural
v) Differences in support services: housing, counselling, etc.
vi) Multiple offices supporting international collaborations
vii) Regular revisions of institutional goals and administration (5 year plans)
viii) Practice of high level administrators of signing memoranda of agreement not necessarily intended for implementation.

Another challenge in developing institutional partnerships between the foreign countries and India is the expectations of students and institutions in terms of student service resources. Many foreign higher education institutions maintain comprehensive student service resources. This includes services that range from support staff for academic advisement in each department to coordinators for student activities, students with disabilities, counseling services, housing, a comprehensive student health center, insurance, athletics, etc. Evaluating the quality of student services on a foreign campus is not a simple process. As with the academic quality, international institutions will end up needing to work to review the quality and quantity of academic services available to find an appropriate match with a foreign college or university.

Student Service Needs

The level of student services provided by foreign colleges and universities may also raise the expectations by foreign students on what they would expect in a study abroad programme or international higher education institution. Following is a sample of some of the service support offices that may be encountered at a foreign college or university. For those foreign institutions providing study abroad programmes, or international institutions hosting foreign students, there may be a need to provide many of these services. Student mobility can be complex when dealing with US colleges and universities. Institutional representatives may play a broad administrative role.

Training is also inconsistent in the student mobility field. In higher education, many student services roles are filled by staff with Master's and Doctoral (Ph.D. and Ed.D.) degrees in student affairs administration and student service roles. There is inconsistent training for those involved in student mobility roles. When looking for a foreign partner, it is important to look at their support service resources, which includes financial and staff resources.

Role of Higher Education Associations

When developing exchange agreements with higher education institutions, it is important to collaborate with both domestic and international higher education institutions. Samples of national, regional, and international higher education institutions that may be relevant in terms of setting up appropriate partnerships include:

i) Association of Indian Universities (AIU)

ii) Association of International Education Administrators (AIEA)

iii) Australia Regional Higher Education Associations (ARHEA)

iv) British Universities Transatlantic Exchange Organisations (BUTEX)

v) California Colleges for International Education (CCIE)

vi) California Community College Chancellor's Office Mega Conference

vii) Council on International Educational Exchange (COUNCIL)

viii) European Association of International Education (EAIE)

ix) German Academic Exchange Service (DAAD)Intl. Association of College Law Enforcement Administrators (IACLEA)

x) International Education Association of South Africa (IEASA)

xi) Interorganisational Task Force on Safety and Responsibility in Study Abroad

xii) National Association of College and University Attorneys (NACUA)

xiii) NAFSA: Association of International Education Administrators

xiv) National Association of Student Personnel Administrations (NASPA)

xv) Risk and Insurance Management Society (RIMS)

xvi) University Risk Management and Insurance Association (URMIA)

Student mobility is a critical component in connecting people from countries around the world. As the US and India are two of the world's most important democracies, one can see the importance of greater understanding by the citizens of each country about one-another. Increases in quality and quantity of student mobility between the US and India will be dependent on cooperation and the sharing of quality practices of higher education in both countries. The Association of Indian Universities and leaders, faculty, and staff at Indian and US higher education institutions can play a critical role in this area. It is important to share quality practices at all levels in developing and implementing relevant, new programmes and evaluating and improving existing programmes.

Developments in Programme and Provider Mobility

In the last five years there has been can emergence of new types of providers, forms of delivery, and collaborative partnerships. Along with traditional private and public higher education institutions, "new providers" include commercial IT and media companies, corporate universities, professional associations, and international conglomerates. Providers use face-to-face and virtual modes to deliver education to students in their home countries through twinning, franchising, articulation, validation, and joint or double degree arrangements. Some also establish branch campuses, independent institutions, teaching and testing centres, and acquisitions or mergers with local higher education institutions.

Given below are examples of developments in programme and provider mobility established in the last two years in all regions of the world.

Middle East

The Middle East is an area rapid developments. Poland has established a new private medical institute in Israel where students study for three years before moving to the Medical University in Gdansk for three more years of clinical study. They then return to Israel for an internship. Saudi Arabia is establishing new private universities that involve foreign institutions and investors. For instance, the University of Arizona and UNESCO are involved in establishing the Prince Sultan Private University. The Stevens Institute of Technology is cooperating in founding the Dar-ALFaisal University, with financial investment from the Boeing Company and the French defence firm Thales. Harvard is planning to set up a branch campus in the United Arab Emirates.

The University of Hanover (Germany) is planning an affiliation with a new Euro University in Bahrain. Egypt has an American University established more than 80 years ago. But the German University in Cairo and the L'Université Française d'Egypte have been established in the last three years, and a new British University is under development. The American University in Egypt is franchised to offer the distance MBA programme of Heriot-Watt University from the United Kingdom.

Asia Pacific

In Vietnam is an emerging centre of activity, RMIT from Australia owns 100 per cent of a branch campus, while Troy State University from the US established a foreign branch, the International College of IT and Management.

The number of active partnerships between local and foreign institutions is steadily expanding. For instance, the University of Hue in Vietnam recently developed a franchised and joint-degree bachelor's programme in tourism with the University of Hawaii. The Hanoi University of Technology offers master's and bachelor's degrees with higher education institutions from Belgium (1), France (8), Germany (1), Singapore (2), and the United States (1). The Vietnamese government recently announced development of the "International University in Vietnam", another initiative to increase national capacity for higher education. While half the university teaching staff will be Vietnamese, the other half will be from foreign universities.

Foreign institutional involvement will build on and expand from the current links of Ho Chi Minh City National University. Australia, China, Egypt, and the United States are increasing cross-border education to Thailand. The Egyptian Al-Azhar University and Jinan University from China are planning to open a branch campus, while Swinburne University of Technology (Australia) has operated a branch campus since 1998, though it is changing its focus to industry training only. Troy State University has a teaching site in Bangkok for its MBA programme; students can transfer to the US depending on funds and visa requirements. The Thai-German Graduate School of Engineering, 13 Australian universities, and nine UK universities also operate in Thailand.

The University of New South Wales (Australia) plans to establish the first 100 per cent foreign-owned higher education institution in Singapore after receiving government approval, offering undergraduate and graduate programmes and developing a strong research capacity. Other respected foreign institutions offer education and training programmes in Singapore through joint ventures, exchanges, and branch-campuses, including the University of Chicago Graduate School of Business, Shanghai Jiaotong University, Stanford University, John Hopkins University, the German Technische Universität München, and the Technische Universiteit Eindhoven (Netherlands).

Singapore institutions, on the other hand are noteworthy exporters. The National University of Singapore and Fudan University developed a joint MBA, aimed at Chinese and Singapore students. The National University is also planning to setup a new graduate school initiative for Chinese students to be located in Suzhou Graduate Town, part of the Suzhou Industrial Park. Raffles LaSalle Limited, a publicly traded Singapore company, provides programmes in fashion and design in many Asian countries. It is described as "a remarkable instance of international partnership, combining a Singapore firm with branches in Australia, China, Malaysia and Thailand, accreditation from an Australian state and a Canadian province, degrees from an Australian and a UK university, and a number of in-county university and college partners."

India's higher education sector imports and exports programmes and services on a large scale. One initiative is the partnership between the Caparo Group—a UK firm with interests in steel, engineering, and hotels—and Carnegie Mellon University (US) which will set up a new campus in India.

Africa

Africa, with the partial exception of South Africa, has the fewest international and cross-border initiatives. The private Universiteit Nienrode (Netherlands Business School) recently established a branch campus in Nigeria in partnership with the African Leadership Forum, a non-profit organisation founded in 1988—one of the first cross-border initiatives on the continent outside of South Africa. Kenya is home to two private non-profit universities. Pakistan's Aga Khan University opened a branch university campus in Kenya in 2002 specialising in nursing education, and Alliant International University (United States) provides education in social sciences and the humanities.

The number of foreign programmes offered in South Africa has decreased, due to strict new government regulations and accreditation processes. Only a few foreign institutions have branch campuses, including Bond and Monash from Australia, De Montfort (UK), and the Netherlands Business School. Monash will remain as will the British-based Henley Management College, primarily a distance provider.

Mauritius, in the process of calling itself a "cyber island" attracts foreign IT firms from the West and India. A knowledge centre considered as a world-class integrated education and training complex is a key aspect of its plans. More than 50 foreign universities and professional bodies offer local programmes, mostly at the diploma or certificate level and in specialised fields. Attracting foreign education providers to support the education and training needs of a new cyber island may help in stimulating brain gain, but local education institutions may pay a price.

Europe

Russia's major economic reforms have important implications for the higher education sector. Many higher educational institutions—for example, the Moscow International Slavonic Institute and the Moscow State University of Industry—operate programmes abroad, such as in Bulgaria. But Russia is also the site of joint and double degree programmes, twinning, and franchise arrangements. The Higher School of Economics has a double degree programme with the London School of Economics. The Stockholm School of Economics operates in St. Petersburg and the University of Oslo's Centre for Medical Studies is located in Moscow. The British Open University runs 80 business-training centres across the country. The University of Southern Queensland has collaborations with Far Eastern National University in Vladivostok for programme delivery. The Pune-based International Institute of Information Technology (India) plans to offer its master's and Ph.D. courses through the newly established Russian-Indian Centre for Advanced Computer Research in Moscow.

The University of Indianapolis, active in Greece for more than a decade, has an articulation arrangement whereby students would start their studies in Athens and complete the programme in the US. The model evolved into a campus in Greece called the University of Indianapolis, Athens.

Laureate Education, a private company, owns part or all of the Universidad Europa de Madrid in Spain, Les Roches and Glion Hotel School in Switzerland, and the L'ecole Superieur du Commerce Exterieur de Paris in France. Apollo International offers its courses in the Netherlands, and Raffles La Salle

(Singapore) has recently agreed to offer bachelor's and master's programmes in fashion and design to Middlesex University.

North America

George Washington University is seriously considering a South Korean branch, since the South Korean government has changed its regulations to permit foreign providers. Other US universities are partnering with Korean institutions and companies. Syracuse University, in conjunction with Sejong University in Seoul, offers a specially designed MBA programme for Korean students.

Duke and Purdue Universities also offer courses in MBAs in Korea, and Stanford University delivers online graduate and postgraduate courses, using alumni as local tutors. US higher education institutions sponsor similar cross-border activities in China, India, Malaysia, Philippines, Singapore, Thailand, Vietnam, and the Middle East. The University of Missouri at St. Louis helped to establish the Gulf University of Science and Technology—the first private university in Kuwait—and the Modern College of Business and Science in Oman.

As an example of US cross-border activity increasingly involving private and publicly traded companies, the Global Education Index, developed by the Observatory on Borderless Higher Education, classifies many large, active publicly traded companies that provide education programmes and services. The Apollo Group owns the University of Phoenix, now the largest American private university, and aggressively seeks to broaden its foreign investments and holdings. Since 1995, Apollo has also owned Western International University (WIU), which runs a branch campus called Modi Apollo International Institute in New Delhi through a partnership with the KK Modi Group, an Indian industrial conglomerate. WIU has an agreement with the Canadian Institute of Business and Technology (CIBT) permitting CIBT to offer WIU programmes through its three business schools in Beijing.

Northface Learning Inc. has established Northface University, an IBM and Microsoft-backed initiative offering degree programmes in IT and business. The University of Northern Virginia, another small private university offering programmes in business and IT, recently opened a branch campus in the Czech Republic and created delivery partnerships in China and India.

The Canadian International Management Institute (CIMI) signed a memorandum of understanding with the Chinese Scholarship Council in 2004 to offer a foundation and credit transfer programme to students in China wanting Canadian university degrees.

The Al-Ahram Canadian University in Egypt is the only example of direct Canadian university support for a new foreign university. McMaster University, Ecole Polytechnique de Montreal, and the Université du Quebec in Montreal are cooperating with the Al-Ahram Organisation, owner of the Egyptian daily newspaper, to establish this private university.

The Serebra Learning Corporation, a publicly traded Canadian company, offers generic and tailor-made software plus more than 1,800 courses mainly in IT. It works with the Consortium for Global Education to provide quality-assured IT training in the developing world. It also played a key role in creating the Pakistan Virtual University.

Latin America

The University of the Incarnate Word (UIW), a private institution in San Antonio, Texas, opened a new campus in Mexico in 2003. Endicott College, Alliant Intentional University, and Texas A&M are other American institutions with Mexican campuses. In 2000, Laureate Education purchased the Universidad del Valle de Mexico and plans to open a new branch in Guadalajara. Laureate also owns Universidad Interamericana, a private university with campuses in Costa Rica and Panama, and part of three private universities in Chile. Bologna University, in Italy, is one of the few foreign institutions with a branch campus in Argentina. The Technical Institute of Monterrey, in Mexico, is known for its online education programmes, especially the MBA, delivered to many Latin American countries.

These various initiatives are examples of how conventional higher education institutions and new commercial providers promote, exchange, link and predominantly sell higher education across borders. Australia and the United States dominate the list of participating countries, though India and China are increasingly active. But cross-border activities also involve risks warranting close attention.

Regulatory Recognition

Many countries lack the regulatory systems to register or evaluate out-of-country providers. Regulatory frameworks for quality assurance or accreditation, even when they exist, usually do not apply to providers outside the national education system. This lacuna permits bona fide and rogue foreign providers avoid compliance with national regulations in many countries, and makes monitoring their activities difficult.

Historically, national quality-assurance agencies did not assess the quality of imported and exported programmes, with notable exceptions. But Hong Kong, Israel, Malaysia, and South Africa, as receivers of cross-border education, have developed systems to register and monitor the quality of foreign provision.

Accreditation

The accreditation process is becoming internationalised and commercialised. Bona fide national and international accreditation agencies now work in many countries. But new self-appointed networks of institutions and organisations also accredit their members—a positive development when academic quality improves. But some of these networks and organisations may be more interested in racing for accreditation "stars" than in improving quality. A related, more worrisome development institutions the growth of non-recognised, illegitimate accreditation institutions that "sell" accreditation without any independent assessment. These institutions resemble "degree institutions" that sell certificates and degrees with no or minimal course work. Students, employers, and the public need to be warned about these accreditation (and degree) institutions, which are often web addresses outside the jurisdiction of national regulatory systems.

Mechanisms for Recognising Qualifications

Students, employers, and the public must be made aware of the quality and validity of the programmes and awards. The mechanisms for recognising qualifications must be national, regional, or international to accommodate the mobility of students and professional labour.

Quality Assurance

Social confidence in higher education demands giving priority to defining the roles and responsibilities of all players involved in quality assurance—including individual institutions and providers, national quality assurance systems, non-government and independent accreditation bodies, professional associations and regional or international organisations. Their roles defined, these players must collaborate to build a system that ensures the quality and integrity of cross-border education. These issues have special importance for higher education institutions. Quality assurance starts with the programme deliverer—domestic or international. Many higher education institutions have adequate quality assurance processes for domestic delivery. But these processes do not cover the challenges inherent in working cross-culturally, in a foreign regulatory environment and, potentially, with a foreign partner. These challenges encompass academic entry requirements, student examination and assessment procedures, faculty workload, delivery modes, curricular adaptation, assuring quality teaching, academic and sociocultural support for students, and title and level of award. While attempting to balance quality issues with the financial investment and return, higher education providers must consider intellectual property ownership, choice of partners, division of responsibilities, academic and business risk assessments, and internal and external approval processes.

References

Altbach, P. and Teichner, U., Internationalization and Exchanges in a Globalized University, *Journal of Studies in International Education,* Vol. 5, Issue 1. 2001.

Austin, A. E. and D.W. Chapman (eds.), *Higher Education in the Developing World.* Westport, Ct.: Greenwood Press, 2002.

Dhar, B.B., Internationalisation in India: To What Extent?, in K.B. Powar (Editor), *Internationalisation of Indian Higher Education,* AIU, New Delhi, 2001.

Etaat, J. "Education and development". *Economic and Political Information, 143-144*(13), 208-225, 1999.

Institute of International Education, *Open Doors 2001: Report on International Educational Exchange,* HE, New York. <http://www.opendoorsweb.org>. 2001.

Knight, J. and DeWit, H., *Internationalisation of Higher Education in Asia Pacific Countries*, European Association of International Education, Amsterdam, Netherlands, 1997.

Neef, D. (ed.), *The Knowledge Economy*. Boston: Butterworth-Heinemann, 1998.

Powar, International Providers of Higher Education in India, in K.B. Powar (Editor), *Internationalisation of Indian Higher Education*, pp 69-75, AIU, New Delhi, 2001.

Sarkarani, M., "The challenges of higher education in developing countries". *Political and Economic Information*, 184-197, 2007.

Wit, H. D., *Internationalization of higher education in the United States of America and Europe: A historical, comparative, and conceptual analysis*. Westport, Conn.: Greenwood Press, 2002.

Yang R., *Third delight: The internationalization of higher education in China*. New York London: Routledge, 2002.

Zolfaghari, A., *The role of education in social development*. Open University, Shahreza, 2003.

6. ISSUES IN INTERNATIONAL HIGHER EDUCATION

Internationalisation is one of the most revolutionary developments in higher education at present. Fuelled by the processes of globalisation and regionalisation of economies, finances and trade, by the unprecedented advances in communication technologies and by the array of factors and features pertaining to the information society, internationalisation assumes new forms, becomes more accessible and enables higher education to better meet current challenges: broadening access, promoting the modernisation of systems and institutions and strengthening links with the world of work. The WCHE convened by UNESCO in October 1998 welcomed the new internationalisation drive in Higher Education as a positive development. At the same time, it made appropriate recommendations for action to assure that it is guided by internationally accepted principles and values, is evenly distributed for the benefit of all and seeks common objectives.

Internationalisation touches all aspects of today's life. Its most important drivers are the academic institutions of the world. Universities worldwide have been the locus of revolutions and when it comes to internationalisation they are no exceptions, they in fact are the drivers of this revolution which seeks to flatten the earth. Irrespective of the geographies involved colleges and universities have to collaborate to make this knowledge-based society a functional and thriving one.

Internationalisation has been happening in academia from the time since centres of higher learning existed. Visiting scholars from abroad or student mobility across borders is nothing new, and was prevalent even in the 5th and 6th centuries. The universities of Nalanda and Taxila in India were centres of higher Buddhist learning and teaching in logic, grammar, astronomy and medicine which attracted scholars from China like Hsüan-tsang, besides knowledge seekers from Tibet, Korea, Japan, Indonesia, Persia and Turkey. Similar cross-border scholarly migration has taken place in ancient times at most centres of higher learning in the world. But what was perfectly sublime and purely for knowledge centuries back has now turned into a search for opportunities of not just knowledge, but also of trade in knowledge, rather than an ennobling search for truth and learning.

Internationalisation has got entangled in the globalisation web, which is intricately interlinked with GATTS, WTO and GATS. Internationalisation refers to physical mobility, academic cooperation and knowledge transfer, while globalisation implies that borders are ephemeral, the nation-state gets diluted and may ultimately cease. Thus globalisation, in contrast to the higher level academic transactions of internationalisation, is often associated with competition and market-steering, transnational education, and commercial knowledge-transfer.

Internationalisation at the national, sectoral and institutional levels is defined as the process of integrating an international, intercultural or global dimension into the purpose, functions or delivery of postsecondary education. Internationalisation is influenced by globalisation and both have impacts on higher education.

Iinternationalisation can be seen as the increasing interconnectedness between national education systems, in which borders and national authorities are not questioned. Globalisation, on the other hand, relates to the process of increasing convergence and interdependence of economies and to the liberalisation of trade and markets. Internationalisation is seen as a response to globalisation but it is a questionable proposition because the former has been in practice even before the latter idea germinated.

With the introduction of the WTO agreement in 1995 at Marrakech in Morocco and the related agreements like the General Agreement on Trade in Services (GATS) and the Trade-Related Aspects of Intellectual Property Rights (TRIPS), education has taken on a role as a tradeable commodity, with stakeholders and customers, and corporate entities vying with traditional universities for a piece of the pie. The traditional role of nation-states as the purveyors of knowledge and the supporters of universities through which this knowledge seeped into society, thereby creating a liberal environment of higher academic learning and teaching, elevating societal skills and thoughts to a higher plane is gradually being replaced, following GATS, by global players who are not bound by borders.

The type of education, how it should be administered and how society should view it are all being changed and are now being attuned to global aspirations, and decisions are often based on agreements that are not confined to any one state or nation, but often pan-continental in dimensions, like the Bologna process. This is one process which has brought in change in traditional European educational structures from outside. It has forced most European nations to discard their centuries old educational system to conform to a system that has been enforced collectively from outside, even though that collective body includes themselves.

GATS and Higher Education

GATS uses four modes of supply viz., cross-border supply (distance and on-line courses or franchised courses), consumption abroad (education abroad), commercial presence (institutions opening their branches abroad or joint ventures with local institutions), presence of professors and researchers working temporarily abroad. The most vociferous demands for differentiated fee structures in the UK were made by the Dept of Trade and Industry rather than the education ministry in Britain, pointing to the new nature of education.

Australia is a good example where globalisation of higher education has seen its biggest economic success. Income from the export of higher education services has a major impact on Australia's balance of payments and on the rate of growth in Australia's national income and Australia draws a very large pool of students from abroad, almost 95 per cent paying full fees. Things have gone to such an extreme, but following the principles of GATS, that anybody can start an educational institute in Australia abiding by certain conditions.

The drawbacks in globalisation is that a few countries that wield enormous clout in economy, innovation, and knowledge might overpower the ideals of lesser nations. These countries will have the best universities, the most successful corporates, the best research centres. Example include IBM and Microsoft, Nokia and Motorola, Elsevier and Springer Verlag, Merck and Pfizer etc. Developing countries have very little freedom of action or competitive advantage in a globalised world.

GATS does have a cascading effect on all socio-political transactions and it decisively influences a nation through its higher education. Internationalisation of education, cross-border collaboration, or equitable trade in education is not opposed by GATS opponents. The original concepts of internationalisation that involved overseas study, collaboration in research and cooperation between institutions involving student-teacher exchanges are accepted. But three underlying elements of the GATS approach to higher education are suspect viz., the market-driven nature and consequent competitive commoditisation of higher education, the idea that higher education is a private good to be purchased by the 'users' i.e. the students, and the idea that higher education is a common commodity, transferable from one country to another.

Often internationalisation can be used as a façade for globalisation in its role as trader in education, e.g. some private universities in India have collaborations with 30 or more foreign universities, which is used to encourage higher enrolment into very expensive engineering Bachelors and Masters courses. Private universities often have ambitious goals and have set out to become 'global universities' by setting up student exchanges, collaborative research programmes etc., with universities the world over.

A recently concluded Accra Declaration on GATS and the Internationalisation of Higher Education in Africa caution against the reduction of higher education, under the GATS regime, to a tradable commodity subject primarily to international trade rules and negotiations, and the loss of authority of national governments to regulate higher education according to national needs and priorities. It further resolves that continued support for multiple forms of internationalisation in higher education, which bring identifiable mutual benefits, should be promoted. It also recognised commitment to the strengthening of national institutional capacity and to developing national and regional arrangements for quality assurance, accreditation and the recognition of qualifications. It exercises caution on further GATS commitments in higher education until a deeper understanding of GATS and the surrounding issues is developed and a more informed position is arrived at.

The Accra declaration perhaps reflects the uncertainty around the internationalisation of higher education triggered off by the GATS. Developments since NPE, 1986, have been on a very large scale. The emergence of education services under GATS and the emergence of private providers of education- domestic as well as foreign, in particular, have necessitated clear policy guidelines and regulations. There seems to be a tension between the objectives as set forth in the 1986 policy guidelines relating to access, equity and quality and the importance that it attaches to public provision of education and the recent trends of commodification and internationalisation of education that may set up forces acting against those objectives.

GATS allows sufficient 'safeguards' and also argues in favour of eliminating 'barriers' to trade in services. How to draw a line between the two? What may be seen as barriers from another country's perspective many very well be safeguards from domestic countries' perspective? For example, US in its requests to India, says, 'Remove ownership limitations on joint ventures with local partners' as it is a barrier to trade. However, from India's point of view it may be a necessary safeguard and hence the requests may not be worth considering.

The point to note is that indeed India should make as many barriers as possible, which it considers as necessary safeguards from national point of view. But if benefits to trade have to be derived it is also necessary that make limited offers, which are in the country's interests. It may also be desirable to derive maximum advantage by exporting education services in which India has comparative advantage. This means entering into negotiations i.e. making requests to countries to allow Indian education providers to operate abroad. The only caution that is necessary to take is that export of education should be a secondary concern. The overriding concern should be to increase access to higher education within country. Any body that is willing to enter into higher education should not be constrained to do so because of supply constraints. Only when there is excess national capacity, country should be prepared to export.

Making the Sector Globally Competitive

A policy on competitiveness of higher education sector needs examination of various complex issues. One such issue is that higher education, unlike other services, was never viewed as a private good and as a commodity to be traded and as earner of foreign exchange. Complexity of the topic arises from the confusion that a category of 'competition' used in the case of private, traded good is invoked to a situation where the category is not applicable i.e. to a case of non-traded higher education scenario. In most developing countries this theoretical issue remains unresolved and competition is used in a loose sense to improve the efficiency. But it creates problems when measures to improve competitiveness are suggested, as measures to improve demand and supply come into conflict with policy standpoint on higher education.

Theoretical difficulties aside, it is worth noting the fact that globalisation of higher education has produced compulsions to treat it as a commodity to be traded. Firstly, the countries like US treat higher education as major earner of foreign exchange. Secondly, GATS provisions invoke higher education sector to lead towards progressive liberalisation. Thirdly, even within a country the expansion of private sector and reduction of the role of public sector produces the compulsions that universities must devise the curricula to suit demand conditions i.e. be oriented to meet changing employment needs of the industries. Internally, the resource crunch, too, produces compulsions to improve efficiency, on the one hand, and to raise resources by offering attractive educational programmes, on the other. Fourthly, there is too much of protection inherent in the public provision of education, which has led to inefficiency. The higher education, therefore, must be subjected to some norms of efficiency. The upshot of the argument is that in a changed circumstance the norms and some policy towards invoking efficiency is imminent.

Shying away from this issue would invite problems of higher magnitude later.

The issue of competition creates complexity from another point of view. Efficiency must go together with equity. However, if competition is allowed then user charges will increase and subsidy to the higher education may be curtailed. Reduction in subsidy will be a step against the objective of equity in higher education. Thus competition should not be the focus of education policy. Education in developing country should be guided by the equity objective, many academicians maintain. Proponents of liberalisation, however, maintain that resources withdrawn with reduction in subsidy may be utilised in providing support to the needy sections of the society. On the other hand, there will be a net gain by promoting efficiency through invoking competitiveness. Therefore, the measures promoting competitiveness must squarely confront the issue of competitiveness rather than evade it.

There is also an aspect of maintaining international equilibrium through following competition but the burden of adjustment may fall on domestic higher education sector throwing it into disequilibria. Competition, by allowing free inflow and outflow of students, resources and institutions, may match excess supply of developed countries with the excess demand of developing countries leading to the maintenance of international equilibrium. However, given the high cost of education, it may be difficult to raise the participation rate in higher education. It is against this background that making India's higher education sector globally competitive may be considered.

Framework

It is necessary to consider the framework of competition before considering the measures for making higher education sector globally competitive. First, given the framework of education policy, the participation of private sector may be considered but not the commercialisation of higher education. Pricing should not be the basis of efficiency in public universities. The non-price factors such as the improvement in quality, governance, infrastructure, library, research facilities, and relevant curricula should be the prime concern in raising efficiency. The private sector may be guided by the price efficiency but only to the extent of meeting the cost or expansion or improvement in education services. This demands some regulatory mechanism to ensure that private sector practices fair competition within policy guidelines.

However, it is a little vexed issue to suggest the framework of competition for foreign education providers. Foreign universities can invest only when there is profit in investing in education services. Hence allowing free competition in higher education by permitting foreign universities amounts to the violation of present policy. Hence a rather difficult issue is entry of foreign universities in India. However, the issue is not without solution as foreign universities may be allowed only in collaboration with public or private universities in India with the majority stake in Indian partner. Thus foreign universities can only repatriate the earning for the services that they offer but cannot repatriate the profit, if any, as this has to be invested in India in improvement and expansion of educational facilities.

Context of GATS

It is noted in GATS agreement that it will facilitate developing member countries to expand services exports through the strengthening of their domestic services capacity and its efficiency and competitiveness. Issues of competitiveness pervades through the different articles of GATS since one of the basic objectives covered under GATS is to expand export potentials of say education services by internationalising curricula, by making it relevant and through measures which promote the competitive strength of the education providers; colleges, universities and technical and professional institutions. While, on the one hand, WTO has to address the issue of multilateral framework on competition policy, the respective member countries have to put in place competitive strength of the institutions to promote export in areas of strength or where competitive cost advantage can be obtained and member countries have also to protect their own institutions from the onslaught of international cartels, on the other. Therefore, there are three important issues in relation to competition under GATS.

i) What should be the multilateral, rule-based framework? The discussion on these issues is continuing?

ii) Measures for enhancing competitive strength of educational institutions need to be considered.

iii) There must be sufficient safeguards to protect our educational institutions from the unfair competition of educational institution abroad.

The objectives of competition law and policy are to ensure efficiency and help to put scarce resources to their best use. Without competition law and policy, the scarce resources of developing countries would be wasted.

Competition is an aspect of free trade. Competition policy allowing for free flow of education services would benefit developed countries to get an access to large market. The various clauses relating to competition under GATS with relative autonomy to the decision-making bodies promotes free trade. It has bee argued that developing countries should promote supply responsiveness, may be through mutual trade among them or by allowing private participation under state control and supervision. This requires change in the mindset of individuals and the institutions so far enjoying excessive protection.

From a practical stand point enhancing competitiveness implies:

i) Establishing university industry linkages.

ii) Internationalising curricula.

iii) Identifying universities and specific courses.

iv) Developing appropriate curricula, method of transaction of knowledge and evaluation of students of international standard.

v) Removal of procedural impediments to opening of foreign campuses by Indian institutes.

iv) Allowing arrangements between India and foreign universities for offering academic programmes at both ends.

vii) Making efforts at mutual recognition of degrees and credits.

viii) Developing infrastructural facilities in identified universities/institutions.

Competition Policy

Competition policy refers to law and framework of rules and regulations to foster the competitive environment. It also refers to fostering of competitive market and removal of control. State must assume the role of regulator of market. Should competition policy, so far the domain of private product and services, exist for the higher education? The objective of such a competition policy is to foster efficiency and also protection of and welfare of students.

Alternative Providers of Services

Competition exists when there are multiple alternative providers of education and the buyers of services are free to choose among those alternatives. This essentially means that among public institutions supply of institutions for courses having excess demand be promoted whereas those courses, which are in excess supply, must be closed down. Hence restructuring of courses and alternative providers of high tech courses producing knowledge and skill should form part of an effective competition policy. The private provision of education should increase. However, there must be a regulatory body to ensure that private sector practices fair competition within policy guidelines. Similarly the foreign providers of education may be provided entry subject to the control and other conditions that do not violate the national policy on education. The basic principle of growth of institutions should be ability to innovate, upgrade and become efficient.

Improvement in Supply and Demand

In economic theory, increasing demand leads to an increase in price. Higher education scenario in India is already one of excess demand and higher education is supply constrained. Then the question is why do we say that promotion of demand is necessary for improving competitiveness? Improvement in demand is talked about in two senses. First, it refers to measures for increasing international demand for Indian education to promote the inflow of foreign students and secondly, it also refers to raising relevant demand for education to meet the needs of employment market that demands diversified skill development.

Regulatory and other measures to promote demand relate to the following:

i) Maintenance of international standards in universities and courses.

ii) Introducing a system of registration of foreign educational institutions and accreditation to ensure quality.

iii) Establishing nodal agency to assess the genuineness, quality and relevance of the programme of study offered by foreign universities.

iv) Identifying universities and courses of study to attract foreign students in India.

v) Internationalise the curricula and orient the education system to the emerging demand pattern of industry.

Improving supply conditions:

i) Improving the supply of trained educational manpower.

ii) Government to improve general infrastructure.

iii) Removing procedural impediments to the opening of foreign campuses by Indian institutions.

iv) Removal of controls on supply must go hand in hand with stopping the sub-standard institutions.

Domestic Regulation

Regulations promoting government control and monopoly have resulted in inefficiencies due to 'state failures'. However, since the market, too, is liable to failures the domestic regulation must pave the way towards control on free market in services without eliminating protection wherever that is required. The proponents of GATS argue that free market supporting regulations will result in efficient outcomes. This is the major premise in domestic regulation under GATS.

Article VI of GATS on domestic regulation along with market access and national treatment articles, can be seen as the third complementary measure to ensure free trade in services. Article VI requires that "in sectors where specific commitments are undertaken, each Member shall ensure that all measures of general application are administered in a reasonable, objective and impartial manner". The article aims to create more transparent domestic regulatory decision-making, implementation and administration. There is explicit recognition of the right of service suppliers to information on regulatory and administrative decisions and to judicial and administrative review and appeals processes. Article VI calls for the development of disciplines to ensure that measures relating to qualification requirements and procedures, technical standards and licensing requirements do not constitute unnecessary barriers to trade in services.

On the other hand, the National Policy guides the national regulation on education within a country. Education is a social sector. It is still not considered as a commodity to be guided by the profit motive. The overriding concerns in the national policy are access, equity and quality. In fact discriminating protection is also offered to the weaker sections of society. Besides regulations are made at least at the three levels in the higher education sector at the university level, at the state and at the national level. University has the academic autonomy to determine the course structure, course content, teaching hours, qualification for admission of students. The affiliation, disaffiliation, admission policy and fees structure for universities' statutory bodies and government regulate various courses. As per the recent Supreme Court judgement the state regulation over unaided privately managed colleges has been diluted and brought down to minimum. There are various apex bodies at the central and state levels, which perform different roles and functions for promoting and regulating higher education and research in India.

Freedom to Regulate

One of the principal concerns is that whether domestic regulation under GATS leads to a loss of nation's freedom to regulate its education service in the manner it deems appropriate. Since the former is guided by commercial consideration where as the national regulatory framework protects public interest, there is bound to be conflict between the two. The Council for Trade in Services has been given a particular negotiating mandate in article VI. It allows the Council to develop, in appropriate bodies, any necessary disciplines to prevent domestic regulations (qualification requirements and procedures technical standards and licensing requirements) from constituting unnecessary barriers to trade. It is thus feared that GATS leaves government regulations open to WTO disputes challenge through MA & NT commitments and directly challenges the crucial role that local and national governments play in regulating services.

To remove the 'loss of freedom' threat it is argued that 'domestic regulation' be conducive to economically rational policy making while preserving the regulatory autonomy required to pursue and achieve domestic policy objectives. For example, if the universal access to higher education is a declared goal of National System of Education, the regulations may contain measures to achieve the stated goals. However, these regulations, "whether for economic or social purposes, can be designed, implemented or enforced in more transparent and efficient ways with positive overall effects in terms of domestic governance". Given this, the GATS explicitly recognises "the right of Members to regulate, and to introduce new regulations on, the supply of services within their territories in order to meet national policy objectives and given asymmetries existing with respect to the degrees of development of services regulations in different countries, the particular need of developing countries to exercise this right".

It should be possible to ensure that certain services sectors, which may be important from the social point of view, may not at all be brought within the purview of GATS regulatory disciplines and even if brought by way of bound commitments other means exist to protect the social sector. For example,

— Schedule of commitments follows positive list approach. Hence only those education services are within the GATS purview in which MA and NT commitments are made.

— Limitations to MA and NT – horizontal as well as sectoral – may be mentioned to limit GATS purview.

— Measures relating to licensing, qualifications and technical standards which discriminate between foreign and domestic suppliers whether formally or in fact, would need to be scheduled as NT limitation in the sector where GATS commitments may have been made.

— Members are required to apply their domestic regulations in a way that would not nullify or impair specific commitments.

Threat of Commercialisation

Internationalisation of higher education poses the threat to the public system of higher education. Education is fast becoming a tradable commodity and private providers of education are fast becoming active even within a country. Mushrooming of private institutions for making fast bucks is alarming and is a cause for concern. Draft Guidelines for a Model Act, UGC, 2003 admits that "... Due to the commercial nature of their activities, their number and nationwide spread are likely to increase in the coming years."

Presently national regulation in India allows that only charitable registered societies, non-profit public trusts or foundations can run educational institutions under section 35 of the company's act. Thus within the control of public authorities non-profit private initiatives are permitted. Furthermore, the scope of private institutions/universities is also restricted to offering of such degrees specified by the UGC. The prevailing practice of offering 'disguised' degrees is creating a state of utter confusion and their employment prospects, too, is being restricted to private and unorganised sectors.

The point to note is that globalisation is providing, overtly or covertly, an impetus to the private initiatives in education that will invite commercial interests to grow violating the spirit contained in the National Policy on Education. Selected private institutions in India, however, have catered to the specified parameters of quality. It is important that the education sector be vigilant about domestic regulations that are seen as safeguards for the importing country but barriers for the exporting country wanting access to the market.

The scope of regulation whether through central or state legislation must have effective enabling clauses to limit pure commercial interests as well as disguised degrees but it may very well promote private initiatives in higher education that stand for reputation and academic excellence. In this respect it is important to note that the scope of control and regulation of private enterprise in India should be carefully determined to not only limit the commercial interests but also to guarantee the principles of equity and norms of quality. As such the review of admission policy, fees, infrastructure and quality parameters by the regulating authority should be under the purview of government.

If such laws are not made, domestic regulation provision under GATS may have serious implications in terms of regulating the entry and operations of foreign education providers in India.

Foreign Education Providers

Under National Treatment clause all educational institutions in India whether domestic or foreign should be equally treated. There should be no discrimination simply on the grounds that a particular educational institution is a foreign institution. Hence there is a danger that if domestic regulations do not properly regulate the private education providers in India then foreign education institutions through collaborative arrangements with private institutions in India or by establishing campuses in India may also indulge in commercial activities, as under the clause discrimination cannot be allowed.

It is important to note that in determining the national regulation a clarity in approach towards the treatment of 'for profit' and private universities should be made otherwise contradictory situations may emerge. Under section 35 of the Company's Act profit making cannot be the criteria of establishing educational institutions under private sector in India. On the other hand if under the central or state legislation private universities are allowed to be opened under private sector that begins to pursue commercial interests overtly or covertly, then it amounts to the violation of company's act. Hence in accordance with the present policy on education national legislation on control and regulation of foreign education providers in India should be framed to restrict operation on profit lines. In India institutions such as UGC, NCTE, National Open School, IGNOU are in the process of framing regulations to regulate the operations of foreign education providers in India. AICTE has already framed the regulation to regulate the foreign educational institutions.

However the asymmetries in education policies and practices, too, cannot be disregarded. The present situation is one of dejure non-acceptability but defacto acceptability of 'for profit' and private institutions in India. Even though given education policy the regulation must forbid 'for profit' institutions yet the operations of the same cannot be reversed unless state takes upon itself the responsibility of higher allocation of resources for higher education. Internationalisation of education thus calls for pro-active role of the state, strategic planning and innovative approach to seek private initiatives at all levels of education. Before making any regulation clarity of the role and responsibilities of private enterprise in education is highly required. An ambivalent stance would invite more troubles if the GATS domestic regulation clause comes into effect.

It is also important to point out that regulation in education must be followed by an appropriate FDI policy. For example, if the earnings by the foreign institutions are repatriated abroad, there is no guarantee to ensure the investment of the earnings into education sector in India. Thus if the domestic regulation allows foreign institutions to operate on the condition that surplus earned is further reinvested in educational activities then any transfer of earnings abroad should be prohibited through an appropriate FDI policy.

Equity Concerns

It is important to address equity concerns in any national regulations on education. An important reason to protect the public system of higher education is to enhance the access to education and to provide the discriminating protection to girls and the socially deprived groups. An important way in which this is affected is through providing subsidy. Article XV on subsidies under GATS notes the distortive effects of subsidies on trade in services. However, the article also notes its importance in development programmes and takes into account the needs of Members in providing subsidy.

The distortive effects of subsidies are explained in terms of excessive protection and consequent inefficiency of public sector educational institutions. On the other hand, the benefits are in terms of higher social returns by providing access to social sufferers. It is argued that the withdrawal of subsidies would generate efficiency in the educational institutions and the resources so saved could compensate for the loss in equity. Needless to say that the policy of subsidy in the past has served equity objectives but the public sector institutions have suffered from inefficiency. Further the resource constraint has severely restricted the autonomy of the institutions to improve the quality of education. As such there is the need to provide greater autonomy to the institutions and the regulations on education should allow for the same.

At present there are three types of educational institutions in India- government, private aided and unaided. While subsidies in the form of grants are received by the first two categories of the institutions by the government and they follow the regulatory disciplines relating to equity by the government, the last category presents a chaotic picture as some approved institutions are regulated although others evade any regulatory discipline. The point to note is that whether unaided categories should be subjected to regulation concerning equity. If not, then foreign institutions, too, cannot be subjected to regulations concerning equity. If the government feels that unaided institutions, too, should be subjected to regulations concerning equity then possibly the right to subsidy must also be reserved for them irrespective of whether they are domestic or foreign institutions.

Scope of National Regulation on Education

There are following issues that need to be settled in a national regulation on education for the private education providers in India.

Private Education Providers

There is the need to regulate the private education providers in India. A comprehensive legislation by the UGC/AICTE to regulate private educational institutions promoted by an Indian/NRI is needed for an orderly growth of institutions. The legislation should clearly lay down the process of registration of institutions. Whereas the academic autonomy to the private institutions with respect to the admission policy, the course and the curriculum, the teaching learning process and the methods of evaluation may be granted, team of experts appointed by UGC/AICTE should periodically scrutinise them. The continuance of the course after three years be subject to the minimum accreditation grade granted by NAAC. It is also important to review the fee structure as and when considered necessary by the UGC/AICTE.

Foreign Education Providers

At present the strategy of foreign education providers in India is to attract a large number of Indian students for studies abroad. The foreign institutions in India have been largely active in collaboration with private institutions promoted by an Indian/ NRI/Corporate group, although few have opened branch campuses as well. The nature of collaboration is mainly the twinning arrangement whereby Indian students may be allowed to receive part education in foreign universities at the high price charged by them.

The national regulatory framework for education in India may also have separate regulation for foreign educational institution. The scope of regulation should be to cover the registration procedure, admission policy, course structure, the academic faculty and the minimum infrastructure. Besides the quality of education imparted by these institutions should also be within the purview of regulation. There should also be compulsory accreditation by NAAC and degree awarded by them should also be recognised in the foreign countries.

Apart from the issue of national regulation the issues relating to subsidy also acquires importance, as the grants are available to the aided private educational institutions in India. All government or aided institutions are fully within the purview of government regulation. The subsidy is reserved for these institutions only. The foreign educational institutions should not be provided such concessions and this should be specifically mentioned in the schedule of commitments.

FDI Policy in Education Sector

The implications of FDI into higher education is not a simple question as it has its bearing not only in the higher education *per se* but also on the education sector and more broadly on the whole process of generation of knowledge. Development being dependent on knowledge the implications of liberalisation have far reaching consequences. In the era of globalisation, nations cannot simply remain isolated. The pros and cons of liberalisation need to be understood before any policy decision.

According to OECD, a FDI enterprise is an incorporated or unincorporated enterprise in which a single foreign investor maintains an effective voice by covering 10 per cent of ordinary shares or voting power in an enterprise or covers less than 10 per cent and yet maintains an effective voice in the management. An effective voice implies ability to influence the management and not absolute control. Thus FDI could be desegregated into components of equity capital, invested earnings and intra firm loans.

The threshold equity usually chosen ranges between 10 per cent and 50 per cent of equity shareholding, which allows effective voice in the management. Ways of acquiring effective voice, other than equity share holding are turnkey arrangements, franchising, leasing, subcontracting, licensing and production sharing.

Foreign capital can enter into the Indian market in any one or more than one of the following ways:

i) *FDI*: Companies may be formed in other countries with the specific purpose of operating in India, companies may start their subsidiary offices or branches and affiliates in India or foreigners may subscribe to stocks and debentures of concerns in India.

ii) *Foreign collaboration:* It may take place between two private parties in India and abroad or between foreign firms and Indian government or between foreign government and Indian government.

ii) *Other means* by which foreign capital can enter the Indian markets are through intergovernmental loans, loans from institutions and external commercial borrowings.

In the current wave of liberalisation there has been worldwide shift in the forms of foreign capital. Firstly, direct foreign investment through involving equity capital of an existing or new undertaking has been rising. Secondly, intergovernmental loans and loans from institutions have been declining and external commercial borrowings have been rising implying a shift towards free market based system of attracting foreign capital. Thirdly, technical collaboration involving payments for technology is not a much-favoured mode. Indian firms are apparently opting for equity linked technology transfer.

The policy of FDI in sectors of education services is through automatic route. In the absence of any policy in this sector foreign capital may flow in or out by means of offshore foreign institutions' campus or through the tie-ups with the private partner in India. There is also no limit to foreign capital investment in education services. Since the foreign education providers are coming in unregulated manner, an unregulated inflow of foreign capital particularly in education sector is a cause of great concern. It is now felt that FDI in education must be guided by certain norms and control as it is a sensitive sector and its implications should be examined before any FDI policy.

Traditionally education is considered to be non-tradable. The government is used to fund education through domestic resource mobilisation. Recently UPE and UEE required large foreign capital to be funded through World Bank loan. In the Higher Education 90's. is the decade of falling percentage budgetary allocation on secondary, higher and technical education. The resource crunch in these sectors have adversely affected the public sector and promoted the private sector participation at almost all levels of education. To raise the participation rate from 7 per cent to 10 per cent targeted by the end of tenth plan is also an uphill task in view of impending financial shortage. It may be argued that FDI may be used as a source of investment at least in some selected sectors. Against this view academia in education sector argue that foreign investment in education might lead to cultural imperialism. Therefore, education should be national agenda purely funded through domestic resources.

Higher Education: Modes of Supply

GATS defines services trade as occurring via four modes of supply all of which are relevant to education:

- *Mode I: Cross Border Delivery*: delivery of education services via internet (distance education, tele-education, education testing services).
- *Mode II: Consumption Abroad*: movement of students from one country to another for higher education (foreign students in US universities).
- *Mode III: Commercial Presence*: establishment of local branch campuses or subsidiaries by foreign universities in other countries, course offerings by domestic private colleges leading to degrees at foreign universities, twinning arrangements, franchising.
- *Mode IV: Movement of Natural Persons*: temporary movement of teachers, lecturers, and education personnel to provide education services overseas.

The modes are essentially defined on the basis of the origin of service supplier and consumer, and the degree and type of territorial presence, which they have at the moment the service is delivered. The following table illustrates the four modes of supply under education services.

Table 1. Modes of Supply

GATS—Mode of Supply	Explanation	Examples in Higher Education
Cross Border Supply	The provision of a service where the service crosses the border (does not require the physical movement of the consumer)	Distance education E-learning Virtual universities
Consumption Abroad	Provision of the service involving the movement of the consumer to the country of the supplier	Students who go to another country to study
Commercial Presence	The service provider establishes or has presence of commercial facilities in another country in order to render service	Local branch or satellite campuses Twinning partnerships Franchising arrangem-ements with local institutions
Movement of natural persons	Persons travelling to another country on a temporary basis to provide service	Professors, teachers, researchers working abroad

Cross Border Supply

In education service, cross border supply covers all types of service that is provided through distance or through telecommunications or mail and through services embodied in exported goods (i.e., services supplied in or by a physical medium, such as a computer diskette or drawings). In all such cases, the service supplier is not present within the territory of the member where the service is delivered.

Under mode I, there are two possibilities of trade. The first is through distance education offered by universities or through national open universities either through print or telecommunication or through computer diskette or through all. The second of course relates to all education services supplied by other than universities or national open universities.

The competitive strength of IGNOU in marketing education programmes abroad is the reputation, quality and the low prices. It charges 250 US dollar for its prestigious management course. Similar course from a developed country would cost at least ten times that of above charge. IGNOU is already a recognised distance education provider in gulf region- Dubai, Abu Dhabi, Sharjah, Doha, Muscat and Kuwait. Its courses are being offered in Mauritius, Maldives, Seychelles, Nepal and Sri Lanka. Staff Training and Research Institute of Distance Education (STRIDE), IGNOU has also collaborated with the International Institute of Capacity Building in Africa (IICBA), Addis Ababa to provide distance education programme to students in Ethiopia and Liberia. Students from Commonwealth countries have also been offered IGNOU programmes through distance mode.

The competitive strength of IGNOU can be realised when it can make right strategies for the offer of courses and for marketing the programmes abroad. India can make requests to other countries to allow IGNOU to market its programme. An assessment of the strength of IGNOU in marketing education abroad vis-a-vis international open universities is necessary for making offers. The general principle should be to make partial commitments restricted to public providers of distance education from abroad.

Some of the concerns are:

i) Capability of national authorities to regulate the content of programmes delivered through this mode.

ii) The temptation of overseas suppliers using distance learning as a medium for dumping upon developing countries modules, courses and degrees that are no longer marketable in their own economies are very high.

iii) In the absence of auditing capability distance learning programmes may be introduced without linking them to development objectives and because there are many people in developing countries who need a degree of any sort to advance their career such courses may become very popular. But their contribution to capacity building for development may be limited.

iv) Limited rigorous mechanisms for quality assurance that can ensure courses are taught by tenured faculty with a record of publications and with hands on knowledge of their fields of specialisation.

v) Intellectual dumping—freelance experts, consultants and retired soldiers offering distance learning courses and materials is increasing.

Movement of Students

This mode of supply is often referred to as "movement of the consumer". The essential feature of the mode is that the service is delivered outside the territory of the member making commitment. Often the actual movement of the consumer i.e., students is necessary as in education services. It should be noted that a member might only be able to impose restrictive measures affecting its own consumers (students), not those of other members, on activities taking place outside its jurisdiction. For example, if India opens mode II, then it may impose limitations with respect to mode II on market access or national treatment that affects the students coming from abroad to India (i.e., its own consumers). India cannot impose restrictions affecting students going to say, United States, for studies there.

Reasons for the outflow of students include the following:

i) Many very able students are unable to obtain entry into local universities because of lack of space and sometimes very competitive entry requirements. Such students often find it easier to gain entry to good foreign institutions than to local schools.

ii) Many of the world's brightest students seek opportunities abroad because there are few world-class institutions in much of the world, especially in developing countries.

iii) Students also leave home when the specialisations they want to study, from astronomical physics to aspects of zoology, are unavailable in their own countries, especially at the graduate and professional level.

iv) Some students feel that the prestige of a degree from a foreign university, especially an American degree, is greater than that of one from a local institution.

v) A significant number of international students go abroad to study with the aim of staying in the host country to work and make a career.

Educational institutions of developed countries have competitive advantages in relation to the educational institutions of developing countries. Advanced countries taking full commitment in mode II have been able to attract foreign students and earn huge amount of money. Do our educational institutions have international curricula, world class, infrastructure and facilities such as library, hostels, and equipment? Let it be known that even IITs in India, though may be world class in terms of academic standards, do not have facilities in terms of hostel, classroom, etc., by international standards. Statistics reveal that the number of foreign students coming to India is falling in recent years. Since restriction under Mode II by India does not restrain the flow of students to any other country, but only to its own country, there is no point in restricting the mode II. Taking full commitment and developing institutions in India to offer world-class higher education services may have immense potentials to attract foreign students in India. Of course, the present scenario is that countries like US, UK, Canada and Australia are making vigorous advertising and sales campaigns to attract Indian students abroad.

Commercial Presence

It refers to the actual presence of foreign investors in a host country. The important ways in which this mode can be activated are opening an institution or branch campuses abroad or franchising or through twinning. Indian higher educational institutions may offer programme or qualification abroad and may allow the outside educational institutions to offer educational programmes and qualifications. Opening of this mode, too, has various implications and therefore, it is in the interests of developing countries to make only partial commitments and impose various limitations so that Indian higher education structure is benefited from trade through this mode.

India has some competitive advantages in certain area of education such as yoga, Ayurveda, Sanskrit. Besides it has also potentials to develop many areas such as engineering, management, medical institutions or their branch campuses abroad. India can make requests to other countries to allow an access to Indian providers of education. India can also make offers where quality institutions are required. They may be permitted to establish institutions provided reputed foreign education institutions provide quality education. Off shore campus requiring minimum amount of investment in infrastructure and quality education may be permitted. Foreign education providers should also be subject to regulation by the government. One limitation that a country like India should impose is that only public education providers should be permitted through the mode III provided various other conditions such as mutual recognition of degrees are fulfilled. Of course developed countries want this mode to exploit the market of developing economies and therefore prefer to have minimum limitations or restrictions to be imposed by developing countries.

Some of the negative implications of opening mode III may be pointed out.

i) Commercial presence may entail welfare distortions. Usually foreign institutions tend to give better and more attractive packages to their staff. This allows them to employ the best leaving the others to share the rest. Consequences may be the creation of wage havens employing and retaining a very happy few while at the same time creating conditions for internal brain drain

ii) One of the negative consequences of market driven for-profit education is that the number of 'diploma mills', 'canned degrees' and 'accreditation mills' will increase.

iii) Foreign institutions can create duality of quality, standards and access.

iv) There may be the rise of inefficient and languishing public sector and a dominant private sector.

The presence of foreign providers signal to government that they can decrease public funding for higher education, thereby jeopardising domestic publicly funded institutions.

On the positive side the following implications of inflow of foreign institutions in India are pointed out:

i) Possibility of stopping outflow of students.

ii) Study programmes will be cheaper in relation to foreign degrees earned abroad.

iii) Diversification of study programmes. Of course this diversification is a very limited one.

iv) Process of integration of an international dimension into the teaching/service/research functions, competitiveness will be promoted and it has its implications on the foreign exchange as well.

Status of Foreign Education Providers

NIEPA is at present conducting a research study on foreign education providers in India. As per the information so far collected there are over 100 institutions/universities providing foreign courses/programmes in India. There has been a spurt in the demand for the courses/programmes offered by Indian institutions working in collaboration with foreign universities. However, off late it is being observed that in the absence of a simple and transparent approach to recognise, supervise and monitor the foreign education providers in India, the students feel threatened to join the courses offered by the foreign educational institutions.

It was observed that most of the foreign institutions in India have twinning or franchisee arrangement with Indian partners. Under the former the foreign institutions in India attract Indian students for a year or two in their own countries. Under the franchisee the foreign institutions permit Indian partner institutions to execute the programmes and conduct the examination. It is said that the foreign institutions supervise quality control, curriculum design and the capacity building of faculty. Revenue is shared on a 50:50 basis. Off shore campus mode of foreign institutions' operation is not very popular. Hence there is a little of FDI inflow to the country and more of the outflow of foreign exchange due to twinning and fees charged on account of franchisee. The diversification offered by foreign institutions is too thin and is confined to courses in business management, hospitality management, information technology and some vocational courses such as nursing, tourism etc. All courses are job oriented and hence attract the limited number of high fee paying students. There is no doubt there are private partners in India who are active in collaborating with foreign institutions, however, public universities, too, have few tie ups with foreign universities.

The most worrisome feature is that any foreign degree offered in India is not recognised if the Indian partner institutions are not recognised by UGC or AICTE or any other recognising bodies such as National Council of Teacher Education (NCTE), Medical Council of India (MCI), Dental Council of India (DCI), Council of Architecture, Distance Education Council of IGNOU. Regulation and processes of recognition, monitoring and supervision of such foreign education providers need to be brought out urgently. There are institutions, which have applied to the AICTE for recognition of programmes, but even before any such recognition the institutions have already begun to operate with the collaboration of Indian partners. AICTE's present regulation is said to be too restrictive.

Export of Indian Education

Export of education from India results from Indian institutions operating abroad and foreign students joining educational institutions in India. Many Indian institutions are opening their branch campuses abroad and are rated high in quality. However, the number of such institutions abroad is lesser than foreign institutions in India. In the higher education segment some deemed universities such as BITS Pillani and MAHE, Manipal and private institutions such as NIIT India, besides some public institutions like Delhi university, IGNOU, SNDT college, Mysore university and Madras university are making their presence felt abroad. There are good prospects of popularising Indian education abroad by enlarging the participation of Indian universities by taking pro-active policy measures.

BITS, Pilani, set up its Dubai campus in September 2000 in association with ETA-NET, a member of ETA - ASCON group. Students of BPDC will obtain their degrees from BITS, Pilani-India, after the successful completion of 8 semesters of programme. Thousands of students study in Manipal institutions situated in Sikkim, Mangalore, Nepal, Malaysia and Dubai. At present 2081 foreign students are enrolled at MAHE. Most of the students are in the medical, mainly from USA, GULF, Sri Lanka and Malaysia. Indian origin students from 49 English-speaking countries are at present studying at MAHE.

Form BITS Pilani experience at Dubai, it is clear that initially it faced visa problem for students. There was also a compulsion to go for collaboration with a local partner. It was not possible for BITS Pilani to purchase land for developing sufficient infrastructure. Initially introduction of courses based on UAEs Islamic laws was insisted upon there was also problem of getting government job either in Dubai or outside, including India, for students having BITS Pilani degree. Sharing of revenue did not pose a problem. For branch campus BITS Pilani pays 15 per cent royalty per student.

Over time many problems were resolved as Dubai broadened the concept of export free zones where any university of world repute can come. The problems that still remain relate to:

i) Visa restrictions.

ii) Mutual recognition of degrees by both the government.

iii) Important lesson is that understanding domestic regulation of different countries where India wishes to export education is necessary so that limitations or restrictions to open branch campus can be overcome through negotiations.

From MAHE experience in Malaysia, it was clear that mutual cooperation of India and Malaysian government was crucial in establishing branch campus abroad.The problem is that MAHE medical degree got recognition in Malaysia, but Medical Council of India does not recognise the degree. What should be the process of recognition of degree in India provided by reputed Indian institutions abroad is a vexed issue up till now.

There are also issues relating to Indian institutions collaborating with foreign universities and imparting education in India. Issues related to:

i) Recognition of degree in India by the government.

ii) Ensuring the registration and quality assurance and thereby regulation of foreign education providers.

iii) Immediate concern is that there is no regulation except for AICTE. The terms of regulation should include issue of accreditation.

An important aspect with respect to the co-ordination among different institutions may be pointed out. As an example, UGC and AICTE must co-ordinate in framing regulations. If AICTE frames the regulation allowing foreign institution/university on certain conditions, UGC should also move together as the right to grant a degree rests with the university which should be recognised by UGC only. Similarly if UGC grants a deemed university status to any institution thereby permitting the authority to grant a degree then MCI or DCI should also recognise the degree. It requires a process of prior consultation or removing of legal distortion that causes overlap of authorities. Co-ordination between state government and the central government and the regularity authorities is also important in matters of education policy.

Movement of Natural Persons

This mode covers natural persons who are themselves service suppliers as well as natural persons who are employees of service suppliers. Mode IV in GATS refers to the 'Supply of a service by a service supplier of one member, through presence of natural persons of a member in the territory of any other member' 'The annex on the movement of natural persons' in the legal texts of the Uruguay Round of Multilateral Trade Negotiations specifies that the mode 4 service suppliers are those natural persons who seek non permanent rather than permanent residence or permanent access to the employment market of foreign countries. They also do not intend to obtain permanent citizenship.

Analysis of the responses of the developed countries indicates that, the movement of natural persons should be linked to mode III i.e., through commercial presence in the developing economies. Since India has got capabilities to provide various professional, technical, skilled services at various levels, it would be in the interests of India to liberalise the trade in education services through mode IV without linking it to mode III.

Since developed countries want to restrict the movement of natural persons through mode IV, they want restrictions such as economic needs tests, labour market tests pertaining to mode IV. Secondly, they also like to process all applications distinguishing work permits from residency permits. It would then be easier to identify work visas under mode IV from residence visas. While later categories may be denied access legally under GATS rules, it would be easier to restrict and regulate work visas. Thirdly, developed countries want to open the movement of natural persons to a select category of specialists only.

Furthermore since developed countries want the movement of natural persons for commercial presence, they have a liberal approach to respective commitments. Firstly, they want under mode IV all those business persons, to be treated as natural persons, that may have to stay within own or affiliate company for career development or training in business practices, even though these business persons are not service renderers or educators in the strict sense. They also want the commitment to allow for the automatic granting of spousal work rights for the spouses of intra corporate transferees. Secondly, the developed countries also want the 'service sale persons' to be treated as natural persons by virtue of not being based in the territory of the member service. Sales persons are basically the negotiators of sales, although not direct sellers to the public. For example, under this category, they may organise business services for education such as 'education fairs', seminars, etc., to attract students for studies abroad. India has a large supply of manpower with varying skills and professional and technical experts. Therefore, India's strategic approach should be to make firm stand on the liberalisation of the movement of natural persons.

References

Altbach Philip, "Higher Education Cross Borders", *Change*, March-April, 2004.

Anandakrishnan M, "Internationalization of Higher Education: Policy Concerns", paper presented at a conference at NIEPA on 26 and 27 August, 2004

Chanda Rupa, "Social Services and the GATS: Key Issues and Concerns", *World Development* Vol.31, No.12, 2003.

Knight Jane, *GATS, Trade and Higher education: Perspective 2003-where are we?* Report, The observatory on borderless higher education UK., 2003.

Kumar Ravindra, "Privatisation of Higher Education and Regulatory Mechanisms in University", *University News*, Vol.42, no. 7, February 16-22, 2004, AIU, New Delhi.

Parhar Madhu, Internationalising Indian Higher Education through Distance, *Indian Journal of Open Learning*, 2001, 10(3) pp. 339-348

Powar, K.B. *WTO, GATS and Higher Education: An Indian Perspective*. Paper prepared for meeting convened by the Association of Commonwealth Universities. Perth Australia, 2002.

7. CHALLENGES OF INTERNATIONAL ENGAGEMENT

There are currently several ongoing reforms aiming at increasing the strengths, quality and attractiveness of Indian higher education system and enhance the training and quality of researchers and research infrastructures. Changes in the international operational environment and the increasing multiculturalisation of society create expectations on higher education institutions. Internationalisation of higher education, research and innovation systems is at the core of societal renewal. Moreover, internationalisation of higher education institutions promotes diversity in the society and business community, international networking, competitiveness and innovativeness, as well as improves the well-being, competence and education of the citizens.

Internationalisation has long been among the key aims of the Indian science and higher education policy as well as at the core of higher education institutions' own strategies. Long-term investments in higher education and research and development activities have led to a rise in the level of our higher education institutions and research and an increase in international cooperation. India has been ranked high in international education, research, technology and innovation activity comparisons.

Despite our progress, the low level of internationalisation is still one of the key weaknesses of the Indian higher education and research system when compared with our competitors. India has built its competence base and success very much with its own means. When compared with the speed of change in the operating environment and the development of globalisation, India's internationalisation development has been slow, and has completely stopped in some fields. The risk is that Indian higher education institutions are losing their position as an interesting cooperation partner.

Great changes experienced in the last decades include the rapid increase of higher education crossing national borders, integration of the higher education systems and increased variety in the forms of higher education. The demand for internationalism touched increasingly the activities of all higher education institutions. Its benefits can be examined from the perspectives of students, teachers, researchers, institutes, individual higher education institutions and the whole system, as well as that of the whole nation. Internationalisation of the higher education system is particularly important for the following reasons:

- Our own mental and financial resources are limited and a significant part of the information we need comes from abroad.
- Higher education institutions are key to the internationalisation of the economy and society. They attract a highly educated labour force and foreign investments. By international networking higher education institutions consolidate the development potential of their region, their overall competence level, available resources, competitiveness and innovation ability as well as make business life in the region more varied.
- Nurturing and promoting Indian culture as part of the diversity of global cultures is among the duties of educational and research institutions in civilised countries.
- International mobility provides opportunities to work and network with the top experts in the field, to participate in their teaching and utilise high-quality infrastructures as well as to become acquainted with the most recent research methodologies, fields of research and ideas.
- A non-Indian researchers and teachers bring new kinds of competence and new influences in the operation of the higher education institutions.
- Studying and working abroad improve the individual's language skills and position in the labour market and increase understanding between cultures and societies.
- A great deal of tacit knowledge is connected to diverse international networking, which is necessary for the

development of education and research as well as societal renewal.

- Internationalisation promotes the mental growth and understanding of global responsibility in an individual.
- The solving of global problems requires international cooperation.
- Participation in the globalisation of education, science and technology and influencing it in the EU, OECD, UNESCO and in other international forums is in the best financial and cultural interest of India.

There are significant differences in internationalisation between different fields of education and science. Also, obstacles to internationalisation and opportunities afforded by it vary. However, there is a consensus among the higher education and business communities about the fact that our higher education institutions do not offer the students, researchers, teachers and other personnel genuinely international and multicultural operating environments.

Changing Operating Environment

The international operating environment of higher education institutions is changing rapidly. Indian higher education institutions must compete increasingly harder to retain their position as producers, conveyors and utilisers of competence and new knowledge. The status of the higher education institutions is particularly affected by changes in knowledge production, international competition for talent, demographic changes, globalising labour markets, increasing mobility of students and researchers, increased influence of policies pertaining to knowledge and competence, the ongoing Asia-wide modernisation of the higher education system, and expectations directed at higher education institutions to provide answers to global problems.

- *Research and innovation activities are becoming international.* The production and wide-ranging utilisation of research information is increasingly a collective and international objective. During the last ten years, the number of internationally co-written publications in the world tripled and the share of international patents of all patents almost doubled.

- *Competition for experts is getting stiffer.* International cooperation and interaction is on the increase, and it will find new closer and deeper forms. Knowledge and new ideas are increasingly produced in global networks. Higher education institutions are channels for such networks. States and regions compete for experts and enterprises with their research and educational systems.
- *Emerging economies.* The rapid economic growth in populous fast developing countries and their engagement with the global economy affect the direction that internationalisation takes. The focus of the world economy and politics is shifting towards Asia.
- *Significance of quality is emphasised.* Success in competition for experts requires that research and innovation environments are of high quality and are internationally well known. High-quality teaching and research attract competent people, knowledge, enterprises, investors and make them put down their roots in the operating areas of the higher education institutions.
- *Work-based immigration.* The ageing population makes it necessary to attract a larger foreign workforce and competition for competent workers is stiffening. The share of the workforce engaged in research and development activities of the whole workforce is growing. Many countries have reviewed their policies and selection measures with the aim of promoting immigration of research and development experts and other highly educated workforce members. In India, the workforce will start diminishing earlier than in competing countries. Promotion of work-based immigration and education of already existing immigrants in India are among the most urgent tasks of internationalisation.
- *The structure of student, researcher and teachers corps has changed.* Due to the increasing number of adult students and the ageing of the researcher and teacher corps, organising work and study periods abroad has become more challenging.

- *Key competences in internationality.* Functioning in internationalising working life requires that all individuals with higher education qualifications have interaction skills, good language skills and diverse cultural competence.
- *The new structures of research and higher education institutions.* In recent years, several new structures have been created and new initiatives launched to consolidate research, education and innovation activities.
- *Student mobility and educational exports.* In three decades, the international mobility of students has quadrupled. The number of mobile students is increasing more rapidly than the overall number of students. Demand for higher education is growing rapidly in developing countries where domestic supply cannot meet demand. The sale of educational services has become an important export product for many countries. New activities have sprung up alongside traditional student and researcher mobility, such as branch campuses, franchising, commissioned training from abroad, bilateral training agreements, twinning, joint degrees, e-learning and corporate universities.
- *International recommendations, instructions and guidelines.* Increased mobility has made it necessary to provide international guidelines and norms. There are already approved guidelines to safeguard students in higher education and other stakeholders against low-quality educational services and erroneous information.
- *Global responsibility.* Globalisation changes the economy and society. Higher education institutions are expected to participate within the scope of their basic duties in the analysis and presentation of scientifically grounded alternative solutions to global problems, such as climate change, infectious diseases, poverty, limited national resources, violations of human rights, wars, and terrorism. While developing new forms of international cooperation, the higher education institutions need to consider more carefully than hitherto the global implications of their activities.
- *Status of national languages.* The dominance of English as the language of trade, science and higher education has

strengthened. Increasing attention has been paid to teaching and publication in national languages outside the Anglo-Saxon language area. It is necessary for the development of science, culture and society to ensure the availability of research-based knowledge and to support the cultural development of the whole population.

Global Challenges and National Response

Higher education worldwide is beset with dilemmas that need to be addressed soon. In higher education, often bound by the constraints of national thinking, a comparative perspective is especially valuable because academic institutions worldwide stem from common traditions, and the issues facing higher education around the world have many common characteristics.

Higher education has witnessed profound changes in the past two decades, and those in the academic field have yet to come to terms with the implications of these changes. While academic systems function in a national environment, the challenges play themselves out on a global scale. We can learn much from both national experiences and international trends. Ideas and solutions suitable for one country or region may be relevant in another.

With academic institutions worldwide sharing common historical roots and facing common contemporary challenges, it is especially appropriate that international dialogues take place. A comparative and global approach to thinking about higher education benefits everyone

Global Perspective

Though higher education has not yet become a global system, yet there is considerable convergence among the world's universities and higher education systems. The basic institutional model and structure of studies are similar worldwide. English has assumed a role as the primary international language of science and scholarship, including the internet. Now, with more than one million students studying outside their borders, with countless scholars working internationally, and with new technologies such as the Internet providing instant communications, the international roots and the contemporary realities of the university are central.

Importance of Universal Access

In North America, much of Europe, and a number of East Asian countries, academic systems approach universal access, with access thereby has become increasingly available for non-traditional students. In some countries, however, access remains limited. In China and India, for example, despite dramatic expansion, under 5 percent of the age group attends post-secondary institutions. In some countries with relatively low per capita income, such as the Philippines, access is high, while in some wealthier nations, it remains a key point of challenge. Throughout Africa, access is limited to a tiny sector of the population.

Access is an increasingly important issue everywhere, as populations demand it and as developing economies require skilled personnel. Demands for access come into conflict with another of the flashpoints of controversy of the present era—funding. Higher education involves heavy funding and there is much debate concerning how to fund expanding academic systems. Current approaches to higher education funding emphasise the need for "users" to pay for the cost of instruction, as policy makers increasingly view higher education as something that benefits the individual, rather than as a "public good" where the benefits accrue to society. This new thinking, combined with constrictions on public expenditures in many countries, have put financial pressures on the academe. These difficulties come at a time when higher education systems are trying to provide expanded access.

Financial Constraints

Higher education's problems have been compounded in many poorer parts of the world by the idea, stressed by the World Bank and other agencies, that basic education was most cost-effective—as a result, higher education was ignored by major lending and donor agencies. Now, higher education is back on the agenda of governments and multilateral agencies just as academe faces some of its most serious challenges. Academic systems and institutions have tried to deal with these financial constraints in several ways—loan programmes, the privatisation of some public institutions, and higher tuition being among the alternatives to direct government expenditure. In many parts of the world, enrolments have risen, but resources, including faculty, have not kept up with needs. Academic infrastructures, including libraries and laboratories, have been starved of funds, hence less expenditure on basic research. Conditions of study have deteriorated in many of the world's best-developed academic systems, including Germany and France. Students have taken to the streets in large numbers to protest declining budgets and poor conditions for the first time since the 1960s. There has also been a dramatic decline in academic conditions in sub-Saharan Africa and in some other developing areas.

Development of Educational Forms

The formal structures by which education systems prepare students for tomorrow are weakly developed. Models developed in Germany, through the linking of post-secondary education and apprenticeship arrangements, or the US community college system are currently being explored in several areas. Professional education often links well to employment in many countries, but education in the arts and sciences is less well articulated.

With rapid changes in technology and the creation of employment categories workers and employers must continually attend to the educational dimension. This has led to the development of a variety of educational forms beyond the bachelor's degree. In Germany, recent changes in the degree structure have led to the modularisation of graduate degrees. In the United States, certificate programmes and short-term courses of study are being rapidly developed. In many countries, especially in the developing world, graduate education is coming into its own as the need for advanced skills and for continuing education becomes increasingly clear.

Impact of Technological Developments

Many of the dislocations in school-to-work transition and the press for lifelong education are partially the result of technological developments. More directly, however, technology has widened the scope of distance education that has important implications for the accreditation of educational institutions and assurance of quality in such circumstances. It is also beginning to have an impact on teaching and learning in traditional universities. Though this technology is expensive, subject to rapid obsolescence, it requires high initial investment simply to start the process. For many developing countries, cost is at present prohibitive, and it is precisely these areas where technology can provide the greatest short-term improvement. Technology is also central to the communication, storage, and retrieval of knowledge. The traditional library is being revolutionised by web-based information systems, as are the management systems of many universities.

International Mobility

As the market for individuals with transnational competencies has grown, so have opportunities for individuals with marketable skills in other countries. Currently, mobility of talent has been from developing countries, such as India and China, to the developed world. If nations are to develop, a means must be found by which talent can flourish in the soils that originally nurtured it. Related issues of internationalising the curriculum and providing a global consciousness to students, including instruction in foreign language, and ensuring that the academic profession is linked internationally are central to any discussion of the internationalisation of higher education.

Expansion of Graduate Education

One of the areas of greatest expansion worldwide has been graduate education—the post-baccalaureate training for the professions as well as for science, technology and teaching. Graduate education offers great opportunities for international links and cooperation. Countries can take advantage of graduate training capacities elsewhere, and the new technologies can provide key links. Highly specialised and advanced-level teaching and research deserve careful analysis.

Privatisation of Higher Education

The privatisation of higher education has worldwide. In Latin America and some parts of Asia, the fastest-growing parts of the academic system are private institutions. In Central and Eastern Europe public universities are in some places being "privatised" in the sense that they are increasingly responsible for raising their own funds. The expansion of the private sector brings up issues of quality control and accreditation since in many parts of the world there are few controls as yet on private-sector expansion. As some developing areas, such as sub-Saharan Africa, will soon be experiencing the growth of private institutions, understanding in a comparative context the problems and possibilities of private higher education is an urgent need.

Need for a Committed Academic Profession

The academic profession is in dire straits almost everywhere. There is a rapid growth of part-time faculty members in many countries, and traditional tenure systems are under attack. The teaching faculty is being asked to do more with less, and student-teacher ratios, academic salaries, and morale have all deteriorated. The teaching faculty is being asked to adjust to new circumstances but is given few resources to assist in the transition. Without a committed academic profession, the university cannot be an effective institution.

Problems of Access and Equity

Access and equity remain central factors, but in the current policy context are sometimes neglected. While academic systems worldwide have expanded dramatically, there are problems of access and equity in several parts of the world. Gender, ethnicity, and social class remain serious issues. In many developing countries, higher education remains mainly an urban phenomenon, and wealthier segments of society benefit. Although women have made significant advances, access for women remains a serious problem in many parts of the world.

Accountability and Expansion

Accountability is a contemporary watchword in higher education. Demands by funding sources, mainly government, to measure academic productivity, control funding allocations, etc. are increasingly a central part of the debate on higher education. Governance systems are being strained, sometimes to the breaking point. To meet the demands for accountability, universities are becoming managerialised, with professional administrators gaining increasing control. The traditional power of the teaching faculty is being weakened.

This is compounded by expansion which brings with it increased differentiation and the emergence of academic systems. New kinds of academic institutions emerge, and existing universities serve larger and more diverse groups. In order to make sense of this differentiation, academic systems are organised to provide coordination and the appropriate management of resources.

The Role of IITs

Universities in independent India are equipped with facilities for undergraduate and graduate education, in the full range of disciplines available at universities in developed countries. At least one agricultural university has been established in each state. Additionally, new national-level apex institutions—such as the Indian Institutes of Technology (IITs) and the Indian Institutes of Management (IIMs)— were established to provide world-class education in fields such as engineering, technology, management, and medicine, research in different fields which are considered critical to development. These were established in consultation with and assistance from some of the best-known experts and institutions of higher learning in Europe and North America. The government has, thus, invested heavily in revamping higher education.

India has the world's third-largest pool of scientifically and technically trained personnel and hence required none from development countries. These personnel are accepted for employment worldwide. Students from other countries, particularly the African countries, come to India for higher studies. Research, which was altogether absent in British India, is now well established. Since the past two decades serious problems have surfaced. Highly qualified Indians, particularly the products of prestigious institutions such as the IITs, have been migrating to Europe, North America, and recently to Australia. Initially celebrated as India's successful entry into the international market for employment it is now resented that, while the migrants prosper, the country is deprived of returns from its massive investment in technical, technological and professional education. Institutions of higher education, particularly the apex institutions, are blamed for their failure to cultivate, among their students, a commitment to serve the country.

Compounding this problem is that of underemployment and unemployment of graduates. Attributing this to economy not growing at on the scale required to absorb all the manpower that the institutions of higher education produce, yet, many positions in industry, in government administration, and surprisingly even in educational institutions, lie vacant for want of suitably trained persons. This is in partly because qualifications for employment are narrowly and rigidly defined. But it is also due to a measure of mismatch between what higher education produces and what the country needs.

Keeping Pace with Global Advances and Market Forces

With challenges facing higher education from the grassroots and by the indigenous culture, it is hard-pressed to keep pace with global advances in the development of both manpower and research. The government is unable to provide adequate funds to maintain facilities at the level required—even at institutions such as the IITs and IIMs, internationally recognised for the quality of education.

Other problem too have to be dealt with for instance, in order to make their mark in their disciplines, Indian academics prefer to do research and to publish on issues that are of international import. Which are not always relevant to the country's needs. In the international network, they are often exploited by being invited only to provide data from the Indian subcontinent. Meanwhile market-driven demands force institutions of higher education to concentrate on the short-term objective of providing employment-oriented courses, at the cost of their mission to advance knowledge. With few careers in research, very few good students opt for courses that lead to the advancement of knowledge. While the academic purpose is thus taking backstage there is no room for a good all-round liberal education either.

With the liberalisation of the country's economy, global market forces have generated new fears and dilemmas for higher education in India. In order to take advantage of the low cost of educated labour, multinationals have been locating many of their labour-intensive operations here. While institutions of higher education are pushed to produce appropriate manpower, observers are unsure about whether this will contribute to the country's economic progress or toward its colonisation by the economies of the developed world.

Higher Education as an Instrument of Equality

The government's policy is to provide opportunities for higher education to all those who aspire to it. Hence facilities have been massively expanded—fees have been kept low; vernacular languages have been introduced as the media of instruction; several universities offer fee waivers to women students. Further, in a bold move to extend access to sectors of the population known to have poor access to university education, the government has instituted a policy of "reservations". According to this policy, which makes it mandatory for all institutions of higher education that receive government funding (and almost all do) to reserve a quota of admissions as well as faculty and administrative positions (a) for the castes that are considered to be low in the caste hierarchy and that were therefore traditionally denied the right to education, and (b) for the aborigines or tribes who were traditionally excluded from education because they functioned outside the mainstream of urban and rural life. Scholarships and other facilities have also been liberally provided for these two categories.

Together, all these provisions have yielded spectacular growth. To finance the expansion, the Government of India has consistently increased its share in the total expenditure on higher education—from 49.1 per cent in 1950–51 to more than 90 per cent today, although government allocations to education have declined to 3.8 per cent of GDP, the lowest in South Asia. Despite these impressive statistics the enrolment in higher education in India today accounts for barely 6 per cent of the relevant age group, as compared to 30 per cent in Europe and 50 per cent in North America. This is partly because the expansion has been offset by the growth of the population in the relevant age group. Nevertheless, the fact illustrates how difficult it is for developing countries to bridge gaps and to keep pace with the developed world.

Decline in Quality

The increased facilities fall short of demand. For some professional programmes, there are more than 500 applicants per seat. To meet the demand, facilities are constantly stretched beyond capacity at the cost of quality. For instance, when classes were small, teachers were able to encourage questions and stimulate interaction, in spite of teaching by the lecture method, extensively used in the country. But now, as they lecture to large numbers, this is no longer possible. Also few students are academically motivated. Most pursue a degree for the status it carries and because it is a required qualification for employment.

Students in the professional stream take courses that are relevant to their future work. But more than 70 per cent of the students are enrolled in the traditional faculties of arts, science, and commerce, in courses that have little relevance to the occupations they will eventually take up. They are aware of this and therefore indifferent, certificate oriented, and examination driven, as are their teachers. Meanwhile, institutions are weighed down by the bureaucratic requirements of the government and their own rules and regulations, designed to cope with large numbers. As the academic purpose has thus receded in importance, malpractice and corruption have grown. Professional education, hitherto relatively safe from these forces, is being slowly sucked in.

Transformation of the Structure of Opportunities

New inequalities have emerged as professional education has steadily grown in prestige. Among professional institutions, such institutions as the IITs and IIMs are considered to be in a class apart. Students who succeed in the competition for admission to professional courses in general, and to these institutions in particular, largely come from more well-to-do, educated homes and superior schools. They enrol in private colleges that charge hefty fees, and European, North American, and Australian universities peddle expensive courses that have no dearth of students. Apart from this, parents who can afford to do so send their children abroad for further education, earlier after completion of the first degree. But with institutions becoming highly competitive, many students are sent abroad for the first degree.

There is effort to provide equal opportunities for higher education but facilities for schooling are highly uneven and unequal. Barely 65 per cent of children in the relevant age group complete primary school and that less than 30 per cent complete high school. Reservations for the disadvantaged castes and tribes to advance significantly in education as well as in employment, have become highly politicised. For instance, the performance there candidates at institutions such as the IITs is significantly lower than the cutoff point for open admissions, but attempts to bridge this gap with remedial courses are rejected as discriminatory. In Parliament these institutions have been criticised for trying to maintain international standards at the cost of addressing national realities. And these institutions are neck deep in litigation over reserved admissions, as well as reservation of faculty and administrative positions.

In spite of higher education in India failing to have functioned successfully as an instrument of equality, yet there is visible, as well as statistical, evidence of a complete transformation of the structure of opportunities in the country—for the traditionally disadvantaged castes and tribes, for women, and for the classes that not very long ago had little or no access to higher education, and to the futures that education opens up.

Government Policy on Privatisation

The expansion of higher education has been criticised for the escalating academic and social costs. But the government is unwilling to renege on its initial promise, as it recognises that people's aspirations for higher education are so intense that it would be suicidal to curb access. It is also ambitious to achieve enrolments comparable to those in Europe and North America, legitimised by the fact that bodies such as the World Bank consistently emphasise the high rates of return from higher education. Finally, there is also the consideration. Also noteworthy is the fact that by expanding opportunities to improve qualifications it is able to contain the frustrations in society because of underemployment and unemployment.

However, public demand and political pressures to accomplish universalisation of primary school education at least by the end of the century, have forced the government to acknowledge that it cannot afford to subsidise higher education as it has for the last 50 years. At the same time, a section of the population clearly has the capacity to pay for the expensive higher education facilities provided by some private institutions and by foreign universities. The government is, therefore, considering privatisation. However, equality might be placed in jeopardy if the facilities available to those who are able to pay are superior to the facilities available to those who cannot pay. Also, higher education could be commercialised to the point that it is almost entirely market driven. The government is, therefore, thinking of extending a system already in operation in some states during the last decade.

Many private bodies owns run a large number of institutions of higher education in the country are owned and managed by private bodies. Most are "aided" with government funds that fully cover the costs of their maintenance and operation. Regardless of this fact, all private institutions charge the same fees. Moreover, in academic as well as administrative matters, all of them are very closely controlled by government and university rules and regulations.

In some states, selected and preferably new private unaided institutions are allowed to charge substantially higher fees, approved by the government. The selected institutions are given a few concessions in administrative matters. But, by and large, they are closely governed in the same manner as are other institutions. It is unfortunate that India is considering this brand of privatisation—one that does not allow for the space, flexibility, and freedom required for the advancement of knowledge, quality, and relevance.

Towards a Genuinely International HE Community

In a genuinely international higher education community, all the students, teachers, researchers and members of staff have the opportunity to achieve the competence for international cooperation and to participate in international activities. The international competence of students is consolidated by well-executed mobility periods abroad and high-quality course selection including international elements in India. The creation of international competence is systematically taken into account in planning the studies at all levels. Completion of studies within the target completion period requires that the development of international competence and the mobility of students are realised in a systematic manner. The ways and means of internationalising are different in different disciplines and areas.

Higher education institutions are responsible for the quality of mobility and recognition of acquired competence. The basic assumption of student mobility is at least a three-month exchange or trainee period. Imbalance in exchange and differences between fields are corrected by supplementing traditional forms of mobility with alternative forms such as e-mobility, study visits and group mobility. The forms of internationalisation have changed in many ways in recent years and short study and research periods abroad are important ways of increasing the international mobility of adult and postgraduate students. International trainee periods are particularly important both in polytechnics and universities in fields with little in the way of traditional student exchange. The business community and its networks as parts of the international training practices of higher education institutions could be utilised better than is currently the case.

The mobility of researchers, teachers and other personnel is increased. The mobility of personnel promotes the internationalisation of higher education teaching and research, the popularity of exchange studies and the creation of joint and double degrees and international elements of study programmes. Moreover, mobility increases the competence needed for working in an international higher education community by improving the appreciation of other cultures, religions and languages. The prerequisites for increasing the mobility of researchers, teachers and other personnel include flexible working arrangements, career development opportunities and commitment to attaining the goal by the higher education institution administration. The mobility of polytechnic teachers can be significantly increased by active participation in international teaching and R&D cooperation projects.

The number of non-Indian degree students, researchers and teachers will be increased. The international student corps and personnel are a key factor in Indian higher education institutions' internationalisation at home. It is the responsibility of higher education institutions in collaboration with other actors in the area and with student organisations to integrate non-Indian students, researchers and teachers into both the higher education community and Indian society. Internal services, administration and communications of higher education institutions are developed in such a way as to enable the creation of genuinely international study and work environments.

Teaching given in foreign languages in Indian supports the availability of a workforce, enables reciprocal student mobility and offers Indian students an opportunity to participate in foreign-language education in a multicultural environment in their home country. The quality of education given in foreign languages is further improved by developing genuinely international education. The prerequisites for organising internationally high-quality study modules are created with the aid of cooperation between higher education institutions and different fields of education as well as through non-Indian personnel and a multicultural student community. Participation in international course selection and in its organisation requires multilingualism and cultural competence from both the students and the entire personnel. Cooperation with the world of work is increased in international study programmes, which improves the student opportunities to find a place in Indian working life. Improving career prospects increases the attractiveness and completion of international study programmes.

Increasing Quality

High-level research and competence, high-quality basic and further education and competitive education and research environments create a basis for international interaction and for attracting experts. Increasing competition for producers of high-quality knowledge and top-level competence presents new challenges for research and education environments as well as for the development of innovation activities and a human resources policy. From the perspective of the attractiveness of the higher education institutions, it is essential that the services supporting entry and integration in India be developed.

High-level education is based on high-quality research, which is brought about by international research cooperation. Research projects are increasingly realised in international cooperation and they require new joint, effective infrastructures and the utilisation of information technology. Strong infrastructures are also a key competitive factor in international research cooperation and researcher education. The aim is to create world-class research infrastructures and research environments in India in addition to a high-quality higher education system. The attainment of the aim requires making cooperation more effective both at national and international levels as well as significant investment in establishing and continuous maintenance of infrastructures.

The role of the research and development activities of polytechnics in the internationalisation of the regional business community and the higher education institution system is consolidated and R&D projects are constructed in international cooperation. The role of research and development activities can be particularly consolidated with regard to utilising research outputs and competence transfer between higher education institutions and the world of work. Cooperation between higher education institutions is needed in order to create sufficiently large high-quality projects.

Services supporting research and development and innovation activities contribute to the quality and attractiveness of research environments. Cooperation in the development and utilisation of the services (such as services pertaining to information, funding, and innovation and corporate cooperation) and competence improve the opportunities for Indian higher education institutions and enterprises to network and operate within an environment of international cooperation.

Support activities for integrating into the Indian work and living environment have a significant role in increasing attractiveness. This requires the development of permits and practices relating to entry and living in the country as well as services supporting settling down, which take into account the individual needs of the newly arrived. Finding accommodation, organising day care and schools for children, supporting the employment of the spouse as well as accessibility to heath-care services must be flexible and organisable according to the needs of newcomers. Assistance received in taking care of practical matters helps in structuring the everyday life and enables faster immersion in studies or teaching and research.

Taking internationality into account consistently in the human resources policy of higher education institutions consolidates internationalisation. Recruitment procedures of personnel and students must support entry of non-Indian individuals into Indian higher education institutions. Effective utilisation of grass-root-level networks at the level of the whole higher education institution promotes the attracting of experts to India.

Export Promotion

Indian higher education institutions, researchers and teachers cooperate actively with the leading higher education institutions and research institutes in the world's leading higher education and science countries. Moreover, higher education institutions have established mutually beneficial cooperation relationships with emerging and developing countries.

Indian higher education institutions possess high-quality competence, the marketing of which will improve cooperation opportunities with the best international higher education institutions. The higher education institutions also have improved opportunities and legal prerequisites to utilise their competence commercially and internationally. In many of the emerging economies of Asia, the Middle East and Latin America, domestic supply is not sufficient to meet the increasing demand of higher education.

The aim is that the export of competence and education by higher education institutions becomes a nationally significant export product and part of Indian export promotion. The export of competence can serve to support the overall internationalisation of the higher education community, international networking and the visibility of India and Indian higher education institutions abroad. The export of competence and the development of new forms of educational cooperation mean that the perspectives of the student and of the consumer in the activities of the higher education institutions are better acknowledged.

The higher education institutions themselves have a key role to play in marketing their competence. Added income derived from fee-based activities is an incentive for making marketing more effective. The development of educational services must be based on a realistic analysis by the higher education institutions concerning what kinds of educational services will be in demand in the near future, what are the main market areas, and what kinds of products and forms of cooperation are most natural for Indian higher education institutions. Research and surveys into cross-border higher education and export of education must be increased. Indian higher education institutions are small actors internationally. Joint marketing and cooperation in developing competence can be used for attaining added value. Moreover, the development of higher education exports requires cooperation between export organisations and enterprises as well as strengthening of marketing and export competence in higher education institutions.

Sufficient basic knowledge of the Indian higher education system and the opportunities afforded by it are prerequisites of marketing competence and exports. Accessibility to this information internationally is increased. It is the duty of the authorities to see to that basic information about Indian education and research system is available and up to date. Competence, country knowledge and networking of Indians with higher education degrees living abroad can significantly support internationalisation and increase brand recognition of India. Public and private organisations already operating abroad offer cooperation opportunities in increasing the visibility of higher education institutions and in networking. Many higher education institutions are networked abroad through business life. In particular, enterprises with Indian backgrounds in emerging science countries and economies can be utilised better than has been the case thus far in creating contacts as well as for student and personnel placement-in-enterprise periods.

Competition for the best experts and high-quality cooperation partners emphasises the need to develop flexible agreement and cooperation procedures. The most important thing is to agree directly between the actors on the goals, content, procedures and funding of the cooperation. However, in many countries—in addition to expression of intent between organisations—a cooperation protocol or other form of expression of support from ministry level is needed for cooperation between higher education institutions. The Ministry of Education provides flexible and appropriate cooperation documents for ensuring that Indian higher education institutions have good preconditions for succeeding in increasingly stiff international competition.

Increasing fee-based cross-border educational activities requires responsibility and measures to ensure the quality of education by the providers of education. In 2005, the OECD and UNESCO adopted common guidelines for quality provision in cross-border higher education. The guidelines cover all forms of mobility. They include recommendations concerning both the home countries of service providers as well as the countries receiving the services. New forms of cross-border higher education will be a significant part of the international activities of Indian higher education institutions. It is possible also that non-Indian actors will start marketing their educational services on a wider scale in India. On the basis of recommendations by the OECD and UNESCO, it is possible to develop a tool promoting the quality of internationalisation and educational services for Indian actors in the field.

Supporting a Multicultural Society

The higher education institutions support the development of India into a multicultural society, which provides opportunities for intercultural interaction in which the relationship between various population groups is balanced and different social groups can co-exist in equal conditions. The increase in the number of foreign citizens and nationalised Indians with immigrant backgrounds is reflected in higher linguistic and cultural diversity. Immigration based on family relations and work has increased while the number of refugees and other immigrants entering the country on humanitarian grounds has decreased proportionally. The Indian immigration policy has emphasised integration into society while retaining the special features of the immigrants' own culture. Realisation of equality and development of attitudes are preconditions of multiculturalism.

Higher education institutions actively provide students and personnel with the competencies to function in a multicultural higher education community, society and in global education, research and labour markets as well as promote positive attitudes towards multiculturalism. Multiculturalism and plurality are two-way processes that require understanding and an appreciation of people's diversity. In higher education communities this means that people working within them promote equality and equal opportunities to participate. People with immigrant backgrounds and foreign exchange and degree students, teachers, researchers and other foreign personnel of higher education institutions in India are an important resource in promoting internationalisation at home.

People with immigrant backgrounds should have equal opportunities for education as the rest of the population. The share of people with immigrant backgrounds in higher education institutions is low when compared with the overall number of people with immigrant backgrounds in India. Partly, this is due to the low attendance level of people with immigrant backgrounds in upper secondary education. It its crucial that immigrants' entry into higher education is supported as early as in comprehensive school and upper secondary education by developing communications and other focused measures in collaboration between various actors. By improving the availability of open higher education and preparatory training for higher education, the threshold for participating in higher education can be lowered for immigrants and people speaking foreign languages as well as provide them with the content and language skills needed in studies.

The higher education institutions promote the smooth progress of studies and access to employment of non-Indian and immigrant experts by taking into account the effects of various linguistic and cultural backgrounds when organising the education and required support services, and by developing well-functioning practices for the recognition and further development of competence acquired elsewhere. The placement in working life and the integration into society of immigrants and people with non-Indian backgrounds require sufficient skills in national languages and knowledge of Indian society and culture.

Together with working life actors, the higher education institutions develop training practices supporting integration into the world of work, which also promote the transition of people with non-Indian and immigrant backgrounds into the service of Indian business and industry and the public sector. The training model developed in cooperation with the business and industry community supports students' equal training opportunities.

Higher education institutions participate in solving global problems, cooperate with developing countries to consolidate competence in them and build their activities on an ethically sustainable foundation. With globalisation, the world is developing into an increasingly comprehensive system. Operating in a globalising world forces higher education institutions to take a critical look at the ethicality of their operating principles. The activities of the higher education institutions are based on responsibility, sustainable development and understanding and appreciating diversity within the higher education community.

The teaching and research duties of higher education institutions provide opportunities for actively seeking creative solutions to global problems. The higher education institutions support social debate on global issues and expand the general knowledge base. Higher education institutions' national and international cooperation consolidates competence and increases the impact of the activities of higher education institutions as promoters of social, cultural and ecological development.

Students in higher education institutions require competencies to understand global problems and to see their own influencing opportunities to promote worldwide equality and sustainable development. In addition to a perception of global entities, understanding the micro-level effects of one's own field is crucial in this. The higher education institutions and student organisations play a key role in supporting the development of these competencies. Teaching content must be assessed with regard to this goal.

References

Altbach Philip, "Higher Education Cross Borders", *Change*, March-April, 2004.

Anandakrishnan M., "Internationalization of Higher Education: Policy Concerns", paper presented at a conference at NIEPA on 26 and 27 August, 2004.

Garrett Richard, "Foreign Higher Education Activity in China", *International Higher Education*, Winter 2004.

Knight Jane, *Trade in Higher Education Services: The Implications of GATS*. The Observatory on Borderless Higher Education. London: United Kingdom, 2004.

Kumar Ravindra, Privatisation of Higher Education and Regulatory Mechanisms in University in *University News*, Vol.42, no. 7, February 16-22, 2004, AIU, New Delhi.

Lee Molly, N.N., "Expanding the State Role in Malaysian Higher Education", *International Higher Education*, Summer, 2000.

Powar, K.B. *WTO, GATS and Higher Education: An Indian Perspective*. Paper prepared for meeting convened by the Association of Commonwealth Universities. Perth Australia, 2002.

8. FINANCING OF HIGHER EDUCATION

Universities today are key drivers of internationalisation and global communication with regard to intellectual property and knowledge production. Parallel to the processes of globalisation and the advent of the knowledge economy, internationalisation has become a major trend in higher education and a major force in the globalised marketplace. In an age of a global knowledge economy, the internationalisation of HE cannot be immune from the two powerful forces of globalisation and the knowledge economy.

Globalisation has facilitated and quickened the pace of the internationalisation of HE. It has opened economies and borders so that competent individuals have far greater opportunities to live, work and pursue education in other countries. However, the global representatives of neoliberalism, the World Trade Organisation (WTO), the World Bank (WB) and the Organisation for Economic Cooperation and Development (OECD), have narrowed the conception and benefits of the internationalisation of HE by prescribing neoliberal policies in the cross-border trade of educational services globally. Insofar as these policies are exclusively economy-oriented, profit has become the major target and motivation leading to the increasing trade in university education. This neoliberal trend in the internationalisation of HE should not be regarded as a form of internationalisation but a part of the university's neoliberal globalisation agenda.

Likewise, the knowledge economy is an important force that deeply affects the internationalisation of HE. Today the knowledge economy is manifest in the phenomenal increase in the amount of knowledge; the speeding up in the fast flow of knowledge on a global level; the considerable growth in knowledge-mediated industries and services; the alterations in the access to and 'control' over knowledge; and the new ways of thinking about the relations between knowledge and innovation. For instance, advances in information and communication technologies are closely linked with knowledge production and exchanges that cut across traditional disciplinary and cultural boundaries. These advances have led to an important move towards international integration of products and markets. Therefore, obtaining sophisticated knowledge and skills has become the most significant competitive advantage in the international market and correspondingly to educate 'knowledge workers' will be one of the key enterprises of the 21st century.

Nowadays, knowledge has become an industry and HE, as a knowledge carrier and agent, has developed into a central component of that industry. HE is seen as a passport to a successful career in the increasingly competitive global marketplace. Therefore, an increasing number of people are seeking HE particularly outside their home countries in order to procure a profitable future job. This challenges the capacity of many universities worldwide, but also brings about welcome additional income for the universities which are confronting tight fiscal situations.

Economic Reforms and Educational Financing

The growth of the globalisation has increased opportunities for those countries with good levels of education and vice versa. Though the higher education system and the pattern of financing higher education vary a great deal across countries in terms of their size and strength and degree of diversification of higher education institutions, yet they all face a severe financial crisis in the public finances available for higher education.

In this global scenario, India is no exception. As part of globalisation, the economic reform packages were introduced in 1991 in India causing a heavy compression on the public budgets on education sector, more specifically so on higher education. When structural adjustment policies were including macroeconomic stabilisation and adjustment, a fiscal squeeze was experienced in all social sector investments in many developing countries, including in India. This has affected public expenditure on education in general, and higher education in particular. With the changing economic front cuts in public budgets for higher education have been very steep, severely impairing the growth of higher education.

Paradoxically, under the reforming economic conditions, integration of the Indian economy with world economy presupposes efficiency and competitiveness in the domestic front as well as in the international arena. With globalisation being technology, and knowledge-driven, the very success of economic reform policies critically depends upon the competence of human workforce. But, what is observed is the reverse. Even within the education sector, relative priority assigned to higher education has been on the decline.

Apart from severe cuts on the education budget on the one hand, accomplishing the long cherished goal of universal elementary education on the other hand, the government has shifted of its focus from higher to primary education. It can be noticed from the approach paper to the Tenth Five-year Plan and Tenth plan document that "Since budget resources are limited, and such resources as are available, need to be allocated to expanding primary education, it is important to recognise that the universities must make greater efforts to supplement resources from the government".

Given the spillover benefits of higher education, it becomes mandatory for the centre to finance an increasing share of expenditure on higher education. But, this has been declining in the recent years. Even in secondary education, the centre's share of expenditure is minimal, ranging around 5 per cent. However the governments' role in elementary education is on the rise since the middle of 1980s. Universalising elementary education began in the country in 1987 with a centrally sponsored scheme, namely, Operation Blackboard, to improve the educational infrastructure in primary schools all over the country. Around the same time another two important nationwide schemes initiated – on teacher education and non-formal education. As a result of all these efforts and initiatives by the government, the flow of plan transfers from central to states in elementary education have improved since the late 1980s.

While primary education is fundamental to the nation, higher education determines its economic and technological progress in the globalised era, which are essential for growth and development. Even with low enrolment ratios in higher education in India, it is increasingly realised that public budgets cannot adequately fund higher education, particularly when sectors of mass education are starved of even basic needs. Hence, the focus and resources from higher education are being diverted to the development of primary education. But it is stressed that while it is mandatory that the nation achieves universal elementary education and total literacy, it cannot at the same time afford to be relegated to a neglected position to achieve global standards in higher education.

Higher Education: Income Sources

Higher education in India is funded mainly by three different sources, viz., government, fee income from students and other sources of income from philanthropy, industry, sale of publications, etc. Allocation of Government resources for education almost doubled from 1951's resources in 1986-87. On the other hand, fee income drastically declined during the same period. Other sources contribute around 10 per cent throughout the period.

Higher education has been largely a state-funded activity with about three-quarters of the total expenditure being borne by government. The relative shares of non-government sources such as fees and voluntary contributions have been declining. On the other side, the needs of the higher education system have been growing rapidly. It is being increasingly realised that public budgets cannot adequately fund higher education, particularly when sectors of mass education are starved of even basic needs. In recent years, there has been compression in the higher education budget. Indeed, the decline in plan allocations had started even prior to economic reforms. Hence, in the recent decade, the need for experimentation with several alternatives such as student fees, student loans, graduate tax and privatisation is intensified.

While, the demand for higher education has been growing rapidly with comparatively faster growth in enrolment in higher educational institutions there has been a dearth in the growth in number of higher educational institutions. The growth rates are doubled among the students enrolled in postgraduate and research, while the number of institutions for postgraduate and research studies has grown at a slower rate in 1990s than in 1980s.

In absolute terms, only 7 per cent of the population in the age group 17 to 24 attended higher educational institutions in India, as against 92 per cent of the eligible age-group population attending higher educational institutions in USA, 52 per cent in UK and 45 per cent in Japan. Even with very low enrolment ratios in India, it is being increasingly realised that public budgets cannot adequately fund higher education, particularly when sectors of mass education are bereft of even basic essentials. As a consequence, several policy directions on new ways of diversifying resources, resulting from a variety of pressures and opportunities are continually emerging with several alternatives, including student fees, student loans and privatisation. The most serious casualy of all these is undermining equity of access to higher education. Equity and social justice demand that newly emerging beneficiaries from the secondary education sector, who increasingly represent vulnerable groups, are able to afford access to higher education and eventually for an upward mobility. However, little is done to examine the impact of increase in fees on access to higher education.

A number of committees have been constituted to examine the issue of mobilisation of resources. They recommend an increase in all kinds of fee and that at least 15 to 25 per cent of the annual recurring cost per student is recovered from the students in the form of fees and from other sources at the end of ten years.

Educational Funds Allocation in Five-year Plans

The government and UGC are finding it increasingly difficult to even sustain the current level of funding to the institutions of higher education. In the eighth plan itself financially self-supporting higher education was advocated that "expansion of higher education in an equitable and cost-effective manner, in the process, making the higher education system financially self-supporting". The approach paper to the Ninth Five-year Plan says, "emphasis will be placed on consolidation and optimal utilisation of the existing infrastructure through institutional networking ...and through open university system. Grants-in-aid will be linked to performance criteria to improve quality and inject accountability. Fees will be restructured on unit cost criteria and paying capacity of the beneficiaries. Additional resources will be generated by involving industry and commerce and through contribution from community."

The distinct hike in fees and shift of resources from higher to primary education can be noticed from the approach paper to the Tenth Five-year Plan, "Since budget resources are limited, and such resources as are available, need to be allocated to expanding primary education, it is important to recognise that the universities must make greater efforts to supplement resources from the government. University fees are unrealistically low and in many universities have not been raised in decades. A substantial hike in university fees is essential." The Tenth Five-year Plan document notes that universities must make greater efforts to supplement resources apart from the governments contribution.

The plan expenditures on higher and technical education has been on the decline since the Fifth Five-year Plan onwards in the case of general higher education and the Fourth Plan onwards in technical education. Elementary education has got the highest priority in First Plan, which again seemed to gain momentum in the ninth plan. In the First Plan higher education got 9 per cent allocation, which is the case again in the ninth Plan. The financing strategy even under economic reforms seems to be developing one level of education at the cost of another exacerbating imbalances among different levels of education. It should be noted that higher education institutions play an important role in setting the academic standard for primary and secondary education. They are responsible for research and development, training inside the country, provide policy advice, etc. Higher education is no longer a luxury; it is essential to national, social and economic development.

Revenue-raising Measures

The adverse impact of economic reforms reflects upon various revenue diverisification measures such as hike in student fees, student loan programmes operated by commercial banks and privatisation. Various revenue-raising measures take place in the form of:

i) Raising tuition fee as a significant source of revenue for the support of instructional cost.
ii) Full cost recovery of other fees such as institutionally provided room and board.
iii) Sale of research publications, consultancy, etc.
iv) Participation of private sector both non-profit and proprietary providers.
v) Philanthropy for endowments, for direct operations and for scholarship to students.

The World Bank suggests that if public institutions are to achieve higher quality and greater efficiency, governments have to implement sweeping reforms in higher education financing in mobilising private financing for public higher education and fostering efficiency in allocating and uitlising resources among and within public institutions.

There are three important economic justifications for government to fund higher education:

i) Higher education investments generate external benefits important for economic development, such as the long-term return from basic research and from technical development and transfer necessary for competition and globalisation. Hence, public investment on higher education should enhance.
ii) Private investment alone in higher education would be socially sub-optimal.
iii) Increased role of market undermines the participation of meritorious students who hail from economically disadvantageous groups.

Cost Recovery Measures

In recent times there have been dramatic and sweeping changes over the nature and philosophy of education in general and financing higher education in particular. Changes within the economic systems and global interaction have forced the higher education system to opt for a number of cost recovery measures.

Student Fees

The Government of India setup a number of committees to examine the issue of mobilisation of resources for central universities and for technical education. UGC too setup committees to specifically look into the recommendations of Punnayya Committee on unit cost of higher education; to review the norms of maintenance grants for Delhi Colleges; and to formulate the revision of fee structure. All these committees unanimously proclaim that one of the major sources of income is the fees from students, as fees have not been revised upward for decades in most of the universities. Hence, there is an urgent need for upward revision of fees chargeable by universities and colleges from a reasonable to a substantial limit.

Tuition Fees

Tuition fees must be hiked with immediate effect and may be periodically adjusted keeping in view the inflation and rise in costs of higher education, and in a meaningful manner. Full cost recovery is suggested in government and aided institutions targeting that the established government funded/ aided colleges may be allowed to start fresh specialised programmes for specific target groups on self-financing / net revenue earning basis. Tuition and all other fees, which are not to be charged on one-time basis, should be tenable for 12 months. Modified unit cost method, i.e., 3 per cent of the unit cost worked out by Punnayya Committee, should be the basis of fee structure. Annual upward revisions may be made at 2 per cent of the suggested rate and after five years the commission may review the entire issue again for upward revision in the fee structure. It is recommended that certain mandatory provisions be made to ensure that the revised fee structure being suggested by the committee is implemented.

Other Fees

Regarding fees for admission and examination fee, it is worthwhile to recover the recurring cost of operations. As far as library, laboratory, sports and similar other facilities are concerned, it is suggested that these fees must be revised to recover a significant part of the recurring cost. It is recommended to revise the development fee to meet the actual recurring cost on no-loss-no-profit basis.

Hostel and mess fees

It is advised to meet the actual recurring cost and to cover part of the capital cost over time.

Municipal, civil and other services

This involves revision appropriately of recovering costs of transport, phone, postage and stationery, typing, computing, photocopying, etc.

Fees as a Source of Income

The recommendations by various committees suggest that institutions should raise the fee levels to recover least 15 to 25 per cent of the annual recurring cost per student from the students in the form of fees and from other sources at the end of ten years. Government should gradually shift the funding of universities to a system of students funding. The tuition fee for the government-funded and government-aided institutions should be revised to at least 20 per cent of the recurring expenditure per student per year. Fees so fixed may be reviewed and refixed once every three years.

There is a general feeling that fees are extremely low and not revised for decades. In reality most universities have not revised some components of fees, like tuition fees, but tuition fee is only one of the components of total fees chargeable. Many services, especially student welfare services, hostels, water, electricity, food charges and the development fees are revised to a substantial extent.

The fiscal crisis due to reduced allocations and increasing expenditures of the higher education system have forced higher educational institutions to look for alternate sources of revenue and find ways and means of reducing costs. Following the recommendations of several committees, the plan directions and reduced resource allocations, many universities and other institutions of higher education are required to reform their fee structures and introduce few financial reforms. Hence, the first focused source of income is the fee income, which has serious ramifications on equity and access to higher education.

In the decade 1990, there have been modest to steep increases in students' fees of various types such as tuition fees, examination fees, admission fees, registration fees, entrance examination, hostel and miscellaneous services, like application forms, brochures, and so on. Government grants to the universities have declined or remained stagnant in real prices, and sometimes even in current prices. Cost recovery measures, particularly hike in fees, are increasingly resorted to in several universities. Most of the universities have already increased their fee, which covered more than 20 per cent of their recurring income.

Other Income Sources

Other sources of income are from endowments, university press, rent from university land, buildings, space, infrastructure, etc; income from consultancy services and research projects; etc. Income from sale of university publications, self-financing courses, and interest income are some other source of internal income of the universities. The search for additional resources and the introduction of income-generating activities has been on the rise in many institutions.

The recent policy directions in India exacerbate full cost recovery from students even in public higher education institutions through hike in fees and introduction of self-financing courses and seats in tune with liberalisation policies. Under the umbrella of globalisation and competition, important economic rationale for government funding for higher education is neglected.

With economic reforms and other pressures of the government, it has ignored expenditure on education as a social investment and the complementary nature of public and household expenditure on education. It is to be realised that the funding of higher education requires both public and private resources under economic austerity. However, the role of the state and public support to higher education remains essential to ensure its educational, social and institutional missions. It is often resorted to diverting resources from higher to primary level of education.

While it is essential that the nation achieve universal elementary education, it cannot afford to neglect higher education in the period of globalisation. Further, it needs to be realised that all levels of education are interdependent; the growth of one level of education should not be at the cost of another. Private investment alone in higher education would be socially sub-optimal. It is because the private and households do not come forth to invest on non-market oriented courses in higher education and research and development. Further, increased role of market jeopardises the participation of meritorious students from economically disadvantageous groups, women and minorities.

Hefty hikes in fees might compel a good number of students from low and middle income families and women not to go in for higher education, while some rich students opt for studies abroad. Further, it is important to notice that self-financing courses are short term in nature and heavy reliance on them will have repercussions on the equity and quality of the higher education system in the long run. This will also lead to lack of teachers and researchers in pure and basic disciplines in the near future as it is being experienced in United Kingdom.

Student Grants and Loans

Financial assistance and loans are being advanced to maintain accessibility in the face of increasing costs borne by students and families in the form of tuition and fees. No country seems to be either willing or politically able to shift cost onto students and families without some measures to preserve accessibility and equity, hence financial assistance in the form of grants and/ or loans becomes part of the revenue supplementation reform agenda. So the shift of cost burden is to be from taxpayers to parents.

An alternative to recovering expenses from parents is to recover them from the student with some form of loans or graduate taxes, to be repaid as the student becomes employable and productive. The effective recovery on student loans depends on the rate of interest, the repayment period, the rate of recovery, and the cost of servicing accounts. Loan systems that are "generally available" without requirement of co-signatories, and that carry low rates of interest and long repayment periods, are able to recover only very small portions of the original amounts lent. Such systems are largely ineffective in shifting significant higher educational cost burden from governments, or taxpayers, to students.

Student loans are currently in operation in more than 80 countries around the globe. Of late, educational loan is very popular among students because of its simple and appealing logic, despite its inherent weaknesses. It is argued that in order to safeguard poor students from the rising costs of higher education (both tuition fee and maintenance cost), a number of countries in the developing and developed world have established student loan programmes. However, cost recovery cannot be implemented equitably without scholarship programmes that should guarantee necessary financial support to academically qualified poor students. Further, imperfection in capital markets related to the lack of collateral security for education investments restricts the ability of poor students to borrow for education.

There has been a paradigm shift in the attitude towards financing higher education *per se* and student loans in particular. The features of second generation of loan programmes around the world are such that loan is not guaranteed by government; sanction of loan requires 100 per cent collateral security and a guarantor that of co-signatory of parent or family member; the loan schemes are operated by commercial banks / private sector / private banks; the loan amounts are charged at market rate of interest; and marketability of a course scores for high probability of a loan getting sanctioned.

A major shift can be observed from the choice of administering agency from government/agency or institutions/ universities to commercial banks and private banks or private sector. There is gradual shift from a regime of interest-free loans to subsidised interest on student loans. With the changes in economic reform policies around the world, there is sudden upsurge of market rate of interest or even above the market rate of interest being charged for student loans.

Second generation of loan programmes aim at full cost recovery and are not responsive to any equity considerations. It should be reminded that such loan schemes involve a number of risks. Heavy reliance on such student loans will discourage students from low-income families, women and other weaker sections and minorities from participating in higher education. More specifically for women, student loan is regarded as a negative dowry. Further, with globalisation and internationalisation of higher education under WTO and GATS, there is a risk of highest student mobility from developing countries to other developed countries.

Following the wave of changes around the world, the present Educational Loan Scheme was introduced in India following the announcement in the budget 2000-01. The scheme is administered by the commercial banks. The scheme covers a wide range of courses in higher studies from post-matric to research studies, both in India and abroad. Eligibility criterion is that any student who secures admission in domestic/foreign educational institution is eligible for loan. The loan covers both instructional cost and living expenses. A maximum of Rs.7.5 lakhs for studies in India and Rs.15 lakhs for studies in overseas institutions/universities is envisaged under the scheme. For loans up to Rs.4 lakhs, no margins are required and collateral security is not insisted upon.

Loan amounts exceeding Rs.4 lakhs require 100 per cent collateral security or guarantee of a third person known to the bank for the entire loan amount. Margins vary from 5 per cent to 15 per cent for loans above Rs.4 lakhs. Interest rate is charged according to the Prime Lending Rate (PLR) for loans up to Rs.4 lakhs and with one per cent addition to PLR for loans exceeding Rs.4 lakhs. The loan can be repaid in five to seven years and repayment would commence one year after completion of the course or six months after getting employment, whichever is earlier. Simple rate of interest is charged during the period of study and up to the commencement of repayment.

However, it is to be noted that there is no income ceiling on students/parents for the eligibility of this loan scheme. Neither the academic achievement is considered as an eligibility criterion, that is, there is no minimum qualifying marks required. There are no special provisions of any kind for the weaker sections in terms of security, government guarantee, lower rate of interest or repayment period, repayment in accordance with earnings, waivers, etc. It is to be noted that the scheme neither adheres to the efficiency nor the equity principles unlike in many other countries, where merit-cum-means determine the eligibility for student loan.

Given the world experience on student schemes, the new scheme in India is insensitive to the needs of the poor and does not concern equity aspects as there are no special provisions of any kind for the weaker sections. The present loan scheme neither takes into consideration the various details, such as eligibility, interest rates, repayment terms and conditions as recommended by various committees. Hence, an alternative scheme specifically for the weaker sections needs to be evolved as the present scheme is not flexible to the needs of the weaker sections.

The world experience on student loans suggests that recovery rate from student loans is very low. In addition, administrative cost of the student loan programme is quite high. Hence, total cost incurred on default and administration would be much higher and eventually the scheme may not be financially viable. Hence, the idea of self-sustaining student loan schemes in the long run seem to be elusive.

In a graduate tax, students continue to get their usual subsidies in the form of low or no tuition and perhaps living grants. However, they incur obligations for greater income tax payments than would have been the case in the absence of their higher educational experiences. The effect is a shift in ultimate cost burden, but without an immediate reduction of the government's need for taxpayer or borrowed revenue. So far, no country has successfully adopted a pure graduate tax, although the Australian Higher Education Contribution Scheme is close. With a stable income tax system, a politically acceptable graduate tax might support the government's ability to deficit finance in the worldwide capital markets, with the future graduate tax obligations serving as a kind of collateral.

Some forms of delayed cost recovery schemes will continue to be important for countries to establish, partly in support of the larger goal of securing more cost-sharing from students and their families by whatever combination of policies and programmes.

Commercial Private Higher Education

Privatisation of higher education has emerged in several forms and types in the recent decade in India. Privatisation within government higher education institutions take place in the form of introducing self-financing courses within government institutions. Converting government-aided private institutions into private self-financing institutions are on the rise. Self-financing private institutions are permitted to expand with recognition and also without recognition, which may be termed as commercial private higher education institutions.

Commercial private higher education emerges from market forces and are tied to economic and global forces. They thrive on the principles of commercialism, and primarily focus on vocational courses and are highly pragmatic. Their commercial thrust is training jobs, indeed, part of the curriculum is industrial training. Not only training for jobs but they also place their students in well-paid jobs. This indeed speaks about the strong industry-institution linkages. They are narrowly focused, rather micro-specific in designing their course and training which is their strength as well weakness. It is a strength as long as there is demand for such specific nature of the courses and a weakness once such a demand is satiated. Moreover, the built-in set-up/infrastructure do not allow them to diversify. They cater to the unmet demands of the non-university higher education sector.

Ownership of these private institutions ranges between a spectrum of substantially weaker and stronger commercial institutions. Indeed, there are chain of institutions from kindergarten to higher levels of education by well-known business groups and corporate sector. Since 1993 with the Supreme Court judgment, growth of commercial higher education in the name of capitation fee or self-financing colleges is mushrooming. The private institutions include colleges, training centres, etc. Neither the Department of Education nor the University Grants Commission collect, compile and publish the information on the size and growth of institutions and enrolments on this rapidly growing private higher education.

There are also different types of these private institutions. Many of the self-financing engineering colleges and management institutions are affiliated to the conventional universities in which, the course structure, design, curriculum, and the pattern of examination fall within the purview of the national or state pattern. On the other side, several of these self-financing private institutions are also non-affiliating to any universities and cater to the demands of the corporate sector nationally and internationally. Whether the private institutions follow multi-faculty or discipline are decided by the individual institutions. The programmes and courses are market-driven and each private institution decides on its own the course and subjects it offers. Hence, they also have a free hand to introduce new programmes and discard the old.

Plight of Faculty in Private Institutions

Enrolment of more students is the power while the faculty is weak in these private institutions. Indeed, the faculty lack the position, power and autonomy as they traditionally enjoy at universities. Basically they serve to students and their practical orientations in commercial private institutions. These institutions rely on part-time faculty and may be drawn from full-time faculty at public universities. When employing full-time faculty, they pay meagre salaries. Perhaps many of them have neither practical nor academic expertise and they lack training.

Finances of Private Institutions

The finances of these private enterprises seem to be free to raise and deploy resources to meet their own norms. Private universities elsewhere, for instance in USA mobilise the resources of about 30 to 40 per cent of the recurring cost of education from students. The remaining 60 to 70 of the recurring cost are generated from endowments, alumni and other sources. On the contrary, fees in these private enterprises in India are exhorbitant as they fully depend upon student payments. Indeed, these institutions make huge profits, sometimes recovering more than their recurring cost. Such institutions survive as long as there is a demand for their services and the students are willing to pay for such job-directed training.

Government's Proposals

The Government of India in its Prime Minister's Council on Trade and Industry, appointed a committee to suggest required reforms in the education sector, along with other sectors. It strongly suggested that full cost be recovered from students even in public higher education institutions through hike in fees and introduction of self-financing courses and seats; shift resources from higher to primary level of education; that government should leave higher education altogether to the private sector and confine itself to elementary and secondary education. Further, the report urged the private university bill to be passed and also suggested that the user-pays principle be strictly enforced in higher education, supplemented by loans and grants to economically and socially backward sections of society. In addition, number of foreign universities and franchise of multinational educational centres compete in developing their own centres in India at a full cost recovery basis.

Higher Education Comparison between India and US

The focus of private institutions is on, it is important to note that in the US, drive for efficiency and profits are categorically powerful among the private higher education providers. In developing countries like India, the profit, at the cost of efficiency. Further, the important dimensions of complementarity and competition found in the US, private higher education sector boosts the growth and survival of both the public and private higher institutions, which is conspicuously absent in India. There are a number of important factors that led to emergence and rapid expansion of private higher education in India.

Factors Affecting Privatisation

Globally there has been rapid expansion and demand for higher education known as massification of higher education. The conventional university sector is unable to meet the demands of the rapidly growing eligible age group population for higher education. As an alternative, private enterprises are encouraged to accommodate this evolving pressure on higher education in various forms, types and levels.

In conventional university it takes considerable amount of time for a change within the formal higher education/ university system. This academic inflexibility boosted the rapid development of private initiatives in higher education. The conventional institutions lack the responsiveness of higher education to labour market demands implying business participation in governing boards of institutions, the creation of financial incentives for joint industry-university research, corporate-sponsored internships for students, and part-time academic appointments for professionals from the productive sector. Alternatively, such a nexus between academics and industry is met by private institutions with multidisciplinary and/or interdisciplinary courses, which are short-term in nature with a very narrow focus. This has led to proliferation of short-term/market-oriented courses. However, leaving barring a few reputed private higher learning institutions, a majority of them are education shops catering to the majority of the students, who are willing to pay with a desperate hope to get into the job market. In short, these private institutions marketed their service in technology courses varying from hi-tech to fashion technology; management courses ranging from institutional management to hotel management; and promised to produce not only employable youth but also assure them of placement in jobs.

Financial resource constraints of the government on account of economic reforms led to financial privatisation of higher education in various forms, such as reduced allocation to higher education; introduction of cost-recovery measures within public institutions and directed policy measures toward privatisation of higher education. The Government of India introduced the Private Universities Establishment and Regulation Bill in 1995. Which is still pending in the Parliament because the private sector was not interested in several clauses in the bill – primarily on the clause on the provision of scholarship for the economically and socially backward sections of the population. Yet another important factor is the deteriorating quality of the higher education over the years which has indirectly made the students look for alternatives.

While internationalising higher education, foreign universities and institutions have been allowed to come into

India and establish franchise centres in the country, offering degrees or diplomas, which are not necessarily recognised by the parent universities in their own countries. Indian providers have also set up institutions in other countries.

Going by the return analysis, the World Bank's focus is on basic education, whereas its involvement in higher education is guided by calls for equitable and cost-effective financing. It highly favours cost-sharing and the promotion of private higher education to free up scarce public resources for improving basic education. It recommends forcefully that further enrolment expansion in higher education should take place in the private sector. Further, it indicates that the higher education systems in developing countries and the institutions can only thrive if they are flexible for change. More differentiated systems, including private and non-university institutions, can help meet the growing demand and make higher education more responsive to labour market needs. The examples are the successful higher education systems found in Australia and New Zealand other than US. It may also be noted that the European system, are undergoing a series of policy debates on financing higher education focusing on the extent and degree of cost recovery in higher education for enabling the transition from elite to mass-oriented higher education.

To conclude, even though private institutions offer course on any discipline, the viability and sustainability depend upon their demand. However, it should be noted that private institutions in developing countries like India are not efficient, competitive and complement as found in developed countries. The absence of a coherent long-term policy perspective on higher education is reflected on the government's ambiguity to regulate private institutions. The unfettered growth of private higher education combined with the international economic and political events created a surplus in the labour market in the recent years.

Entrepreneurial Activities

Since tertiary education is becoming increasingly diverse several vocational institutions are going into partnerships with potential employers, leading to technology transfer, dual forms of training, apprenticeship schemes, etc. Also, universities are unequivocally more entrepreneurial than they were only a few years ago. In Russia and China, institutional entrepreneurship extends to the factories, farms, and firms that were owned and operated by the institution for the state, or that have been started in joint ventures with foreign interests or new native capitalists. The new ventures seem more for the purpose of revenue supplementation.

Among Mexican universities, since regular operating subsidies from the government will not grow. Hence, they must be entrepreneurial, earning extra income and involving faculty and students in this effort. Some of the departments are beginning to generate income on their own through the sale of services, specialised courses, etc. In Argentina also the resources generated by the universities themselves increased between 1991 and 1996 from 7 per cent to 14 per cent of the total budget. This is very significant given the fact that during that period state funds increased 52 per cent. This reflects that universities in Argentina have made an effort to increase their budget by generating resources of their own.

Some African universities like the University of Zambia and Eduardo Mondlane University in Mozambique have generated significant benefits in enhanced capacity, information and income, by establishing internet nodes linked to local electronic networks which sell subscriptions to non-university business, organisations and individuals. Ghana and Nsukka have been fairly successful in their initiatives. Ghana indicated a profit of 9% on a total income of US$ 22700 in 1991. Its policies and method of operating the consulting centre are very popular and might prove to be a useful model for other universities. While survey reports have concluded that consulting activities are minimal and are mostly concentrated in a few fields, on closer observation a very contrary picture emerges, with a fairly large number of faculty involved in consultancy and not adhering to any specific rules or criteria. Hence, while consultancy can prove to be beneficial, it also needs to follow certain guidelines.

Although it has its' share of problems, there are also several benefits to entrepreneurial activities within the university framework. It helps introduce a market sensitive institutional culture; relevant training experience is introduced for students; cooperative links are established with business partners who might become involved in curriculum guidance, work placements, and part-time teaching arrangements, etc., all of which helps enhance quality of higher education and monetary inflow. However, there should be no compromise on: the proper utilisation of resources, teaching and research; and the personal, departmental, and institutional canons of academic responsibility and integrity.

Restructuring of Higher Education Institutions

Radical change, or restructuring, of an institution of higher education involves fewer and/or different faculty, professional staff and support workers. This means lay-offs, forced early retirements, or major retraining and reassignment, as in the closure of inefficient or ineffective institutions; the merger of quality institutions that merely lack a critical mass of operations to make them cost-effective; and the radical alteration of the mission and production function of an institution.

While public universities resist radical change, they are not immune to the loss of large amounts of public revenue. In fact, the very short-term robustness of the university may be its worst enemy in the competition for increasingly scarce public revenues. These short-term arrangements sometimes allow the government or the ministry to cut the funds to the public institutions without acknowledging the need to close down inefficient campuses, or lay off faculty no longer relevant to the needs of the students, the economy, or for that matter of the university.

References

AICTE, *Report of the High Power Committee for Mobilization of Additional Resources for Technical Education*, All India Council for Technical Education, New Delhi. 1994.

Ambani, M. and K. Birla, *Report on a Policy Framework for Reforms in Education*, Government of India, New Delhi, 2001.

Carnoy, M., *Globalisation and Educational Reform: What Planners Need to Know*, Report No.63, International Institute of Educational Planning, Paris, 1999.

Government of India, *Approach Paper to the Tenth Five-year Plan: 2002-2007*, Planning Commission, New Delhi, 2001.

NSSO, *Attending an Educational Institution in India: Its Level, Nature and Cost*, NSS 52nd Round, July 1995-June 1996, NSSO, Government of India, 1998.

Stewart, F., "Globalisation and Education", *International Journal of Educational Development*, Vol.16, No.2, pp. 327-33, 1996.

UGC, *Report of the Committee Constituted by UGC for 'Formulation of Revised Fee Structure in the central and Deemed Universities in India'*, University Grants Commission, New Delhi, 2000.

UNESCO, Higher education in the Twenty-first Century: Vision and Action, Final Report, World Conference on Higher Education, UNESCO, Paris,5-9, October, 1998

World Bank, *Constructing Knowledge Societies: New Challenges for Tertiary Education*, Washington, D.C., 2002.

9. REINVENTING HIGHER EDUCATION

Globalisation poses challenges to higher education systems of the world. These challenges should be solved through important strategies. In some literatures, these challenges have been classified into two categorisations: individual and institutional. The individual challenges of higher education in these literatures are a lack of competency, negative attitudes, absence of incentives, lack of personal knowledge and expertise. On contrast, institutional challenges consist of a lack of financial sources, scarcity of human resources, and educational structure. It is important to keep in mind that the national challenges of higher education originate from the states' view on education. On the other hand, national challenges are related to the economic, social and cultural problems at the national level.

Tertiary Education Reforms

The modern world of tertiary education is undergoing enormous reforms. This reform agenda can usefully be viewed in the context of five themes:

i) *Expansion and diversification*—of enrolment, participation rates, and the number and types of institutions;

ii) *Fiscal pressure*—as measured in low and declining per-student expenditures and as seen in overcrowding, low-paid (or unpaid) faculty, lack of academic equipment or libraries, and dilapidated physical plants;

iii) *Markets*—the ascendance of market orientations and solutions, and the search for non-governmental revenue;

iv) *The demand for greater accountability*—on the part of institutions and faculty, and on behalf of students, employers, and those who pay; and

v) *The demand for greater quality and efficiency*—more rigour, more relevance and more learning.

Expansion and Diversification

The reform agenda is based on an avowed orientation to expansion and diversification, forced by the demands of a growing, upwardly mobile population and by the needs of an increasingly competitive, technologically-sophisticated economy.

The major forces for this expansion and diversity include:

i) the expansion of basic and secondary education which creates a strong potential demand for the tertiary level;
ii) the rate of growth in the proportion of the above cohort that elects tertiary education—this rate, amongst other causes, is a function of the demand from the labour market, fair rates of return, tradition and urbanisation;
iii) the diversification of higher education and new possibilities for the expansion of tertiary education in order to meet the growing and complex demands of the modern world;
iv) the increasing incentives being provided by governments globally in order for students to have equal access to tertiary education; and
v) the expansion of the amount of tertiary education per participant.

Expansion includes the expansion of knowledge itself, the increasing level of skills and competencies required in a modern, globally-competitive economy, and the need for continuing professional upgrading, supported by the natural tendency of professions to seek enhanced status by requiring ever higher amounts of education for licensure. Contraction includes the relatively greater growth in some countries of non-university sectors featuring shorter training cycles, as well as reforms being instituted to discourage excessive time-to-degree.

Fiscal Pressure

The focus of higher education in the 1990s has been financial distress—the principal condition in the World Bank's declaration in 1994 that higher education was "...in crisis throughout the world." Four major factors underlie this state of affairs today. The first is enrolment pressure, especially in those countries combining growing populations of secondary school leavers with low current higher educational participation rates and inadequate higher educational capacity to meet the growing demand. A second cause is the tendency of unit costs in higher education to rise faster than unit costs in the overall economy, due to the very rapidly increasing costs of technology and by the rapid change in the fields of study in greatest need and/ or demand. The third cause is the increasing scarcity of public revenue. The fourth factor is the growing dissatisfaction in many countries with the rigidities and inefficiencies of the public sector generally, and a corresponding drift toward the market solutions, including privatisation, deregulation and decentralisation of functions still considered "public".

Orientation to the Market

Higher education can not be treated as a purely public good it exhibits conditions of rivalness, excludability and rejection— all of which do not meet the characteristics of a purely public good, but reflect at least some important conditions of a private good. The consumers of higher education are reasonably well informed and the providers are often ill informed—conditions which are ideal for market forces to operate. This has led to elements of the reform agenda such as tuition, which shifts some of the higher education cost burden from taxpayers to parents and students, who are the ultimate beneficiaries of higher education, more nearly full cost fees for institutionally-provided room and board, and more nearly market rates of interest on student loans, all of which rely upon market choices to signal worth and true trade-offs.

As universities and higher education systems pay more attention to good personnel practices, cash flow, market position, product diversification, and accountability, they will look more "private" than the stereotype of "public," even if they remain state owned, substantially tax-supported, and avowedly "public" in their mission.

With taxes increasingly avoidable and otherwise difficult to collect, and with competing public needs—basic education, public health, public safely, transfer payments, and public infrastructure—so compelling in all countries, an increasing reliance on tuition, fees, and the unleashed entrepreneurship of the faculty may be mainly the only alternatives to a totally debilitating austerity.

Accountability

Universities should be accountable in various ways to students, parents, employers, and to the general public. Accountability, though difficult to achieve because the benefits are both multiple and hard to measure, is nonetheless essential to lay down transparent guidelines, to install better measures of outputs, or performance, and to better align both individual and institutional rewards with these performance indicators.

Quality and Efficiency

The World Bank's Lessons of Experience report identified severe quality problems resulting from overcrowding in educational institutions, from insufficient control over the quality or behaviour of the teaching staff, or from inappropriate curricula, unrelated to the needs of the emerging economies. There is a dire need to improve the qualifications of teaching staff and the quality of their instruction, the appropriateness of the curriculum, improved student assessment and selection; and the extent and quality of facilities such as libraries, computers and equipment.

The principal higher educational productivity problems lie not so much with excessive costs, but with insufficient learning. The reform agenda for enhancing productivity, therefore, requires attention to:

i) effective teaching, including good instructional techniques, appropriate instructional resources such as libraries, laboratories, scientific equipment, computers, and internet accessibility;
ii) an appropriate curriculum, including content that is intellectually challenging, up-to-date, and appropriate to the mission of the institution;
iii) effective learning, including appropriate student time-on-task, as well as the ability to focus and concentrate; and

iv) an efficient managerial and administrative structure. Such efforts towards efficiency, cost control, and resource generation can go a long way in helping developing nations solve their resource and quality related problems.

Problems in Higher Education System

Some of the problems faced by the Indian higher education system are loss of primacy of the universities in the scheme of the higher education sector in India, erosion of their autonomy, undermining of undergraduate education, the growing distance between knowledge areas and the isolation of universities from the real world outside and crass commercialisation.

Invisible Walls

There are criticisms that our undergraduate and graduate programmes are too 'theoretical', and devoid of 'practical' experiences. The chasm that exists between theory and practice combined with the fragmentation of the idea of knowledge leads to the confusion that our system of higher education is suffering from. It would be therefore necessary that the universities adopt a curricular approach which treats knowledge in a holistic manner and creates exciting opportunities for different kinds of interfaces between the disciplines. It would also be necessary that the university education is seen in its totality and subject areas not be designed in isolation.

The Indian system of higher education has also kept itself aloof from the real world outside. Within the system, there are distances between disciplines. Within a single campus, disciplines often grow in complete ignorance even of each other's presence. This lack of dialogue becomes more profound when we talk of areas like engineering, medicine and teacher training. While universities award engineering and medical degrees, it is ironic that they do not have the powers to determine whether an institution that claims to train engineers or doctors has the wherewithal to do so nor do they have sufficient say in designing the academic programmes, in professional disciplines, as these are largely influenced by statutory bodies like the Medical Council of India and the AICTE.

Divide between Research Bodies and Universities

Now that universities have become mass institutions and costs of research, especially in the context of science and engineering, have become very high, things have changed. Over the years, there has been an increasing tendency to treat teaching and research as separate activities, being reinforced by separate policies, programmes and structures. This has led to a situation in which, on the one hand, most of the universities have been reduced to the status of centres that teach and examine masses and, on the other hand, more and more elite research bodies are being created where researchers have absolutely no occasion to engage with young minds.

It should be necessary for all research bodies to connect with universities in their vicinity and create teaching opportunities for their researchers and for all universities to be teaching and research universities.

Isolation of IITs and IIMs

The IITs and IIMs brighten up the otherwise dismal scenario of higher education in India. There is no doubt their claim to quality and excellence. They have also fiercely and successfully defended their autonomy over the years.

With the enormous potential they have, they must strive to be models of all-round excellence, like the famous Massachusetts Institute of Technology or CALTECH in the US, without isolation of the study of engineering and management from other knowledge areas. As initiatives some of the IITs aim to introduce humanities and other disciplines, and expand their scope. They have to broaden their curriculum framework and assume the functions of full-fledged universities without losing their unique character. Not far will be the day when IITs and IIMs would be producing scholars in literature, linguistics and politics along with engineering and management wizards who would have substantial motivation for engagement with the local community, and the opportunity to use and enhance learning by solving real-life problems in their immediate environment. While working towards this goal we need to understand that different IITs and IIMs would have different strategies to expand

and diversify, and we must refrain from issuing a uniform diktat to all of them to move in a prescribed direction.

Erosion of Democratic Space

In India, where social hierarchy and divisions are sharp, institutions of learning serve as sites where powerful social forces vie for dominance. The institutional capacity to maintain peace and a democratic process plays a critical role in shaping the ethos of this site. If institutions of higher education fail to ensure peace on their own premises in this sense of the term, they cannot avoid failing in a far greater sense when they claim public money on a gigantic scale and lose public faith.

Following Independence, institutions of higher learning succeeded in providing a space where dialogue between rival social forces and ideologies could take place in a peaceful atmosphere. However, since then certain distinct signs of the erosion of this space have emerged quite often in different parts of the country worsening situation over the last few years. Not only organised youth but the official machinery of the university has been deliberately used to obstruct or subvert the possibility of peaceful debate and inquiry resulting in a long-term institutional damage to their capacity to serve as sites of peace. This is a serious matter not just because it marks the erosion of institutional sanctity, but also because it distorts the idea of a university and its role in the creation of knowledge by free and open inquiry through research and dialogue.

Geo-cultural diversities is another critical area where our universities have increasingly failed to act as spaces where students would learn to respect diversity as a value. In a world where boundaries are disappearing it is important that we learn to acknowledge and appreciate differences and not try to homogenise everything.

Curriculum Issues and Syllabi

At present, the archaic curriculum and syllabi and the examination system, ostensibly used as a means of certifying the ability of students, unfortunately do not really test the kind of skills they require to be successful in either the pursuit of pure theoretical knowledge or in practical real world situations.

The examination system, even in relatively better equipped and less rigid institutions, has remained quite traditional and incapable of distinguishing between different talents of students in a reliable manner. The rote-based 'application' highlights the student's lack of ability to examine and understand the real world, as a result of which their engagement with people or issues remains scarce once they enter the world of work, with implications for their abilities as workers and citizens. As a result of this lopsided emphasis on evaluation of students through examinations, what is considered knowledge in the prevailing set-up is at best a body of facts. This occasionally leads to students gaining 'knowledge' with varying, though usually low, degrees of success.

The syllabi should require the teachers and students to apply what they have learnt in their courses, on studying a local situation, issue or problem. There should be sufficient room for the use of local data and resources to make the knowledge covered in the syllabus come alive as experience. This is required simply because engaging with the world surrounding us is an important aspect of learning, both as a means as well as an end.

Curricular reform should include compulsory exposure and engagement with different kinds of work, in the form of summer jobs or internships, according to the circumstances and surroundings of the particular university, and should include both manual and other kinds of work/occupations, with a certain minimum set of occupational exposure compulsory for all students, irrespective of discipline. Evaluating students on these fronts would necessarily have to analyse how well they have understood, and are as a result capable of applying themselves to work and be problem-solving in these situations.

This process of syllabus designing will need to be worked out in different disciplines, since an engineering or science course will clearly engage with local matters differently from history or political science. For this strategy of syllabus redesigning to succeed, evaluation and examination practices will also have to change, and certainly, there will have to be a change in pedagogic practices used by teachers.

Learning across Disciplines

At present, much of our higher education is uni-disciplinary or within a narrow spread. Wherever education involves inclusion of disciplines other than the major one that the student is studying, it is in the form of 'subsidiary' subjects. By their very nomenclature these subjects are seldom regarded as serious, either for the assessment they carry, or, least of all, for their content. Likewise, the teaching and syllabi of these subjects, over a period of time, also become poor in quality and motivation. Hence, there is no real learning across disciplines happening.

Understanding and application of concepts to worldly questions is an acknowledged aim of education, particularly at the higher levels such as undergraduate education. Integrating a given subject to which the student devotes a majority of her/his time with other relevant subjects is therefore essential to improve the current undergraduate education structure.

Students for whom a subject is additional should be allowed to study along with those for whom the same subject is primary.

Students have to be exposed especially at the undergraduate level, to various disciplines like humanities, social sciences, aesthetics etc., in an integrated manner. This should be irrespective of the discipline they would like to specialise in subsequently.

Teacher Education

Training of teachers for all levels of school education should be the responsibility of institutions of higher education. So far the involvement of universities in school-level teacher education has been confined to secondary and senior secondary-level school—teachers' pre-service training under the B.Ed. degree programme. The state governments manage the preparation of teachers for the primary and pre-primary levels. Although these levels have been recognised as being fundamental to the development of children and the nation, the absence of university-level interest has resulted in poor academic quality.

The quality of teacher education within higher education also needs careful attention. At present, Academic Staff Colleges are serving to provide refresher courses required by faculty to acquire eligibility for promotion. It is necessary to develop full-fledged orientation programmes for newly recruited teachers in colleges and universities. Such courses should orient teachers towards the proposed curriculum framework as well as to impart communication and assessment skills.

Rehabilitating Professional Education in the University

The pursuit of engineering and medicine, in particular, in colleges or institutes, has come at an incalculable social and cultural cost. Young students who move from a higher secondary school straight into an engineering or medical college, with little exposure to any in-depth knowledge of society, its economy, politics and culture, while possibly becoming excellent engineers and doctors in a very restricted sense also have as much potential to become an impediment to holistic social development.

Medical colleges in general have evolved in isolation from the rest of the university, with the latter acting merely as a degree-granting or certification authority. Conversely, there are also universities in certain fields, such as agriculture, medicine and law which are isolated from others and have rarely any interaction with them. While there has been a need for providing depth in specialisation in specific knowledge areas, this process has been trivialised and has now deteriorated to such an extent that universities are being created for narrow areas like information technology, pharmacy, catering, yoga, music and fashion technology.

It would be necessary that the curriculum of graduates is so designed that they could work in partnership with other institutions in their vicinity. Instead of making any prescription in this regard the committee proposes that these institutions should evolve creative ways of engaging with diverse range of knowledge areas.

The vocational education sector is at present outside the purview of universities and colleges. Students who go for vocational and technical education after completing higher secondary education are deprived of any possibility of pursuing higher education after completing their vocational or technical training. Alienation of this sector can be overcome by bringing it under the purview of universities and by providing necessary accreditation to the courses available in polytechnics, industrial training institutions, and so on. Further growth will greatly depend on the guidance and leadership that universities will be able to provide for institutions of vocational and technical education, once they are brought into the domain an all-encompassing system of higher education.

Undermining Undergraduate Education

In our country, the undergraduate years have mostly remained in the precinct of affiliated colleges, i.e., not as part of mainstream university life. By not exposing itself to UG level teaching, university faculty, especially the senior faculty, deprives itself of a rejuvenating pedagogic experience. In all the great universities of the world we know of, great teachers, even Nobel Laureates, prefer to teach undergraduate students.

It should be mandatory for all universities to have a rich undergraduate programme and undergraduate students must get opportunities to interact with the best faculty. While appointing teachers to the universities their affiliation to a particular college should also be specified to emphasise the need for their exposure to undergraduate students.

Performance Criteria

While endorsing the principle of full autonomy for a university, we recognise the need to evolve certain performance criteria on the basis of which universities can assess themselves and can be assessed by others in a transparent manner. The current environment favours those criteria which can generate enumerative data, such as the number of research papers published by the faculty in journals, the number of patents acquired, and so on. Though convenient to use, they often end up becoming mechanical and lose their significance in the context of larger aims of education when the faculty's work gets delinked from national or social concerns and priorities.

The higher education system offers pervasive instances of gender asymmetry. Perhaps no instances are as glaring as the ones we see in our best institutions of technology and management, but the situation is quite grim in several other domains, especially if we extend the scope of our enquiry to cover the composition of the faculty at the highest levels and administrative positions like that of the Vice-Chancellor. In the composition of the faculty, the representation of regions other than the one in which a university is located can serve as a valuable means of assessing a university's resolve to avoid the parochial tendencies we commonly notice.

Our universities and institutes tend to isolate themselves from the social world that surrounds them. In several cities, the contrast between the life and landscape one sees inside the gates and outside is sadly stark. It shows the absence of social responsibility in the concept of excellence. It also shows that the concept of knowledge that such a university does not require engagement or experiential construction of knowledge by learners and teachers. It is necessary that all kinds of documents generated by the university, including its syllabi, the papers and books published by its faculty, the assignments submitted by its students and other products such as audio and video material, be treated as its knowledge products which need to be sampled for independent assessment on the basis of intrinsic merits as well as relevance for the study of problems which are manifest in the university's immediate social and natural milieu.

An institution's awareness of its own problems, its will and capacity to study these problems and to make plans for resolving them are indicators of its overall institutional quality. Therefore, we feel that an important set of criteria can be identified within a university's own targets for organisational improvement and its record of moving towards them within specified timeframes. Priority areas for such self-motivated institutional reforms can be decided and articulated by the university itself.

Internationally, academic institutions and universities set up teams consisting of academics of eminence, recognised internationally for their expertise and integrity to get themselves assessed. Even in India, we have, for example, National Law Schools which have a process of evaluation similar to this. IIMs have a different process. Universities must submit themselves to credible processes of evaluation which would only help them establish their credentials in the academic world and society at large in a transparent manner.

State Universities and Affiliated Colleges

Although state universities are primarily the responsibility of states, because state legislatures create them, development of all young people, be they in state-run institutions or central institutions, is a national responsibility and there cannot be any discrimination between the two. State governments would need to significantly enhance their support to the universities while the centre should make matching incentivising allocations available in a sense of a joint national enterprise.

Many academic planners feel that the colleges need to be treated as the foundation of higher education similar to the way primary schools are for school education. Qualitative development of these colleges should be our priority. Money needs to be made available for the qualitative development of colleges and new universities are created, they should begin with undergraduate education and build on this base their postgraduate programmes, thus becoming not only role models for the colleges in their States but also a resource for them.

The need is therefore to renew and revitalise the college system and also to "lighten the load" of these universities and freeing the better and large colleges to become independent of the university processes. There is a view that the optimum size of a university has not only a quantitative but also a qualitative dimension. The optimality of a university has to take account of a critical level of students, teachers, disciplines, programmers of study and the needs of society and its emergence as a nurture and creator of knowledge, which may vary across universities.

Mushrooming of Deemed Universities

The sudden mushrooming of newly established educational institutes as deemed universities is another area of concern. Between 2000 and 2005, 26 private-sponsored institutions got the deemed university status. Since 2005, the number of private deemed universities has increased to 108. By a notification of the UGC, it is no longer necessary for them to use the adjective "deemed" and they all call themselves simply universities. Though, the deemed universities do not have affiliating powers, many of them have a number of campuses spread throughout the country.

It may be argued that the increase in the number of deemed universities is commensurate with the increase in the number of institutions of higher learning in the country. What has raised the concern of the academic world is the fact that the majority of these institutes are not established with any educational purpose, and they end up only deluding the students.

The institutions, which have somehow managed to secure a deemed status should be given a period of three years to develop as a university and fulfil the prescribed accreditation norms failing which the status given to them would be withdrawn. Every university, large or small, should have the scope to rise up to the prestige achieved through its performance and recognition. While the state could do everything to enable the university to demonstrate higher levels of performance, it is also necessary for the universities themselves to organise their programmers and activities in a manner that would continue to attract the support of the state as well as the private enterprise.

Issues of Affordability

Many private institutions, while charging exorbitant fees in the form of many kinds of levy, are unable to provide even minimum competent faculty strength. The regulatory agencies have been unable to come to grips with the problems of capitation fee and unauthorised annual fees mainly due to deficiencies in enforcement instruments, and partly due to high-level reluctance to sort out this problem. Since the norms for fixation of fees are vague, the quantum of fees charged has no rational basis.

While most of the private investment in higher education is in the field of engineering, management and medicine the majority of enrolment is taking place in traditional disciplines. The private providers are, therefore, not putting their money in areas which attract the bulk of the students, especially first generation university goers. It is the middle class, which has for long benefited from the state education system and is now breaking away from it.

The primary focus should therefore be on making education affordable, either through scholarships or loans. Institutional funding can then be for capital costs and research, and based on the worthiness of the institution. Once a student qualifies to enter an institution of her choice, she should not be deprived of education for want of money. It is the duty of the institution and the state to provide for her education through means as suggested above. Steps need to be initiated to ensure availability of loans and scholarships.

Foreign Universities

Before taking any decision on allowing foreign universities to operate in India we have to be very clear about the purpose it is going is achieve. If the best of foreign universities, say amongst the top 200 in the world, want to come here and work, they should be welcomed. Any decision in this regard has to be taken with utmost care keeping in mind the features which are essential for an institution to be called a university. Such institutions should give an Indian degree and be subject to all rules and regulations that would apply to any Indian university.

Financing

Universities require constant supply of resources to maintain and upgrade their facilities, resources and technologies. State funding for the same has been dwindling over the years and is irregular. Universities are expected to raise their own resources. This has resulted in poor infrastructure –physical and intellectual – as well as introduction of very low quality self-financing programmes that have no relationship with the university curriculum.

While the state cannot shy away from its responsibility of financing higher education, they have to be devise ways to find complementary sources of funds so that our universities can move beyond their current levels of engagement with students and excellence in providing education. Changes in regulatory systems are required to encourage philanthropy from society.

Universities are inadequately, irregularly and inflexibly funded. For every post, whether academic or non-academic, the university has to face inordinate delays before approval, if any, are given by funding agencies. Hence, universities are unable to plan their development on any long-term basis. Release of funds annually is leading to delay in implementation of plans and is an intrusion in the autonomy of the institution. Block grants against a plan should become the norm with universities being competent expend according to their priorities.

There does exist in today's world a large student body that can also afford to pay for their education. No student should be turned away from an institution for want of funds for education. Absence of differential fee has led to subsidisation of a segment of student body that can afford to pay for its education. Guaranteed student loans at low interest rates for those who can take loans and free education for those who cannot afford it at all will be necessary to educate India.

Students from all over the India aspiring to enter universities should be allowed to take GRE tests as many times as they like. Their best test score can then be sent to the universities of their choice which can admit them if they satisfy State Boards of Secondary Education and the Central Board of Secondary Education (CBSE) must seriously think of reviving our faith in each school and its teachers to credibly evaluate its own students. At present, our system manages to attract only a small fraction of this potential clientele. If systemic impediments are removed and academically imaginative and flexible programmes are made available, the participation of foreign students in our higher education can significantly increase. Apart from the benefit it will provide to them, it will enrich the ethos of our universities as well.

Human Resource Management

Higher education has lost a generation of academics due to the inability of universities to find place for their scholarship. The constraints from the funding agency had led universities to stop recruitment of faculty even on approved positions. Positions of retiring academics are lost. Retired academics are rehired to teach and are paid meagrely for each session. This is indeed a national shame and not a strategy of developing higher education in the world's most promising country. Any reform of higher education must give the highest priority to attracting talent from diverse backgrounds and take care not to encourage inbreeding.

Assessment of teachers is another area which has been in discussion for quite some time. It is necessary to remember that while research and publications can serve as important criteria for assessing the scholarly dimension of a teacher's personality, students are in a unique position to provide an experiential assessment of the quality of teaching. Parameters of student feedback can be drawn up so as to avoid distorting factors, such as the tendency to earn cheap popularity by using conventional means like dictating examination-oriented notes. Student feedback at the end of each semester should become a routine, and teachers whose feedback record remains poor in successive years should be required to face formal procedures which might allow a university or college to shed them.

Poor Governance of Universities

The governance structures in universities are archaic and have not changed with changing environment to meet the expectations of its various stakeholders. While most other organisations in society have adapted themselves in terms of organisational design, mechanisms for conducting their business and motivating people, use of technology to bring effectiveness in operations etc., universities have not changed much.

Hard rules that were framed for a past era still prevail. All of these have led to centralisation of decisionmaking and low involvement of faculty and students in most policy decisions affecting academics. These may have been the direct outcomes of low autonomy as well as low management skills amongst administrators at these institutions.

With an urgent need to improve governance by developing expertise in "educational management" and avoid burdening good academics with administrative chores universities have to start programmes in management of educational institutions. A separation between academic administration and overall management may be desirable. In general the governance structure of centrally funded institutions, such as the central universities, IITs, NITs, IIITs, IISERs etc., are relatively more autonomous than the state funded institutions. Even among state institutions, National Law Universities enjoy high levels of autonomy as compared to other state universities.

In academic matters, the teacher should have complete autonomy to frame her/his course and the way she/he would like to assess her/his students. This autonomy should also be available to the students who should be allowed to take courses of their choice in a relaxed manner from different universities and then be awarded a degree on the basis of the credits they have earned.

Loss of Autonomy

Various political or commercial vested interests interfere in the functioning and priorities of the universities comes in many different forms and intensities. It touches all aspects of higher education and involves improper admission of students, pressures in selection of teachers, manipulation in appointment of senior functionaries like vice-chancellors, registrars and deans, purchase of equipment and allotment of construction contracts and so on.

It is gratifying to note that a substantial number of higher educational institutions demonstrate a credible record of quality and ethics. Most of these are centrally funded institutions like central universities, institutions of national importance such as IITs, several higher technology and management institutions and some state-funded institutions. One common feature they share among them is their structure of governance, consisting of eminent persons, excluding practising politicians and including only a limited representation from the government. Autonomy in the true sense is available to these institutions with the guidance and support of such governing bodies.

Similarly, the appointments of heads of such institutions, like vice-chancellors, directors etc., are made by Search Committees with candidates of impeccable credentials, keeping the best interest of the institution in view. In recent years though choosing persons for such high-level appointments is becoming scandalous in several states involving political and financial considerations at the cost of qualifications and competence.

Wherever the higher educational institutions have a governance system that functions with a high degree of autonomy, their performance have earned national and international respect not withstanding financial constraints. The absence of any sense of academic and administrative autonomy, introduces a high degree of educational and social distortion.

Subversion from Within

There is a need for deep introspection by the academia on the origins and the extent of the crisis that the higher education system is going through and on its own role in exacerbating this crisis. This would reveal that there has been a willing abdication on part of the academic community, of the autonomy which was available to it. Education was made subservient to ideological compulsions which led to its loss of respect.

The independence of scholarship from power has failed and resulted in a situation where it has become easy for some of those in power and in the bureaucracy to curtail the autonomy as the academic community has proved itself to be unworthy of practising it.

Multiplicity of Regulatory Systems

The UGC and a few other institutions of learning took major initiatives in fostering educational innovations such as setting up of inter-university centres to facilitate national synergy in research efforts among universities and to optimise the investments in sophisticated research infrastructure. The creation of country-wide educational communication facility through multiple platforms and creating large-scale contents; the setting up of national network of libraries including e-journals for convenient access to higher educational institutions across the country; special incentives to advanced centres of research; and additional resources to institutions with potential for excellence were some of the other initiatives of the UGC in the recent past. Given the national aspirations for greater and equitable access to knowledge a well-designed regulatory system will also help to promote a high degree of professionalism in managing higher education institutions.

The creation of bodies like the AICTE, ICAR, MCI and so on has certainly helped in focusing attention on specialised areas. It has, at the same time, fragmented the higher educational sector in the country from a policy perspective. This has, on many occasions, created situations where different agencies have taken different views on issues of regulation and promotion of higher education. The powers vested currently in these multiple agencies for regulating creation of academic institutions and their content would be also taken over by the proposed apex regulatory body. There have been suggestions to create a coordination council of various existing regulatory bodies, which could ensure harmony in their views. A mechanism, which seeks to defragment policy areas, would need to act like one mind. Co-ordination among agencies which have different views of knowledge and education and which tend to treat knowledge within narrow confines is extremely difficult, if not impossible. A single apex body in the field of higher education would treat all knowledge areas in an integrated manner and work towards convergences which overarching regulatory powers. Only such a body would ensure that there is a live and close interaction among co-thinkers and co-workers and there is no dilution of any idea, which it has to suffer if made to traverse a bureaucratic maze.

Reinventing Higher Education

Over the years, higher education has served the twin purposes of research and teaching. In its knowledge production function, higher education institutions have been the centres of innovation and creators of new knowledge in diverse fields of human activity. It has been assumed that knowledge production is taking place only in higher education institutions; people's experiences and daily struggles in communities produce experiences, not knowledge. This elitist view of knowledge has been challenged over human history.

In their teaching function, higher education institutions have focused largely on the learning of theories in the classrooms. Students are rarely involved in "engaged" learning in real settings, and much of that arises from the orthodox meaning of teaching and education. Alternative approaches to learning are being attempted, largely at the margins of academia. In order to reinvent higher education to make its contemporary relevance more meaningful, it is important to explore how the principles and perspectives of participatory research can be applied in higher education institutions to address the challenges of participatory and sustainable development.

Participatory Research

The essential premise of participatory research is recognition and utilisation of knowledge for purposes of transforming the relations of power in social systems. This perspective allows learning about the dynamics of a social-political system to be closely linked to bringing about changes in that system to achieve certain desirable public values of equity, justice and peace. Participatory research methodologies are thus used to both learn about realities and transform the same towards such desirable public values.

Participatory Research with Mobilisation

Participatory research throughout these three decades has been of linking knowledge production with mobilisation. Mobilisation here is meant in terms of conscientisation, awareness raising, collectivisation, getting together to address a problem, with or without external help. There is a very close link between knowledge, learning and mobilisation to act – to act to solve a problem.

Research vs Teaching

Participatory research methodology and perspective also tend to integrate what are called research and teaching functions – the twin key functions in any institution of higher education. But this is unlike what occurs in institutions of higher education where research functions are seen as separate from teaching; some days of the year you do research, other days of the year you do teaching. Some experts, senior professors, research universities do research; some "lower order", not so eloquent ones are teachers, tutors who do teaching. This distinguishment between research and teaching has become a part of many higher education institutions calling for challenges by changing the concept. The moment you change the concept, the moment you treat research as an act of knowing and make teaching a process of learning, then you see very close connections between the act of knowing and the act of learning, because in a sense they are similar acts. Unfortunately, learning is something that has lost its significance in much of teaching that goes on in higher education institutions. And knowing has lost its credibility in much of research that is going on.

In the last 15 years, attempt have been made to link participatory research methodology to teaching as well as to research. Students and faculty or departments of social work, sociology, political science, public administration, law, engineering, management, geography, planners, etc., go out and work with local communities, local community-based organisations, civil society groups, local governing institutions, like panchayats and municipalities to contribute to their development through micro-planning, resource mapping, studies on the status of malnutrition of kids, issues relating to the dropout of girls from schools; as well as gain knowledge from such an engagement. This approach is now being tried in higher education in Canada, Thailand, Samoa, for example.

Confronting the Challenges

Higher education institutions face several challenges and these required to be booked into immediately. Higher education institutions are sites of high density of Ph.D where power is derived from the exclusive process of certification of knowledge and resources applied to disseminate that knowledge. When you posit this high density, high power expertise in an institution of higher education with a group of indigenous people it is a very big one-sided story. Those who today have power must reach out to those who do not, because otherwise those who are disempowered know only one way – resist, shout, protest.

Another issue is that of authentic participation within institutions of higher education. There are students, researchers, academics and faculty members in all institutions of higher education, who would like to be engaged, who are engaging sometimes without telling authorities that they are engaging. So this work needs to be incentivised and mainstreamed in institutions of higher education.

The question about multinationals funding research is a legitimate one. What about states funding research? In many instances, there is research funded by government agencies that could not be published in the public domain because its conclusions went against the relevant mainstream state policy. We are finding in our societies that the nature of education in higher education institutions is such that today in society the most passive citizens are those who have higher education. They are becoming disengaged from the public sphere and democratic questions and concerned only with meeting private goals. To promote participatory and sustainable development, higher education and higher education institutions need to re-dedicate themselves to deepening democracy through active citizenship.

Responsibility for Sustainable Development

Education plays a necessary and decisive role in the economic, social and political development of a country and impacts each area to a significant degree. Various reports by the United Nations have proved the inevitable links between the role of educational development and economic growth through many statistical and analytical surveys.

Education may contribute to development, but it does not mean that the expansion of school attainment necessarily guarantees the improvement of economic and social conditions. What is important is the quality of education and schooling – whether students are really learning what truly matters. As one of the Millennium Development Goals proposes, the universal access of children to primary school education is the basic condition of development. It is still a target, which cannot be easily reached within this decade. However, in order to drive our education more towards sustainable development, we have to provide quality education that is oriented towards the values and skills of sustainability at the various levels of education.

Universities play a vital role not only in shaping the future by educating the professionals of tomorrow, but also by creating a research base for sustainability efforts, and providing outreach and service to communities and nations, especially related to difficult sustainability issues.

Our universities, still very isolated from society and social reality, need to be more open to the needs of society and more connected with social innovation through partnerships with civil society. But universities in many countries remain in the ivory tower isolated from the challenges of rapid social change through globalisation and technological revolution.

The more serious problem in the field of education is the tendency towards unsustainable, or anti-sustainable, research and teaching by the universities and colleges. Especially many scholars in science and technology institutes and management and policy institutes are inspired too deeply by development ideology, and neglect the principle of sustainability.

Education for sustainable development should be oriented toward the global dimension of the sustainable future, and the interconnectedness of local and global development. However, many research and teaching programmes of the universities are oriented at national developmental goals only and ignore the global issues of a sustainable world such as poverty, illiteracy, war and cultural diversity. In this regard, reorienting universities to address sustainability is an urgent task as much as reorienting teacher education.

For creating a sustainable future and lifestyle sensitising children and youth in basic and secondary education is most efficient and powerful, because their value systems and behaviour can be changed through reoriented education. However, the crucial point is to have qualified and committed teachers who can deliver the reoriented lessons and convince children of sustainable awareness and behaviour. For this to happen, the institutes of higher education – universities – have to be innovated and restructured. Universities should play the role of capacity builder, in terms of training teachers and formulating the conceptual framework of appropriate education for sustainable development.

The establishment of a specialised institute of sustainable development is to be recommended in order to study the holistic philosophy and contextualised methods of education for sustainable development and to maintain access to information and global cooperative networks. As the themes of sustainable development are multifaceted and multidimensional, the research approach on education for sustainable development should be interdisciplinary or transdisciplinary through the formation of research clusters.

Educational programmes of universities should be innovated and improved upon in order to conscientise and sensitise students of sustainable development. Educational programmes for the environment, development and cultural heritage, and peace and human rights can be integrated into the special course on education for sustainable development.

Institutes of higher education have to strengthen the networks of cooperation and exchange with other centres of excellence at the national, regional and global levels in order to create synergies and mobilise greater resources and capacity to ensure sustainable development. In this regard, universities and higher education should be more globalised, and also localised.

Roles of Universities in Sufficiency Economy

Commercialisation of science brings science and technologies as well as higher education into the competitive arena. Innovations, based on science and technologies, serve to form competitiveness. Internationalisation and cross-border services further expand the strength of the knowledge economy.

Scholarship of Teaching and Learning

Scholarly approaches to teaching and learning enable individual faculty members and their institutions to develop better curricular programmes, improve the quality of student learning and professional training, and evaluate effectively the learning strategies that work best under specific contexts. The scholarship of teaching and learning (SoTL), on the other hand, brings scholarly teaching to the next stage of more rigorous engagement by producing and disseminating pedagogical research in peer reviewed contexts, such as journal publications, conferences and other practices of different learning communities.

Many university-community partnerships involve curricular review and development projects, team-teaching projects, peer review of existing and exemplary curricula and/or teaching practices, pedagogical workshops, evaluation of research skills training, internships, manuscript publications, programme evaluation projects and faculty development programmes. There are many lessons to be learned about the conduct of scholarly teaching and learning within university-based, international capacity-building projects; we need to improve more than the pedagogical approaches and evaluation of participant learning outcomes. These lessons can be shared and used to contribute to the promotion of SoTL using international development projects as subjects of study.

In respect of higher education, the utilisation of scholarly approaches to teaching and learning might be conceptualised as a form of "capacity-building" at the individual and institutional levels, while the widespread production and dissemination of scholarship of teaching and learning might have greater potential to contribute to wider "capacity development" of universities and their engagement in international development work.

SoTL takes scholarly teaching to a higher level of rigour and engagement by its sheer multiplier effects and attempts at replication in various learning communities within and outside classroom and university settings. Herein lies the importance of community-university partnerships and the role of universities in capacity development, and the role of capacity development in both scholarly teaching and the scholarship of teaching.

We have not fully understood the capacity-building needs of universities, particularly in the fields of faculty and curriculum development to make them better agents of international development. Universities and university people need to develop so that they can better collaborate with local communities and governments as well as international development agencies to achieve long-term development goals.

As capacity development can have greater ability to incorporate the importance of stakeholders, participatory techniques, indigenous ownership, consensus and commitment, it has significance for long-term human resource development, particularly professional faculty development, within colleges and universities.

Community Service Learning

Community Service Learning (CSL) is a form of experiential learning that integrates service in the community with academic courses and/or extra-curricular programmes. As a form of experiential learning involving adult learners it is more than the systematic acquisition and storage of knowledge and information. It also involves making sense of our lives, transforming not just what we learn, but the way we learn, and it is absorbing, imagining, intuiting and learning informally with others. Adult education sees adult learners in a holistic manner, that is, as individuals with "mind, memories, conscious and subconscious worlds, emotions, imaginations, and physical body, all of which can interact with new learning".

In International Service Learning (ISL) the learning process is as important as the context of learning in which situated learning becomes cognisant of how axes of social difference, power relations and differing conceptions of knowledge and truth shape the context, process and outcomes of learning. While there is a lot of reflection about the processes of teaching and learning that goes on within university classrooms, there is also reflection on whether there is wide acceptance as well as full and effective use of teaching and learning innovations in CSL and ISL. This is because CSL and ISL practitioners tend to focus more on their practice of teaching rather than reflecting on the practice itself. And yet, CSL in international contexts offers many opportunities and promise in integrating innovative and alternative teaching and learning strategies beyond the typical lecture, chalk and talk, approach. They typically involve co-operative forms of adult learning that have positive impacts such as improved teaching, enhanced self-esteem of learners, harmony in the learning environment and greater interest in the subject matter. Cooperative approaches to learning can enhance strategies used in the training and learning component of ISL such as problem-based learning, classroom assessment, curriculum review and development, charettes and on-line

Renewing the Role of Universities

Two historical core functions of teaching and research directed at the production and dissemination of knowledge for the benefit of society and its continuing development are the responsibilities of universities. The focus has shifted to generating knowledge and labour for the capital enterprise instead of developing the capacities of people most in need – especially the poor, deprived and excluded. Universities are beset with competition for world-class recognition and this has led them into techno-bureaucratic institutions as they vie for measurable accomplishments and visibility instead of developing partnerships for people-centred development.

Neo-liberal agendas and government policies have constricted the role of universities which have to meet the demands of the rapidly growing global economy. Hence recognition hinges on their contribution to the global market. Recent trends, especially in developing countries, suggest the emergence of an entrepreneurial model of academic research which is being strongly advocated as "good practice", as a way of fostering entrepreneurship among university researchers to attract industrial funding. Faculty members are encouraged and rewarded to undertake consultancies with the business sector.

As specialisation and up-scaling of certain disciplines have occurred in business studies, engineering and technology, including ICT departments, they have been given prominence while the humanities and social sciences have been put on the back burner. This further accentuates the absence of concern for the social-political aspects of development agendas and disregards the university's social and democratising role in society. The current system of academic assessment and rewards in universities are far from being conducive Engaging with communities to address their problems and needs will involve more time, energy and creativity than just publishing academic research, thus affecting their measurable output in internationally referred journals. Indeed, the role of academia has become irrelevant and unimportant as universities strive for world-class status.

Today, universities are at an important crossroads. They have the potential to make a difference to critical global needs with a student population of 200 million by 2030. The fundamental challenge of universities is to provide an ethical knowledge base responsive to societal needs, and contribute to the common wealth and well-being of its entire people. If universities are to engage responsibly and thrive within contemporary realities, a basic shift needs to be made from relying exclusively on neutral curriculum content and approaches designed to develop market-oriented competencies and values of competition and power, to developing an educational practice that exemplifies and engenders the valorisation of commitment, compassion, responsibility and service.

Civic Mission of higher Education

Internationalisation is an interactive response to globalisation, yet the nature of competitiveness and economic driven orientation is being particularly highlighted in the internationalisation of higher education in the Asian Pacific region. Transnational education will cause the problematic issues of including the hegemony of Western knowledge and pedagogies and commodification of knowledge through which cost and effectiveness and profit are of prime focus. Critical reflection on how the higher education systems in the Asian-Pacific region have been impacted by the international criteria and practices determined by the Anglo-American paradigm can help address the following fundamental questions:

i) What is missing in the process of internationalisation?
ii) What should internationalisation of higher education aim at?
iii) For what purposes should the HEIs exist in the post-colonial era?

It is unquestionable that the notion of international education comprises the primary goal of international exchanges that provide opportunities for countries to learn from one another or for those less developed countries to receive assistance from their counterparts but it does not mean the less developed have to duplicate from the developed. To refrain from being recolonised, scholars especially in the Asian regions must learn from the West and guard against duplicating without proper adaptation and analysis.

Restructuring HEIs by means of adopting Western standards, marketisation and corporatisation are then the salient features in transnational education nowadays. Impacted by the tidal wave of these market driven forces, the most prominent challenge of the higher education policy includes the gradually diminishing of culture values and civic missions that higher education used to promote. Hence, what is missing in the internationalisation process is higher education that should be embedded with the vision of preparing future leaders and citizens to address global issues and challenges like shaping sustainable development, international solidarity and global peace in a highly independent globalised world, but these goals are becoming limited because HEIs would rather incline to the impetus of income generation.

On the other hand, the research conducted by Romm, Patterson and Hill confirmed that failure of social interaction with domestic students was a major source of course dissatisfaction for international students. Research findings inform us that a number factors affecting the study life of overseas students, such as students' aspiration, perception of their courses and institutions, impact of culture and values on learning environments, learning autonomy and styles of learning. For humane reason, therefore, internationalisation should integrate an intercultural dimension into teaching, research and community service in order to enhance academic excellence and promote civic the notion of social responsibility and civic engagement in societies.

We have a deep belief that internationalisation of higher education will be undergoing a "humanising process" that multicultural and intercultural characteristics of mankind in the globe are respected. The creation of a fair, just, tolerant and caring society is not one which can be left to the market. After all, cross-cultural and multicultural understanding, tolerance and the creation of democratic communities do not appear by themselves. There is a need to create a possibility of a citizenship which transcends national boundaries: the citizens of the world. In this regard, it seems that there is need for a more moral and civic tune or to regain balance between responding to market pressures and liberal and civic values in higher education. Nevertheless, "citizenship" and "cultural awareness" as two of the most important aims in the internationalisation process is missing in higher education agenda.

Knight's survey with 526 HEIs in 95 countries on the aims and objectives of internationalisation for the International Association of University (IAU), UNESCO has found that in the area of "Rationales Driving Internationalisation", HEIs around the world ranked "competitiveness", "strategic alliances" as the two most important rationales whereas "cultural awareness" and "international cooperation" were of comparatively low priorities at both national and institutional levels respectively. On the other hand, in area of "Benefits of Internationalisation", "academic quality" and "strengthen research" were ranked as most important benefits but "national and international citizenship" and "brain gain" were treated as least important at both national and institutional levels. The survey shows that many HEIs neglect the important mission of socialising our university students to be active citizens in the civil society of the nation and the globe.

It is believed that HEIs could be motivated by both the finance-driven ethos and the communal aspirations of civic engagement through re-engineering their curricula. Academic values and civic missions in HEIs are also at the heart of the aspects such as human rights, multilateralism and global citizenship. Increasingly, universities around the world are expectedly to play a key role in advancing the cause of humanity and citizenship because international education should be a trading game for students' self enrichment.

Internationalisation of higher education should be motivated by education for global citizenship rather than dominated more by the desire for income than better education. It seems problematic to integrate concepts of citizenship, social justice, ethics and sustainable development within HEIs being oriented to goals of fund generation. The main challenge facing internationalisation and effective education for global citizenship is the HEI. Internationalisation of higher education should be committed to encouraging democratic inclusivity and ethical living.

We need to help HEIs imbedded with these missions and values that will provide the global society with a future. This will affect the way courses and programmes are delivered and life in the campus is conducted. This also demands cultural change driven by educationists inside the campus and policy makers at the system level. At the system level, it relies heavily on the governments' effort to realise the aim of internationalisation of higher education for humane and civic missions that include education for democratic values, global citizenship, world peace and sustainable development. At the institutional level, if learning is linked to social change, pedagogy can help reinvent the HEI as a community as relevant and positive influences in a sustainable future. Therefore, university faculties engaged in internationalisation can assist by designing courses that promote responsible global citizenship.

References

Bohm, A., Davis, T., Meares, D. and Pearce, D. *Global Student Mobility 2025: Forecasts of The Global Demand for International Higher Education,* 2002, IDP Education, Australia.

Chan, W. Y. "International Cooperation in Higher Education: Theory and Practice", *Journal of Studies in International Education, 8,* 2004, pp. 32-55, 2004.

Haigh, M. "Internationalization of the Curriculum: Designing Inclusive Education for a Small World", *Journal of Geography in Higher Education,* 26, No. 1, 2002, pp. 49-66,

Haigh, M., "Internationalization, Planetary Citizenship and Higher Education, Inc"., *Compare, 38,* No. 4, 2008, pp. 427-440.

Knight, J. "Internationalization Remodeled: Definition, Approaches, and Rationales". *Journal of Studies in International Education, 8,* No.1, 2004, pp. 5-31.

Mok, K. H., "Questing for Internationalization of Universities in Asia: Critical Reflections". *Journal of Studies in International Education, 11,* No. 3-4, 2007, pp.433-454.

Scott, P., *The Globalization of Higher Education,* 1998, Open University Press and Society for Research into Higher Education, Buckingham.

Yang, R., University Internationalization: Its Meanings, Rationales and implications, *Intercultural Education, 13,* No. 1, 2002, pp. 81-95.

BIBLIOGRAPHY

AICTE, *Report of the High Power Committee for Mobilization of Additional Resources for Technical Education,* All India Council for Technical Education, New Delhi. 1994.

Altbach Philip, "Higher Education Cross Borders", *Change,* March-April, 2004.

Altbach, P. and Teichner, U., Internationalization and Exchanges in a Globalized University, *Journal of Studies in International Education,* Vol. 5, Issue 1. 2001.

Ambani, M. and K. Birla, *Report on a Policy Framework for Reforms in Education,* Government of India, New Delhi, 2001.

Anandakrishnan M, "Internationalization of Higher Education: Policy Concerns", paper presented at a conference at NIEPA on 26 and 27 August, 2004

Austin, A. E. and D.W. Chapman (eds.), *Higher Education in the Developing World.* Westport, Ct.: Greenwood Press, 2002.

Back, K., Davis, D., & Olsen, A., *Internationalisation and Tertiary Education Institutions in New Zealand,* Wellington: MoE, 1998.

Barron, A., "Designing Web-based training". *British Journal of Educational Technology, 29*(4), 355-371, 1998.

Berge, Z., "Guiding principles in Web-based instructional design". *Education Media International, 35*(2), 72-76, 1998.

Blackmore, J., "Globalisation and the Restructuring of Higher Education for New Knowledge Economies: New Dangers or Old Equity Work in Universities?", *Higher Education Quarterly,* 0951-5224. 56:4, pp. 419-441, 2002.

Blackwell, Fritz, *India: A Global Studies Handbook,* United States of America: ABC-CLIO, Inc., 2004.

Bohm, A., Davis, T., Meares, D. and Pearce, D. *Global Student Mobility 2025: Forecasts of The Global Demand for International Higher Education,* 2002, IDP Education, Australia.

Carnoy, M., *Globalisation and Educational Reform: What Planners Need to Know,* Report No.63, International Institute of Educational Planning, Paris, 1999.

Chan, W. Y. "International Cooperation in Higher Education: Theory and Practice", *Journal of Studies in International Education, 8,* 2004, pp 32-55, 2004.

Chanda Rupa, "Social Services and the GATS: Key Issues and Concerns", *World Development* Vol.31, No.12, 2003.

Collis, B., "Information technologies for education and training". In Adelsberger, H., Collis, B, & Pawlowski, J. (eds.) *Handbook on Technologies for Information and Training*. Berlin: Springer Verlag, 2002.

Dhar, B.B., Internationalisation in India: To What Extent?, in K.B. Powar (Editor), *Internationalisation of Indian Higher Education,* AIU, New Delhi, 2001.

Elder, Joseph W., "Caste System", *Encyclopedia of India (vol. 1)* edited by Stanley Wolpert, 223-229, Thomson Gale, 2006.

Etaat, J. "Education and development". *Economic and Political Information, 143-144*(13), 208-225, 1999.

Garrett Richard, "Foreign Higher Education Activity in China", *International Higher Education,* Winter 2004.

Government of India, *Approach Paper to the Tenth Five-year Plan: 2002-2007,* Planning Commission, New Delhi, 2001.

Government of India, *Programme of Action on the National Education Policy,* Ministry of Human Resource Development, New Delhi, 1992.

Haigh, M., "Internationalization, Planetary Citizenship and Higher Education, Inc"., *Compare, 38,* No. 4, 2008, pp. 427-440.

Institute of International Education, *Open Doors 2001: Report on International Educational Exchange,* HE, New York. <http://www.opendoorsweb.org>. 2001.

Jonassen, D. & Reeves, T., "Learning with technology: Using computers as cognitive tools". In D. Jonassen (ed.), *Handbook of Research Educational on Educational Communications and Technology,* New York: Macmillan, 1996.

Knight Jane, *GATS, Trade and Higher education: Perspective 2003-where are we?* Report, The observatory on borderless higher education UK., 2003.

_______________, *Trade in Higher Education Services: The Implications of GATS.* The Observatory on Borderless Higher Education. London: United Kingdom, 2004.

_______________ "Internationalization Remodeled: Definition, Approaches, and Rationales". *Journal of Studies in International Education, 8,* No.1, 2004, pp. 5-31.

_______________ and DeWit, H., *Internationalisation of Higher Education in Asia Pacific Countries,* European Association of International Education, Amsterdam, Netherlands, 1997.

KPMG, *Transforming Higher Education: At the Gateway of the Knowledge Economy*, KPMG LLP. 1999.

Kumar Ravindra, "Privatisation of Higher Education and Regulatory Mechanisms in University", *University News*, Vol.42, no. 7, February 16-22, 2004, AIU, New Delhi.

Kumar Ravindra, Privatisation of Higher Education and Regulatory Mechanisms in University in *University News*, Vol.42, no. 7, February 16-22, 2004, AIU, New Delhi.

Lee Molly, N.N., "Expanding the State Role in Malaysian Higher Education", *International Higher Education*, Summer, 2000.

Mok, K. H., "Questing for Internationalization of Universities in Asia: Critical Reflections". *Journal of Studies in International Education, 11,* No. 3-4, 2007, pp.433-454.

Moore, M. & Kearsley, G., *Distance Education: A Systems View*, Belmont, CA: Wadsworth, 1996.

Neef, D. (ed.), *The Knowledge Economy*. Boston: Butterworth-Heinemann, 1998.

NSSO, *Attending an Educational Institution in India: Its Level, Nature and Cost*, NSS 52nd.Round, July 1995-June 1996, NSSO, Government of India, 1998.

Parhar Madhu, Internationalising Indian Higher Education through Distance, *Indian Journal of Open Learning*, 2001, 10(3) pp. 339-348

Powar, K.B., International Providers of Higher Education in India, *Internationalisation of Indian Higher Education*, pp 69-75, AIU, New Delhi, 2001.

_______________ *WTO, GATS and Higher Education: An Indian Perspective*. Paper prepared for meeting convened by the Association of Commonwealth Universities. Perth Australia, 2002.

Prabhu, Joseph, "Educational Institutions and Philosophies, Traditional and Modern", *Encyclopedia of India (vol. 2)* edited by Stanley Wolpert, 23–28, Thomson Gale, 2006.

Salmi, J., "Perspectives on the Financing of Higher Education", *Higher Education Policy*, Vol.5, No. 2, pp.13-19, 1992.

Sarkarani, M., "The challenges of higher education in developing countries". *Political and Economic Information*, 184-197, 2007.

Scott, P., *The Globalization of Higher Education*, 1998, Open University Press and Society for Research into Higher Education, Buckingham.

Setty, E.D. and Ross, E.L., "A Case Study in Applied Education in Rural India", *Community Development Journal*, 22 (2): 120–129, Oxford University Press, 1987.

Sripati, V. and Thiruvengadam, A.K., "India: Constitutional Amendment Making The Right to Education a Fundamental Right", *International Journal of Constitutional Law*, 2 (1): 148–158, Oxford University Press, 2004.

Stewart, F., "Globalisation and Education", *International Journal of Educational Development*, Vol.16, No.2, pp. 327-33, 1996.

TFHE, *Higher Education in Developing Countries: Peril and Promise*, Task Force on Higher Education, The World Bank, 2000.

UGC, *Report of the Committee Constituted by UGC for 'Formulation of Revised Fee Structure in the central and Deemed Universities in India'*, University Grants Commission, New Delhi, 2000.

UNESCO, *Higher Education in Developing Countries: Peril and Promise*, The Task Force on Higher Education and Society, World Bank, Washington, D.C., 2000.

_______________, *Higher education in the Twenty-first Century: Vision and Action*, Final Report, World Conference on Higher Education, UNESCO, Paris,5-9, October, 1998

_______________, *Towards an agenda for higher education: Challenges and task for the twenty-frst centuly viewed in the light of the regional conference*, Paris, 1998.

Vrat, Prem, "Indian Institutes of Technology", *Encyclopedia of India (vol. 2)* edited by Stanley Wolpert, 229-231, Thomson Gale, 2006.

Wit, H. D., *Internationalization of higher education in the United States of America and Europe: A historical, comparative, and conceptual analysis*. Westport, Conn.: Greenwood Press, 2002.

World Bank, *Constructing Knowledge Societies: New Challenges for Tertiary Education*, Washington, D.C., 2002.

_______________, *Higher Education: Lessons from Experience*, Washington, D.C., 1994.

_______________, *Technical and scientific manpower development in India*, Draft, The World Bank, 2000.

Yang R., *Third delight: The internationalization of higher education in China*. New York London: Routledge, 2002.

_______________, University Internationalization: Its Meanings, Rationales and implications, *Intercultural Education, 13*, No. 1, 2002, pp. 81-95.

Ziderman, A. and D.Albrecht, *Financing Universities in Developing Countries*, The Stanford Series on Education and Public Policy, The Falmer Press, Washington, D.C., 1995.

Zolfaghari, A., *The role of education in social development*. Open University, Shahreza, 2003.

INDEX